A WRITER'S CHINA

BRIDGES EAST & WEST

PEOPLE'S REPUBLIC OF CHINA

U.S.S.R.

U.S.S.R.

Mongolia

Shenyang

N. Korea

Beijing •

Pakistan

Tianjin

S. Korea

Xian
•

Chengdu•   Wuhan   Shanghai

Chongqing
Leshan•   Yangtze River   Taiwan
           Gorges

Nepal

Bhutan

Guangzhou

India   Burma

Hong Kong

Laos

Vietnam

A

———— BRIDGES ————

WRITER'S

———— EAST ————

CHINA

———— & WEST ————

肯尼斯·林肯

Kenneth Lincoln

CAPRA PRESS
SANTA BARBARA

Cover and book design by Frank Goad, Santa Barbara.

Cover photograph and all interior photographs by the author.
Chinese characters on cover and title page represent the author's name.
Thanks to all the authors involved with this project and their publishers for
permissions to reprint material.

LIBRARY OF CONGRESS CATALOGUING-IN-PUBLICATION DATA

Lincoln, Kenneth
A writer's China : Bridges east & west / Kenneth Lincoln
p. cm.
ISBN 0-88496-439-6 (pbk. : alk. paper)
1. China–Description and travel. 2. Authors, American–20th century–Journeys–China.
I. Title. II. Title: Bridges east & west
DS712 .L538 1999
951.05–dc21
98-54859
CIP

Capra Press
P.O. Box 2068
Santa Barbara, CA 93120

for Kappy and Sam
making wells together

The nameless is the origin of heaven and earth.
The named is the mother of ten thousand things.
– LAO TSU

Table of Contents

Preface
Stone Characters

> *I have noticed that general works about the history of Man*
> *either ignore China altogether or relegate this huge*
> *section of mankind to a couple of paragraphs.*
> – ARTHUR WALEY, *THE WAY AND ITS POWER*

A WRITER'S CHINA charts the journey of ten American writers, their family members, and literary hosts through China, April 1988: Harrison Salisbury, Maxine Hong Kingston, Larry Heinemann, Barry Lopez, Charles Wright, Roberta Whiteman, Alice Fulton, Jay Wright, Robert Rees, and myself. We were the second contingent of American writers touring China, spearheaded by Norman Cousins and Harrison Salisbury, while two Chinese groups reciprocated to the United States in the 1980s. The narrative is inspired by the men and women rebuilding China today, from the bottom up, essentially by hand. From poets, to rice planters, to playwrights, to pole carriers, these Chinese work toward modernizing the character and country of the twenty-first century's largest economy and nation, over a billion people in one of humanity's oldest continuous cultures.

Xian in the sixth century, with some two million inhabitants, was the world's biggest city. Today, the legendary, two-thousand-year-old "Forest of Stele" stands in the city's center, scripted Chinese characters engraved into 2,300 human-size tablets. These stone "characters" speak classically for China—its ancient history, rooted culture, compacted wisdom, and scrappy economy. By World Bank calculations in 1998, the fabled Middle Kingdom is the third largest economic power in the world, after the United States and Japan, and the second largest recipient of foreign investments. Its economy has grown an average of ten percent annually for the past two decades, noted by the Dutch reporter, William van Kemenade, "making China the newest low-wage country with the highest economic growth in the world" (*China, Hong Kong, Taiwan, Inc.*). Just so, the ancestral character of China's people is embedded in daily life today, as its historic literature is incised in stone, from Confucius and Lao Tsu, to writers encountered in this journey, Liu Binyan and Bai Hua, Deng Youmei and Liu Shahe. To be ignorant of them would be like overlooking the Himalayas.

In the 6th century B.C., Lao Tsu left some 5,000 picture-words to point toward the *Tao* or "way," still pondered two and a half thousand years later. For the "Old Master," words were at once transparent signs and opaque mysteries, that is, partial openings toward the ways of natural living. But only partial: pointing toward the moon or "light snatcher," Zen masters would later say, is *not* the moon. So this narrative can only point toward China. Enlightenment comes as the moon reflected on water, Dogen Kigan noted. The moon does not get wet, the water is not broken.

ii

The Chinese love grouping things quizzically. Speaking about the Gang of Four in the late 1970s, they gestured with all five fingers: the Gang, plus Mao's shadow. When officials set out to eradicate the Four Pests during the Red Guard mayhem—mosquitoes, flies, sparrows, and rats—people again held up five fingers. The unnamed "pests" to be purged were artists and scholars, essentially the intelligentsia, especially the writers. Artists were tortured and maimed, locked in closets for years, hung from their wrists by wire, for showing any interest in the West. Anyone wearing glasses or speaking in another language was suspect. An imprisoned musician was beaten for talking English in his sleep. Discounting the human cost in favor of ideological revival, the Italian leftist Alberto Moravia saw Mao Zedong, peasant-born and commoner-named, replanting his feet in Chinese soil by way of the people's egalitarian revolution: "In one year, fifty million Red Guards surged, in a new Children's Crusade, from one end of China to the other. Millions of poster newspapers appeared. There were hundreds of thousands of parades, demonstrations, meetings. More than ten million Red Guards were received personally in Peking. And all China was turned upside down: agricultural and industrial production diminished, the state bureaucracy was overturned, party bureaucracy was destroyed" (*La Rivoluzione Culturale in Cina*, 1967). What is the price of revolution? *Seize the day, seize the hour,* Mao wrote verses in 1963, *Our force is irresistible. | Away with all pests!* Just before his infamous swim in the Yangtze three years later, Mao wrote his Draconian wife, Jiang Qing: "Great disorder across the land leads to great order. And so once again every seven or eight years monsters and demons will jump out themselves."

During those scapegoating times, thinkers capped the enemies of Maoist communism as "The Stinking Ninth." They must "put aside their writing," the state formula decreed, and go "to the country" for "reeducation through labor." Brutalizing his poet-generals of the Long March and unleashing national mayhem, Mao quipped in his dotage, "Intellectuals have the lowest intellects." Poets slopped pigs, essayists dunged out barns, novelists hoed beans, musicians planted rice in the mud, philosophers labored in factories.

The Cultural Revolution incited civil chaos with an anti-intellectual backlash. In some respects it seemed an ethnocentric aftershock of the 1940s purge, when some three million landlords were rubbed out. During the Cultural Revolution, artists were labelled "decadent" or "bourgeois," to be beaten, ridiculed, or locked up. Their spouses were pressed to divorce them: choose allegiance to the party, or marriage to "bourgeois decadence," Deng Youmei's wife was told when the celebrated novelist faced prison. Children were marched out of school to spit on him bowing from the waist by the roadside. Some purged thinkers committed suicide; survivors recanted Western ways.

These men and women outlasted their terrorists. They now comprise China's literary and intellectual masters. Beyond their so-called "scar literature" and renewed "modernism" of the 1980s, they quote Confucius and Du Fu, revive the classical 7-5 character verse forms, and experiment in Westernized "free" verse. Dramatists sample folk wisdom and adapt parables to plays. Still other writers realistically tell China's old and new history in fiction. Miraculously, these literati survive with a bladed sense of humor, from parody to pratfall, comparable with Cervantes or Shakespeare, Rabelais or Joyce. Enduring writers, from East and West, are the heroic characters of this narrative.

iii

A year after our cook's tour of China, the June 1989 Tiananmen massacre bloodied and blocked the country's cultural rebuilding. One hundred acres of the world's largest public square, Tiananmen has guarded the Forbidden City for centuries. The name means "Gate of Heavenly Peace." A 120-foot obelisk, Monument to the Martyrs of the Revolution, fronts Tiananmen Gate, and to the south Mao's tomb stands in the center of the square. The governing Great Hall of the People looms to the west, and the Museums of History and of the Revolution border the eastern square. During the Tiananmen protests, a plaster Statue of Liberty, "The Goddess of Freedom," stood for Western democratic reform. Three thousand fasting students wore white headbands stating, "GIVE ME FREEDOM OR GIVE ME DEATH." On June 4th, 1989, more than 3,000 people were massacred in Beijing, and 120,000 were imprisoned.

No group of writers has since recharged our stalled dialogue, in either direction, and few cultural exchanges have taken place. A fifth of the world's population has been shadowed in fear and silence. A decade later, the stone door is moving from the tomb. The five-foot tall Chinese dictator, who played master bridge and wore a white ten-gallon hat at a Texas rodeo, is now dead. Deng Xiaopeng ordered dissident students shot down under the plaster arms of the Goddess of Freedom. At ninety-two he was blind and deaf. Sixty-five years earlier, Mao called him affectionately a "needle wrapped in cotton." The last Maoist cadre said long ago, "It does not matter whether the cat is black or white, as long as it catches mice." Deng's successor today, Chairman Jiang Zemin, quotes Abraham Lincoln freely, speaks several foreign languages, and is the first Chinese leader with a college degree. Jiang's favorite lines come from the Gettyburg Address, "government of the people, by the people, for the people." Chairman Jiang has visited the United States, and President Clinton has gone to China. The Middle Kingdom is fast becoming our major trading partner, awakening as the world's economic giant.

A renascent Sino-American dialogue, so abruptly begun and broken a decade ago, reopens the door to our collaborative exchange. We need to jump-start the cultural talks and reengage our historical discussions. Chinese and American readers have mutual interests in the twenty-first century, from the stone characters in Xian to Pacific Rim stock markets, Confucius to Maxine Hong Kingston.

Maxine finished *Tripmaster Monkey* on our journey through Xian. She now teaches at the University of California, Berkeley and published *Hawaii One Summer* in 1998. Charles Wright, professor of contemporary poetry at the University of Virginia, was given the Award of Merit Medal from the American Academy of Arts and Letters in 1992, a Ruth Lilly Poetry Prize in 1993, and the Lenore Marshall Poetry Prize for *Chickamauga*, also the Academy of American Poets best book of poetry in 1995. Charles won both the Pulitzer Prize and (a second) National Book Award for *Black Zodiac* in 1998. Larry Heinemann, Bravo Company veteran, published *Cooler By the Lake* in 1992 and continues to write a Vietnam train book from his native Chicago. After releasing his *Selected Poems* in 1987, Jay Wright brought out another book, *Boleros*, in 1991. In 1996 Jay received the 62nd Fellowship Award from the Academy of American Poets. Alice Fulton, teaching at the University of Michigan, won a MacArthur Fellowship in 1991 and published *Sensual Math* in 1995. Roberta Hill Whiteman was awarded the Lila-Wallace Reader's Digest Award and published *Philadelphia Flowers* in 1997. Bobbi teaches American Studies at the University of Wisconsin, Madison. A prolific magazine essayist for *Harper's*, *The Paris Review*, and *North American Review*, Barry Lopez in the last decade has published *Crow and Weasel* (1990), *The Rediscovery of North America* (1991), *Field Notes* (1994), *Crossing Open Ground* (1994), *The Grace Note of the Canyon Wren* (1994), and *Lessons from the Wolverine* (1997). Barry gathered his personal travel essays in 1998, *About This Life*. Harrison Salisbury, twice a Pulitzer-prize journalist, published his first-hand *Tiananmen Diary* in 1989, followed by *Heroes of My Time* and *The New Emperors* in 1993. Harrison died July 5, 1993. After lecturing in Lithuania for four years, Bob Rees relocated to Santa Cruz, California, where he teaches at the University of California. Currently he is finishing a collection of essays and writing a play on Dietrich Bonhoeffer.

A Writer's China draws the lines of an East-West dialogue on the eve of China's rebuilding, a gate into the twenty-first century. Deng Xiaoping's death in February 1997—the last of the military Maoist poet-generals—opens passage to the Middle Kingdom again. July 1st of 1997, Hong Kong reverted to mainland control, and Beijing has since been solidifying economic-political ties with Taiwan. A Pacific Rim trading empire will either include or exclude the United States, now exiled from the European Economic Community. Will China's renewed voices of free inquiry and open exchange be heard in the West? Listen to what Chinese writers were asking the spring before Tiananmen. How American writers were responding may help us understand East-West global events to follow.

Beginning at the End
Refugee on the Couch

Henry in bonsai garden

THE TELEGRAM CAME to my Culver City condo on Thursday morning: "Arrive LAX Sat July 10, 4 pm, United #10. Please to meet you. Henry Chen."

"Who's Henry?" asked my daughter, Rachel, quizzically. She had taken to wrinkling her brow and squinching her small nose at odd events in my life. Bumped up to eighteen, recently graduated from high school and headed for college, Rachel was *out of here,* as LA kids said those days. I'd raised her from infancy, a single-parent dad-as-mom, and we were going through separation anxiety.

"Is this some defector from your China trip?" Rachel demanded to know.

"Henry was one of our translators, traveling around China this spring. His full name is Chen Binyan, but he calls himself Henry. He's married and has twins," I answered, "hardly a set-up for defection. Henry's quite a character, a streetsmart Beijing kid in his early thirties. A Party favorite, a regular guy."

"Don't worry, Rachel," Jeannine tossed in, "he's not coming to live with us. We're already bunched like squirrels into this crackerbox. The only place to sleep is on the couch." Jeannine was nicknamed JJ and had been living with us, going on three years, in a one-bedroom-and-loft condo. In such close quarters, I figured we would either work things out, or self-destruct.

"On the couch, what if?" Rachel shrilled. "My bed is on the other side of that wall! I suppose we get to share the bathroom, then. Sheez, a Chinese communist on the couch."

Well, come to pass, sleep on the couch Henry Chen did, for a few weeks, until I found him a place to house-sit. He'd come for a Master's in American Literature at Kansas State, a last minute release from the Beijing Writers' Association. Since LA was his first stop across the States, Henry showed up on our doorstep. How could I refuse?

"Oh my Gawd," Rachel spasmed, valley-girl style, "oh my *Gawd*."

It felt as though a planet had fallen out of the heavens into our apartment; here was the Beijing translator himself, roosting on our couch. So my friendship with Henry Chen, begun in China, April 1988, deepened and grew into a conversation between East and West. It became the on-going dialogue of an introduction to the fabled Middle Kingdom.

"I feel so bad, Ken, dropping out of sky like this," he said with all sincerity, "but I had no others."

Henry was my youngest brother's age, born in 1953 to educated Beijing parents, thirteen when the Red Guard erupted. To escape more serious harassment, his parents slopped hogs and chopped sorghum with the farmers. Young Henry learned the ways of city streets, in a time when teen-age patriotic hoodlums were throwing old people out of apartment windows, or marching their teachers in dunce hats through squares to public trial. I figured Henry could tell Rachel a thing or two about youthful rebellion.

"Stay out of ways," was all he said, "duck bullets."

Henry was smart enough to escape the Red Guard censure of his parents and crafty enough to lay in a pay-back. By his mid-twenties, Henry had become a budding writer and party translator for the Chinese Communist Writers' Association. He wove through people and politics like a high plains Sioux fancy dancer. Since Chinese has no articles, prepositions, or inflections as Westerners use them, Henry bypassed the non-essentials of English as so much chaff in the grain. His idiosyncratic English was refreshing. When the first contingent of American writers came to visit in 1984—Allen Ginsberg, Toni Morrison, Gary Snyder, Maxine Hong Kingston, Leslie Marmon Silko, William Gass, William Least Heat Moon, and Francíne du Plessix Gray—Henry was assigned as Allen "Ginsberger's" personal attaché and spokesman.

"You know, Ken, Chinese can't swear in public, and no sex talk," Henry chuckled over a cold Tsingtao beer that summer evening he arrived in LA. "It's illegal, like call girl. Ginsberger kept saying he want *get laid with boy* in China, whole people hear. Man, I was in sweat as translator, when Allen came to line in poem, 'America,' *Go fuck yourself with your atom bomb.* So I just make up something, like *America, bad luck yourself, with your atom bomb.*" His eyes partly closed, over a rapscallion grin. "*When I go to Chinatown,* Ginsberger says, *I get drunk and never get laid,* so I just change a bit, *never get paid.*"

Henry looked at me in all seriousness and said, as though to himself, "I could translate, *Asia is rising against me, I haven't got a chinaman's chance,* that was Party line, you know, but then he ends with, *America I'm putting my queer shoulder to the wheel.* So I just say it something, you know, like Greek Ixion, *putting my dear shoulder to the wheel.* Chinese very up-tight about sex. Homos are forbidden in China, Ken, no prostitutes." His face went dark, frowning, then he looked up impishly. "How do you translate in America poem, *That no good. Ugh. Him make Indians learn read. Him need big black niggers. Hah?* Chinese has no tones like that, Ken." With all my Ethnic Studies background, I didn't have a clue.

Henry's grin was infectious. He was slender, though wiry muscled, taller than most Chinese, and open to all comers. He had tousled black hair, a clear forehead, lightly amber-tinted large glasses, a strong noseridge. Henry flashed a grin that let you in on a labyrinth of secrets, part shady joke, part sticky gossip, part clandestine innuendo and bone truth. I liked him immediately. He was the kind of regular guy I used to hang out with in high school pool halls, back in Nebraska—only street-smarter, politically savvy in ways only a survivor of patriotic witch-hunting and pointless violence can be. He knew where he stood and where the exits were, at all times.

Henry's ticket to California cost him two years' salary. The Beijing Writers Association chipped in as a gesture toward his six years of service. He was slated to replace the current director, and she was rightly upset, seeing forced retirement. So everyone "got happy" when Henry asked to study American Literature for two years in Manhattan, Kansas.

"I want to write thesis on John Berryman," he announced that evening over Coca Cola and peanuts. "My real name is not *Henry*, you know, I take that from Berryman's poetry. That trickster guy you talk about, Ken, that coyote-crow guy who smart-talk through crazy times and all bad things. Henry my man, my, what you say, *to-tem?*"

"Yeh, your 'fellow-clansman,' the Ojibwa say, your guardian spirit."

"Yes, and more, *Mis-tah Bones,* you know, he face death head-on, no flinch-back, no chicken off." Henry smiled to himself. "Also Henry is wife's dentist, you know, Ken, old family friend for John Berryman." My translator had done his research. He was in America to learn our ways.

"Trickster get away with sexing lots of women, or like Ginsberger, even mens and boys. You know sex is sinful in China, masturbation punish by law. Doctors all say it lead to blind impotence, loss of manthing. That Last Emperor you hear about in movies, Pu Yi, he was impotent because his ancestors use up their virility. Too much sexing around, they say, too easy."

"Well, I don't know about that, Henry. Here, the Puritans, then the Victorians repressed sex to glue people's noses to the grindstone. Keep distractions to a minimum, as Mao said, when there's work to be done."

"Many have VCR with porn films now," Henry said with a wry look, "imported on black market from Taiwan. China very modern, very American, like that, now." He gave me a funny look and crunched a handful of peanuts.

The next morning we drove to Venice beach for breakfast. The Pacific waves were breaking in slow curls, surfers lazily riding to shore on the froth lip. The palm trees were wafting, blue sky still blue just ahead of the midday smog. We walked down the Boardwalk to Figtree John's. Chen took it all in as he talked—g-string bikinis, roller skaters, weight lifters, Black basketball hustlers, Hispanic t-shirt vendors, street guitarists and break dancers and stand-up comedians.

"I must ask you this," my favorite Sufi head-tripper, Jingles, asked Henry, giving him a five-dollar shoulder massage, "are there MacDonald's in China?"

"Ahaa, three MacDonald's in Beijing and one *Kentucky,* you know, fry chicken, across from Mao's tomb in Tiananmen Square. Colonel's chicken does best business, it cheapest. Eveyone go 'Dutch,' instead of spending month's salary in Chinese restaurant."

Jingles couldn't hold himself back. "Tell me, Mr. Chen, do they eat dogs and cats?"

"Birds and mice, too," Henry said with a straight face, "monkey brains and bear paws in old days. Remember saying called *four don'ts:* 'Only soft things Chinese don't eat are flowers. Only hard things we don't eat are clods. Only four-leggeds don't eat are tables, the only two-leggeds, parents."

"Far out, dude!" Jingles crowed. "Somewhere I read the 'Three Squeals' recipe for eating rat embryos. First squeal when the baby rat is squeezed by chop sticks, second squeal when it's dipped in hot sauce, third squeal when it's popped in the mouth."

"Raise you glasses and forget policy," Henry chuckled and said, "once chopsticks start moving, everything possible."

"Whew, you come a long ways, Mister Chen," Jingles whistled, "a long way across the big waters. Welcome to America."

"China even have Silkworm atomic weapons, Mister Jingle," Henry said. "Government worry if West blow itself up, like in Allen Ginsberger poem." He flashed that Confucian trickster's grin. "You know poem 'America,' Mister Jingle?"

"*America I used to be a communist when I was a kid I'm not sorry,*" Jingles quoted the middle lines, "*I smoke marijuana every chance I get.*"

"Very good, Mister Jingle, very good," Henry praised, "you come to China, be poet, government lock you up, too!"

We strolled on past the racks of cheap sunglasses, gym socks, earrings, backpacks, crystals, dayglo Frisbees, and Mexican blankets to the oceanside cafe and ordered Tecate, chips, and salsa. Henry grew serious for a moment. "Chinese have always squabble over things, money, goods, politics, you name it. So-called 'collective' thinking only a little bit disguise backbiting, power play, gossip jockey into position, betrayal, all that kind of stuff. Everyone suspicious of everyone, just like your government, probably. Bureaucracy wash your brain. All motivated for own self. Common welfare is Communist myth. Today, Chinese want to be free, want to follow own ends, just like you guys." He cracked a tortilla chip and thought a minute.

"Marxism help overthrow landlords, yes, organize people and resources. Mao like George Washington, you know, reshape feudal system, what you call 'fiefdom,' I think. Different regions come into nation, but China too big to work together, collectively, too all-time competitive." He thought a second, dipped a tortilla chip in salsa, and continued. "China Party just too unruly to last forever. There must be reform these days, or reformers be thrown out on bottoms." He gazed out over the Pacific.

"What holds party in place is still fear, fear of reprisal, on one hand, and ambition to make use of fear machinery, on other. Personal need come foremost, personal gain. If party line lead only to Beijing, or take too much sacrifice—like removing spouses, husband work one city, wife another, kids in collective school—is too much, finally. Party outstay welcome, even may be over now." He dropped his gaze to the empty chips plate. "Liberal moves seem sign that our leaders catch drift, want to address modernization on local level. They may be willing to bend Marxist dogma line toward capitalism, or not. That put more chickens in pots, less suffering across China. Chinese not fools: remember, long time pragmatic, proud, *ethno-*, you say, *centric.*" His face brightened and eyes narrowed. "China cultured for thousands of years, deep in agrarian—the people still hold grounded values of peasant workers, keep loyalties low to ancestral soil. This make them hard fool to uproot, hard to disregard own terms."

Next day, on the way to UCLA, I dropped Henry off at Pico and Veteran, to get a job. "There's a Chinese restaurant, Henry. You're on your own. See what you can come up with. I'll pick you up on this corner at four."

Two hours later, the phone rang in my office.

"Ken, I've got job!" Chen fairly sang out over the telephone.

"Great, Henry, where?"

"Parking cars where you drop me off at China West, four dollars an hour, maybe seven hours all day, all summer. I get rich! This America great!"

*

So Henry starts making $28 a day, plus a tip here and there. He notices that the Lionel train shop next door closes at five and has spaces for about ten cars. After checking with the management, he sees that the burger joint on the corner needs additional parking, so Henry charges a dollar a car and pockets the overage.

"Chen, for a communist, you make a great capitalist," I kid him.

"Oh, very funny, Ken, very funny, you make good comrade."

In the mornings, when business is slow, Henry translates Viktor Frankl's Holocaust memoir, *Man's Search for Meaning*, borrowed from my library. He's also reading Aristotle, Plato, and Heraclitus to bone up on Western culture. Henry makes the word "industry" pale beside his self-help inventiveness. In China, work is work. Here the profit motive sparks his capitalist fancy. No looking back for Henry. He's not very homesick, he says, because there's no time to be. And "no time to have breakfast on the beach," he tells me poker-faced. "I need to finish my translation."

Henry is riding a borrowed, bent-pedal, ten-speed bike. He doesn't know how to shift, so he pumps around West LA in high gear. With a can of WD-40, I oil the moving parts and show him the lower gear mechanisms.

"Good-bye, for the day," he waves, wearing his UCLA camouflage t-shirt, "don't wait for me, I'll get free ham-bur-ger at Islands, for parking their cars."

Chinese children start school at age seven and study calligraphy for six years. There are no private typewriters. Government secretaries who can manage vast sets of alternate keyboards, for the many dialects, are hard to come by and costly, so most writing is done long-hand in China. Some three hundred writers are state funded. In three weeks, Henry has *Man's Search for Meaning* copied in Chinese characters on a ledger notepad.

"Maybe I translate Chinese writers in English," Henry says reflectively. "Sheng Cong just died. He write realist literature until 1949, when the Reds take over. Elegant, simple novels about people's lives. He refuse to write in political formulas. So Sheng denounced as rightist—friend of landlords and Western decadents—and he take up stage costuming, from scholarly angle. Sheng have chance at Nobel prize, everyone think. No Chinese ever get one."

Henry finds Los Angeles, except for the weather, much like what he imagines the rest of the cities in the States to be—larger-than-life people driving everywhere, buying things, hurrying. A cocaine-high lawyer, threatening our man with a lawsuit for charging a dollar to park, made Henry fantasize busting the BMW window with a rock. He studied the situation—when the lawyer stalked off without paying—thought of wearing a glove, and running away from the police, then thought twice and went back to translating Viktor Frankl.

"Maybe you could just let the air out of his tire," I volunteered.

"Ahh, you have many good ideas, Ken, I like these thinkings."

Henry gets me rereading from *Chinese Profiles*, a couple hundred statements by contemporary fellow workers translated into English: "If we don't clinch a deal," one says, "it's the old story: big brother gets the noodles, second brother drinks the soup, third brother has the dishwater, and little brother goes hungry because he's left with nothing."

"You've got to realize that we're all bullshitters," says an express train commuter. "We get on the train like gentlemen, and get off like blind men. We do our job like children, and go home like con-men. It's a hard life. And what's in store for us? Tongues worn out, shoes worn through for no good reason, a whole basketful of crimes to our name, and the black house. The black house? Clink."

Two months later, Henry went as he came without fanfare or ripple. I drove him to the Greyhound bus station, gave him a bear hug and handshake. *Zaijian*, my friend, bye-bye.

"We meet soon, Ken, not like LA to Beijing now. Henry go American."

"Just be sure to come back, Magic," I tell him, "*Bao-zhong*, Xiao Chen, take care." I'd nicknamed him back in China.

Some weeks later, we received a letter from the Midwest. Henry's written English was quickly sounding more Western:

Dear Ken and JJ,

I got to Kansas safe and sound. After hectic time for the first couple of days, I settle down and get ready to crack the hard nut of literature.

I just don't know how I can thank you enough for all you have done for me. Without your help, I wouldn't been been able to go to LA in the first place, my stay there could have been a nightmare. Sometimes, I felt ashamed of myself for giving you so much trouble. A real American solves his own problem, as they say. So more often than not, I had to take Dutch comfort by thinking that I'm not an American and excuse myself for doing what an American wouldn't do.

The two month's stay in LA benefits me a lot. The goals I had set before I left for LA were all obtained. I got more familiar with the American society and the American people. I made some profits by bluffing people into what they hated to do at the expense of being bluffed, too. The American way of life and its social customs are no longer what I can only read of in books and magazines, but something real and tangible. They're part of my life already. So, I can say as proudly or foolishly as Nietzsche said: "What doesn't kill me, makes me stronger." However, but for you, I could not have survived in a place where even Angels lost.

"A journey of ten thousand Li begins with a single step," Confucius once said. Now that I've got over the first wave of cultural shocks—one of the worst things for a stranger on a strange land. I'll have nothing to be afraid of in the future. The mere thought of your help and support ready at hand gives me enough strength to see all troubles in their face. I'm now fully prepared for an on-coming fight with all the headaches of literary subjects and wrestles with John Berryman in years to come. *If all must hurt at once, let yet more hurt now, / so I'll be ready, Dr God. Push on me. / Give it to Henry harder.*

My thoughts are always with you.

Looking forward to meeting you in the near future. I haven't seen any BMW or Mercedes Benz or even Buick. Oh, LA, I miss you!

Say hello to Rachel.

with love, Chen

PS. In *Henry's Fate*, remember John Berryman's last line before he jumped?

"*—Kitticat, they can't fire me—*"

The letter ended there, where Berryman axed his own fatal punchline, *I quit.* I got the point: Xiao Chen quit China. From our couch to Kansas, Henry had defected.

So this story of American writers touring China opens with Henry in the Midwest. Let's go back to the beginning with Xiao Chen, and see where we've come, my friend, where we're going, now.

I

Gathering the Characters

A journey of a thousand miles starts underfoot.
—LAO TSU

DELEGATION OF AMERICAN WRITERS, April 1988

Delegates	*Traveling Companions*
Harrison Salisbury Head of the Delegation	Charlotte Salisbury (wife)
Robert A. Rees Deputy Head of the Delegation	Robert S. Rees (son) Maddox H. Rees (son)
Maxine Hong Kingston	Earll Kingston (husband) Joseph Kingston (son)
Charles Wright	Holly Wright (wife)
Jay Wright	Lois Silber (wife)
Alice Fulton	Henry De Leo (husband)
Larry Heinemann	Edith Heinemann (wife)
Barry Lopez	Sandra Lopez (wife)
Roberta Hill Whiteman	Ernest Marcus Whiteman (husband)
Kenneth Robert Lincoln	Jeannine Stewart Johnson (companion)

Translators/Facilitators
Sue Fan
Shu-mei Shih

MEMO, 28 March 1988
University Extension, UCLA, Department of the Arts
To: Members of the American Delegation, Chinese/American
    Writers' Conference
From: Robert A. Rees

As we make final preparations for the visit to China, here are some last minute details:

1. The Shanghai hepatitis strain is type A, in case your physician needs to know. Gammaglobulin shots should be made as close to departure as possible.

2. The Chinese have graciously offered to pay for all expenses of spouses or traveling companions within China.

3. There have been some changes in the delegation. Tillie Olsen had to withdraw because of family matters, and Carolyn Forché had to withdraw because she had an automobile accident. We have found two excellent writers to replace them: Kenneth Lincoln and Alice Fulton. Attached is an official list of those traveling with the delegation.

4. The Chinese have suggested the following subjects for the Conference: characteristics of artistic approaches by American and Chinese writers; contemporary problems confronting writers of the two countries; and influences from national tradition and abroad. Judging from past experience, these suggested themes are only catalysts to begin exchanges at the conference.

I just received a late notice from the Chinese Writers' Association to ask each writer to prepare a ten-minute introductory statement, handed to the Beijing group when we land. I am sorry we were not given more notice about this request. Your statement could serve as an introduction to your position as a writer and address those things that characterize your work. The Chinese will probably expect you to read your statement at the conference.

5. Sue Fan, our translator, says you should bring clothing to "layer up," since the climate will vary, colder in Beijing and Xian than in the South.

6. Because of the size of the group, we have changed the dinner/reception from Norman Cousins' house to the UCLA campus. We will meet you at the Guest House and walk you to the initial gathering. Please keep the receipts for your cab fares and other incidental expenses, so you can be reimbursed. Your passports and visas will be returned just prior to final departure from China.

7. We hope to have our exact itinerary, complete with hotels, by the time you arrive in Los Angeles.

I look forward to seeing you on Saturday. *Ni hao!*

Harrison Salisbury and Robert Rees

Beijing Birdmen

The Forbidden City

Beijing Traffic

Imperial Palace

A WRITER'S CHINA

Beijing Streets

Parabolic Flight

LOS ANGELES, APRIL 1988

Awake at dawn with the birds. Still the ten thousand things nagging: clean house, give daughter advice, park cars, box keys, pay utilities, sign federal tax check. The daughter-sitter has a flu, so we ask a neighbor to drive us to the airport. Rachel is still in bed, as I'm vacuuming the rug and the phone rings.

"Do you know what time it is, Kenny?" Hal calls out singsong.

"Yeah, 8:40."

"An hour later, my friend. Happy Easter, it's daylight savings time. Spring forward, you don't want to miss your plane."

We dash for the door with two hundred pounds of luggage and gifts—American books, tapes of classical, blues, rock-and-roll, and country-western music, Indian beadwork and silversmith broaches, horsehair jewelry, zoom lens camera, electrical adaptors, clothes, and presentation Lakers t-shirts. My great gifts to China are Magic and Kareem grinning as "world" basketball champions.

"Bye, Rachel," I call out, "be good."

"By, Dad," she smirks, "I love you."

A dash out the door, sun glasses at the ready. Downstairs, Hal waits in a grubby t-shirt. "You artists live in another time zone, sheezz."

"Just drive, Hal, and get us there before the big bird lifts." Luckily, the streets are empty, and we hope the planes are running late.

LAX passenger lines serpentine like cold spaghetti on Easter morning. The Beijing flight will be full of returning Japanese tourists headed for Tokyo. A Korean teen-ager fondles his Fender guitar, as another strolls by with two Louisville sluggers, booty from the New World. Our Orient is around the global corner, a dip in the horizon, under a full Passover moon.

"Some of these guys creep me," JJ grouses when we meet the assembling group, "running around yowling about being writers. They remind me of tomcats in heat." I suspect she includes me, but can't muster a defense. My housemate is not fond of being pushed or rushed.

"Oh my God," JJ shrieks, "we've forgotten our tickets!"

"Not to worry," Bob reassures us, "it's all taken care of. You're checked in with the group."

"Oh great," JJ fumes under her breath, "we're a *group*."

"Just get in line, sweetheart. We better get used to groups for a while. In China nobody does anything alone." Last minute invitees, after Carolyn Forché had a car wreck, we're lucky to have made it with all our stuff, even without the tickets.

Our winged Conestoga wagon lumbers out across the Pacific. We head far north over the Arctic Circle to fly east. The light angles low across the azure ocean, chasing the sun all day, twelve hours to Japan, another five to China. Since 1956, no American could enter the Middle Kingdom for thirty years, and now the rocking cradle struggles with rebirth. China is getting *modernized*, as they say. Remaining fond of folk parables and popular slogans, the Chinese buzz words these days are *reeducate*, the *four modernizations*, and *slackass*. Bottom line, the work ethic is a passion. A straight-faced crematorium laborer in a book I'm reading, *Chinese Profiles*, puts it on the line, "All jobs are alike. They need doing, don't they?"

Fifteen minutes into flying, we hover at six thousand feet over the California coast, circling. Something's definitely wrong.

"Ladies and gentlemen, this is your captain. We are experiencing a pressurization problem which we think can be corrected, rather than returning to Los Angeles."

The Arapaho sculptor, Ernie Whiteman, winks and handsignals that we're turning around. Coyote in the stratosphere. My ears feel like heated peyote drums. JJ takes a deep breath and frowns.

Last night, our send-off banquet was catered by Norman Cousins with salmon poached in champagne, the West's little seductions. No wonder so many Asian travelers, for tens of thousands of years back, found homes along the Pacific Rim. The Mono Indians settled in the Sierra foothills 5,000 years ago. What we now see as "California" below housed a tenth of the country's native population. Today, some 232,000 Native Americans live in the Golden State. People have been coming and going between hemispheres for some time.

"Buddhist scrolls back you up," Barry Lopez adds to my musing, as we sip tea over plane seats. "Five Chinese beggar monks set adrift on the Japanese Current in 458 A.D. They ended up in Central America, calling it the *Kingdom of Fu-Sang*."

I recall that UCLA archeologists think Caucasoid migrations to the

Western Hemisphere, 40,000 years ago, were followed by Mongoloid peoples 20,000 years back. There were successive migrations, down to 12,000 and 7,000 years ago. During the various ice ages, the sea lowered some two hundred feet along the Bering Straits, and hunters followed animals across the land bridge. Agglutination in the so-called *Diego blood-type* shows that 90% of North America's *Indians* were originally Caucasoid. The Athabaskan and Southwest natives more recently—Navajo, Apache, Papago, Pima, Pueblo—appear to be blood-related to Mongoloid genes in Central and South America.

"Tribal peoples combined everywhere," Barry says, "as they swept across the contintent."

"The Lakota started in the Appalachias, then drifted up through the Smokies," I remember reading. "They migrated west into the Great Lakes by the fourteenth century and onto the Great Plains in the sixteenth century."

"That's about when Ming dynasties ruled China and rebuilt the Great Wall," Barry puts the time frame together. "The Wall was already two thousand years old. You know, that wall and coal mine pollution in the Navajo Four Corners area," he adds, "were the only manmade artifacts the first moon-walkers could distinguish on earth."

These histories layering together fascinates me. As Europe was emerging from the Dark Ages, the Navajos swept down from western Canada into the Southwest. The Pueblos, part of the Southwest Anasazi complexes, had been settled in the Rio Grande Valley for some 2,000 years, back to a time when the Chinese were codifying Confucius in stone tablets. The Chaco Canyon ruins were more architecturally advanced than the Romans. The Anasazi built four-story structures without mortar.

"Remember how Norman Cousins called us cultural 'pioneers' the night before we left LA?" Barry reflects, sipping tea, cold by now. "In 1959, as I recall, he convened Russian and United States writers at the Dartmouth Conference. They wanted to open Soviet-American relations under Eisenhower. Norman was stumping for a World Federalist Doctrine—primarily trying to end the threat of nuclear war and address mass hunger. He was also attacking terrorism, pollution, and the exhaustion of natural resources. A big order, eh? Norman and Harrison Salisbury thought that writers might spark a dialogue among themselves that would carry over to politicians, maybe a global melting of the Cold War tensions." Barry looks up hopefully. "It helped with the Russians, thirty years ago."

"And two centuries before that," I remember, "Lord Dartmouth heard Samson Occom, a Mohegan minister, spreading God's word around England. Dartmouth decided to fund a New World college to educate natives. Not a bad idea the other direction—educating non-Indians tribally. Indians can still go to Dartmouth tuition-free, if they pass entrance standards."

"Yeah," Barry says with a grin, "in Norman's parting words, *Delight awaits.*"

"Ladies and gentlemen," the pilot interrupts, "we have solved our pressure problem and will proceed now to Tokyo."

Our American perspective downsizes in the greater scheme of things. Here's a bird's-eye glimpse that two-thirds of the world is covered with sea. We've been told that a fifth of humanity lives in China.

Across the aisle a Japanese businessman types on a Toshiba laptop.

He points at his personal computer, and says beaming, "Weighs ten pounds!"

"How do you get hard copy?" I ask.

"Printer only about that big," he gestures the size of a loaf of bread. "Runs on batteries too."

"Pacific Rim investors own the Brentwood Country Club," JJ whispers, "and every other office building in downtown Los Angeles."

This trip may give us some idea why.

*

West to the East
Watchful as men crossing a winter stream.
Alert as men aware of danger.
Courteous as visiting guests.
—Lao Tsu

Landing in Tokyo, twelve hours along:
It's midnight in L.A., as late afternoon shadows pine trees around the Japanese airport, all so civilized. The smell of prosperity holds here,

civility, manners, wealth. Eighty-nine MacDonald's crosshatch Tokyo.

Charles Wright, a lanky poet from the University of Virginia, introduces himself with a Tennessee cadence and boyish innocence. His wife, Holly Wright, is a visual artist from California.

"We have a mutual Italian friend, my translator, Gaetano Prampolini," he says quietly. "He tells me you two trimmed the family vineyards in Spello a few years back. Gaetano's making family wines again, as his father did before the war. We drank some of the chianti this fall."

"Ahh, Gaetano," I remember with affection, "gentleman paisano. We drank a lot of his uncle's grappa. Told stories late into the night. Did he ever get you to smoke one of his Tuscano cigars?"

"I'm allergic to tobacco," Charles says diffidently.

"You're lucky," JJ tosses in, "they're vile, like outhouses on fire."

"When the army stationed me in Italy as a college drop-out," Charles offers, "Pound's Confucius got me interested in writing. Changed my entire life."

"Italy does that to you," I agree. "Did you know that Gaetano's mother, Elsie, was Spello's first woman mayor?"

"And a Communist doctor," Holly recalls. "Quite a woman, quite a country."

"Did Gaetano ever tell you of driving Robert Lowell to visit Pound in Rapallo?"

"Yes," Charles brightens, "said Ezra had those steel-grey eyes that bore right into you, like a ghost walking through locked doors. Only in Italy—boy, do I miss the mother country."

On the opposite side of the globe, we're far from his native South and my Plains, blinking in the spring grey of Japanese dusk.

Harrison Salisbury, the eighty-year-old *New York Times* war correspondent, has been to China eight or nine times with the "finest" translators, he says. JJ flinches. His wife Charlotte looks conspiratorially at my companion. On sight, the older and younger women are quizzically in cahoots.

"I'm going back to promote *The Long March,* the story of Mao's 1934 retrenchment," Harrison says. "My publisher insists—it was last year's best-seller in China. The communists don't exactly like what I've said about Mao and his cronies, but I'm no softer on Chiang Kai-shek. They were all a bunch of armed goons, vying for power. Couldn't trust a one of them, all in it for their own gain." Harrison's latest history caps half a century of political journalism and some twenty-five books about Russia, the States, and China. He's won two Pulitizers, the second retracted for political reasons, Bob tells me.

I'm carrying a copy of *The Long March,* which declares early on: "Between October 16, 1934, and October 1, 1949, China's stage was filled with heroism, tragedy, intrigue, bloodletting, treachery, cheap opera, military genius, political guile, moral goals, spiritual objectives, and human hatred. Shakespeare could not have written such a story. It is not yet finished. Perhaps it never will be." And there is Harrison in the flesh, continuing the story.

"Lady Macbeth would come off as Mother Goose in the Chinese revolution."

Standing around the Tokyo airport, Barry Lopez and Earll Kingston joke to lighten the travel fatigue. "Ever hear the Winnebago tale of Wakdjunkaga humping a dead tree?" Barry quizzes Earll, an actor married to Maxine Hong Kingston.

"If it's not in Powell's Colorado River journals or Mamet's *American Buffalo,*" Earll confesses, "frankly, no." He's a Bay Area professional actor who each summer at the Grand Canyon does a one-man perfor-mance of John Wesley Powell.

"Well, to make a long story a bit shorter," Barry launches the tale, "in the old times Wakdjunkaga, the Foolish One, has this epic phallus. It's so big he carries it in a box on his back. When Old Man sees a pretty maid-en, he takes Big One out and sends him off to ravage her virginity."

"Hmm," Earll muses, "you mean Indians tell stories like that?"

"Oh, they get much worse," Barry shakes his head and repeats dryly, "much worse. Now Wakdjunkaga goes around desecrating all the villages until he runs out of maidens. He tries holes in hills, vulvas made of cooked acorn mush, slabs of venison, helpless animals, any-thing he can violate. Finally Old Man comes to a hollow tree and spies an opening. 'Quick,' he says to Big One, 'go do your stuff with that dead oak tree.'"

Earll lights a cigarette and keeps listening. An airline stewardess with a drink tray leans in to eavesdrop.

"So Wakdjunkaga starts to defile the tree. Only on the inside, a chipmunk has made its nest. Seeing this ugly thing busting in the door, the chipmunk takes a bite out of Big One and 'Phew!' spits it out because it tastes so bad, like dead wolverine in a slough."

"That bad, eh," Earll pokes at the story.

"Yeh, *that* bad, really awful." Barry keeps a straight face. "But, you know, a funny thing happens when the chipmunk spits out a mouthful of Big Penis. UP pops a pine tree! Damndest thing . . . So he takes another chomp, 'Phewoo!' spits it out, and UP pops a deer. And another, 'Phewey!' and UP pops a badger. And so on, and so on, a squirrel here, a buffalo there, swamp onion to the first stinkbug. That way, Old Man's penis gets chewed way down to size and everything gets started, just by that chipmunk defending home."

"Well, whadda ya know," Earll drags on his smoke and exhales.

"But, you see," Barry winds up the tale, "the Winnebagos say that's why a man's penis is all shriveled up today," he holds his thumb and index finger a couple inches apart, "and only about that big." JJ nods with a wry look, and the stewardess, frowning, walks away stiffly.

"Mao had an imperial bed filled with books and young girls," JJ says scowling.

"You don't say," the Vietnam vet, Larry Heinemann, joins in. "Reminds me of a story I heard in Hanoi after the war."

Edie, his wife, shushes him. "Not now, Larry, save it."

Larry hangs his head. "Aw, c'mon, Edie, let's have some fun."

Her round face flushes under Irish red hair. "Behave yourself, Larry."

Charles Wright and Jay Wright, two of our four poets, hang back with their wives. Holly has battled diabetes for years, and she and Charles seem skittish of public places and group behavior, rightly so. Bob has warned us that the trip is no Best Western excursion. Jay is the only black among us, a former baseball catcher for the St. Louis Cardinals farm team, Guggenheim and MacArthur fellow, jazz bass musician on the side. Jay and his wife, Lois Silber, live quietly in Vermont, no teaching, little schmoozing, minimal exposure. Jay smiles shyly when we're introduced and doesn't say much more than, "Pleased to meet you." Little I can do with poetic diffidence, except respect it, back off.

Maxine Hong Kingston plays the puckish owl, currently putting the finishing touches on *Tripmaster Monkey*. "Don't tell anybody," she whispers conspiratorially, "but I'm using this trip to complete the manuscript. I got the idea for a book about a transplanted trickster in Berkeley, a Frank Chin kind of guy, before we came to China four years ago. That was my first return, since growing up in California. I began to see the stretch, from Asia to America—that I'm neither one nor the other, but both." She plans to end the book when we reach the Grey Goose Pagoda in Xian.

Roberta and Ernie Whiteman, Oneida and Arapaho native artists, introduce themselves with a quiet gentility. "Call me Bobbi," she smiles broadly and shakes my hand. Grinning down from a six-foot-four frame, Ernie says, "Hi, I'm Ernie, portable sweatlodge salesman." Found objects fascinate him, old Zen accidents leaking through natural art. "My art is a kind of mobile process," he answers my question about his sculpture. "I gathered up some scrap auto parts along the highway in Wyoming," Ernie tells me, "and made a sculpture called 'Rusty Cat.'"

"No kidding," I invite him to keep talking, "that's wild. I'm trying to write a book these days on Indian humor. *Trick or treaty*, as Charlie Hill says. Do the Arapaho still have ceremonial clowns?"

"You betcha," Ernie laughs. "These guys are called 'Crazy Warriors.' They used to harrass people into their teepees, shooting arrows at anything that moved. They policed the tribe with a kind of crazy humor. Don't your Lakota friends have *heyokas*, those contrary clowns, or *winktes*, the 'would-be woman' healers?"

"Yeh, those crazy Sioux—we have a *heyoka* in my extended family, George Lone Wolf. Uncle George comes into a room like a jaybird and leaves like a wolverine. He'll say and do anything, just to get a response."

"A sense of humor," Ernie says, "allows Indians to survive, you know, it always has. If you can't laugh, the medicine's dead."

Alice Fulton, the Michigan poet, and her artist husband, Hank De Leo, seem playfully curious about our trip as itinerate writers. She is an auburn-haired woman with a sharp tongue and hawk-eye for detail, he a genial sidekick with a genius for natural design. Hank paints abstract art "without borders." JJ and I take to them immediately. I get the sense that Earll, Hank, Ernie, and my girlfriend will be a rump parliament to our writerly parade. We trade stories and jokes in the Tokyo airport to pass the hours. I find a poem, "Scumbling," in Alice's new collection, *Palladium*, and read it to Jeannine:

> *All night*
> *I pretended night was an unruly*
> *day. I pretended*
> *my voice. I pretended my hair. I pretended*
> *my friend. But there it was—"I"—*
> *I couldn't get rid of that.*

"Sounds familiar," JJ says, "not exactly locker room talk, go on."

> *What could I do but let it learn*
> *to tremble? So I watched feelings hover*
> *over like the undersides*
> *of waterlilies: long serpentines*
> *topped by nervous almost-*
> *sunny undulations. I had to learn*
> *largo. I had to trust*
> *that two bodies scumbling*
> *could soften*
> *one another. I had to*
> *let myself be gone*
> *through, do it in the arbitrary light*
> *tipping and flirting*
> *with seldom-seen surfaces.*

"Scumbling?" JJ puzzles. "Is that a painter's word?"

"It is now."

Harrison and Charlotte Salisbury lead our literary troops into China. Mao's first poem of the Long March celebrated arriving at Loushan in 1934, where peasants were busy fermenting *maotai* white lightning from sorghum and wheat:

> *Idle boast that the stout pass is a wall of iron,*
> *We are crossing its summit,*
> *The heaving hills sea-blue*
> *The dying sun blood-red.*

Bob Rees, our spokesman and my UCLA colleague, shepherds the crew, assisted by his college-age sons, Bobby and Maddy. Bob is one of those leaders who doesn't say a lot, but means it, no question, when asking us to do something or to go somewhere. I trust him implicitly. Feeling like a tag-along, JJ suspects a chauvinist bent.

"Women hold up half the heavens," I remind her that Mao advised his people.

"What about selling, smothering, and drowning baby girls," she asks me stone-faced.

So I leave my common-law mate to her suspicions and scribble away in my ubiquitous blue notebook. Jeannine bites her tongue and reads Marilyn Robinson's *Housekeeping*.

According to Harrison's *The Long March*, Mao turned his "Three Main Rules of Discipline" into 1930s marching songs for his troops: *Obey orders in all your doings. / Don't take a needle or a piece of thread from anyone. / Turn in everything you take.* The "Eight Points of Attention" were metered into singing cadences:

> *Speak politely.*
> *Pay fairly for what you get.*
> *Return everything you borrow.*
> *Compensate for any damage.*
> *Don't strike or curse at people.*
> *Don't damage the crops.*
> *Don't take take advantage of women.*
> *Don't abuse captives.*

The Red Army was looking for converts and recruits, not conquest, from workers whose life expectancy was only thirty. Their goal was to free peasants from landlords and revolutionize China, uniting the vast Han majority and some fifty minorites. "I hated Confucius from the age of eight," Mao Zedong professed, but at twenty-five he graduated from Changsha Normal School, June 1918, versed in Chinese classics, Buddhism, and Western great books. Like Sitting Bull among the Lakota, he was an eloquent speaker, a gifted singer-poet, a budding philosopher, and a political genius, still a Chinese peasant who looked to George Washington as a role model. Mao grounded his political vision in the stone-cut epigram over his school's outer gate: "Seek Truth from Facts."

We leave the Tokyo airport and climb back aboard the 747 to Beijing. There are rows of empty seats. Our flying LA companions had all been wealthy Japanese, none traveling on to China. It's early morning on old California time, time for dinner over the China Sea: linen menus, computer-designed with two storks in classical-modernist postures, the calligraphy showing ancient split lines for "man," a box of light for the "sun," a roof for "house."

"What do we have here," JJ pokes at the aluminum foil, "filet mignon! Let's settle in," she says with a grin. "Nothing like edibles to lift the spirits."

"Don't forget Mao's favorite dish," I add as a blessing. "Moon and Four Stars recipe."

"What's that?" she asks, sipping a dry bordeaux.

"Layers of chicken, fish, lamb, vegetables, and a special taro root. The mound is drenched with rice flour and steamed all night."

"Sounds like stewed pizza," she muses and attacks her steak.

The sea edges the Japanese land, thatched in very small swatches, sewn and requilted by endless ancestral hands like an old patched blanket. Below us, Japan invaded China in 1937, precipitating eight years of war. Then Mao's communists battled Chiang Kai-shek's nationalists for popular support and national unification. Millions died, millions more suffered deeply, for now over half a century. Blood and time have flowed in rivers under us. The Red Army banner, a credo of sixteen Chinese verse ideograms, led Mao Zedong's early success:

> The enemy comes near, we retreat.
> The enemy halts, we pierce.
> The enemy tires, we charge.
> The enemy retreats, we chase.

We'll enter Beijing by night.

*

Beijing Airport
A revolution is not a dinner party,
Or penning an essay, or painting a picture, or stitching embroidery:
It cannot be so genteel, so leisurely or gentle,
So tempered, kind, gracious, restrained and giving.
A revolution is an upheaval,
An act of violence where one class overthrows another.
—LYRICS FOR RALLIES, MAO'S LITTLE RED BOOK

"Linking China with the world of Trade and Finance," announce the bilingual neon signs. Political observers, since Napoleon, refer to China as *the sleeping giant*. The country is relatively poor, but rich in natural resources, eager labor, and Party control. Accenting restraint, the flat flourescent lighting certainly cuts down on airport electricity.

We make a smooth entry, surprisingly no red tape. A mix of Chinese racial stocks floods the luggage pick-up. "There are fifty or more native minorites in this country," Harrison says, as we scramble for our bags. "The Mandarins have held dynastic power for centuries."

Everyone is a bit dazed from the seventeen-hour trip, but wide-eyed. A defected Russian comedian on our flight checks his luggage through customs with us.

"*Ni hao!*" The bus driver flashes a grin.

"You well," the Chinese commonly greet. Or they inquire cordially, "*Ni hao ma?*" more or less, "How are you?"

Two weeks ago, my UCLA colleague, King-Kok Cheung, coached me in a few essential phrases for thanks, please, sorry, correct (yes), incorrect (no), where, good-bye, and the first ten numbers. The four Mandarin tones baffled me.

"Now say *ma* as I do," she coaxed singsong; alas I proved tone deaf. *Ba-ba* for "father" worked a little better than *ma* or "mother" to my Oriental tin ear.

"The jokes will be hardest to get," King-Kok warned me. "I could understand Shakespeare when I came to Berkeley, but not *Laugh-In*." My Barron's *Chinese at a Glance* says that *shi*, spoken in different tones, can mean variously poem, lion, history, teacher, envoy, market, life-time, test, style, ten, stone, to show, or to be.

Little traffic shows up on the drive into Beijing. The two-lane concrete slab road is laced with alder cousins to European plane trees. White painted concrete markers line both sides of the road. Everything is orderly, a touch old-fashioned. Our bus driver straddles the center white line to give the bicycles plenty of room.

Entering Beijing is no grand parade. Vendors' stalls dot the widened highway just outside Tiananmen Square. A new Star Wars-style hotel has just been raised across the way, and then—the Great Hall of the People, the Forbidden City, with Mao's round mosaic face. His tomb stands just beyond a turn down the boulevard into the Tiananmen parade ground. Our bus rolls slowly by this monument to monumentalism, and everyone is quiet, observing, thinking. Mao declared the People's Republic in 1949 from these stairs and reviewed a million marchers in a single parade.

KENNETH LINCOLN

"Five hundred thousand years ago," Bob Rees tells us, standing in the bus aisle, "people lived in caves just south of this capital city. Think about it, our senses of history are surely different from the Chinese, two and a half thousand times older than the United States. Yet their revolution is forty years in the making, as ours only two hundred."

Our hotel is "modernized," but not plasticized in the American interstate style of throw-away glasses and Gideon Bibles. Instead, the room is quaint with all the niceties of old-world, hands-on China—cold beer, water and soda in a small fridge; hot water and tea in thermos bottles; cookies and cakes set out on the coffee table. There's piped-in radio playing a bilingual *Tess of the D'Urbervilles* and an old-style TV, but no stations broadcasting at 10 p.m. The shower water is very hot. I'm delighted to find a 110 watt-plug for my contact lens cooker. JJ marvels at the hand-embroidered sheets and silk quilts. The landscape painting on the wall—a mountain scene with drifting clouds—adds natural graces, human touches.

In 1982 Chinese writers convened at UCLA with American counterparts. I sat in the audience wearing headphones for the translated dialogue through simultaneous interpreters, tight security, and much guarded fanfare. The ping-pong team also made the headlines. Two years later, American writers reciprocated in China with Bob Rees again trail-bossing the group. After the trip, Maxine Hong Kingston dug into *Tripmaster Monkey,* and William Gass published a monograph on Chinese walls. Gary Snyder wrote a poem of Allen Ginsberg writing a poem on an ancient Buddhist bridge near the Han Shan Temple bells:

> AT MAPLE BRIDGE
>
> *Men mixing gravel and cement*
> *At Maple Bridge*
> *Down an alley by a tea-stall*
> *From Han Shan temple;*
>
> *Allen on the bridge arch*
> *Writing down his poem*
> *Where Zhang Ji heard the bell.*
>
> *The stone step moorage*
> *Empty, lapping water,*
> *And the bell sound has travelled*
> *Far across the Sea.*

"In Beijing that spring," Bob tells me in the hotel corridor, "Bill Least Heat Moon and I thought we'd play a joke on the group. Gary Snyder had jumped up behind a boulder in Xian and scared Bill one day. So on the Fourth of July, Bill and I set off firecrackers in a banquet hall, which triggered the sprinkler system, and we had to evacuate! Bill and I had some apologizing to do, but the Chinese took it all in good humor." He looks quizzical, then adds, "They invented firecrackers, you know."

Liu Binyan, attending the first meetings at UCLA and in China, said at our spring send-off that everyone sensed "not having gotten enough." Western artists were baffled trying to fathom such a "formidably ancient and complex country as China." The Chinese, in turn, were "fascinated with the West," especially Disneyland. In 1979, Liu had addressed the Fourth Congress of Artists and Writers in Beijing and advocated three points: face life squarely, while listening carefully to the people's voices; take stances on social issues; regard "literature as a mirror." Liu lamented the writers' silence during the disastrous Great Leap Forward: "Had writers during 1958-60 been able to hold their heads high, to speak out in behalf of the people, to uncover mistakes and to expose the destructiveness of our enemies, this would, in fact, have been the best way they could have upheld the party and socialism." He added the familiar warning, "Power corrupts, and absolute power corrupts absolutely." Liu knew this lesson all too well. He joined the Communist Party in 1943, the year of my birth, and taught himself Russian to read Lenin in the original. Denounced as a liberal rightest in 1957, Liu spent twenty-one years in and out of labor camps. He told the 1979 gathering of writers, "Fate brought us into intimate contact with the lowest levels of the laboring masses; our joys and worries became for a time the same as their own. Our hopes were no different from theirs. This experience allowed us to see, to hear, and to feel for ourselves things that others have been unable to see, hear, or feel." Liu was twice expelled from the Party for listening, seeing and feeling with the people, and speaking his mind. "It is mystifying that this piece of land called China, always so inhospitable to the cultivation of 'rightest opportunism,' has nonetheless allowed revisionism with a 'leftist' tag to grow so wild." In ancient times, Confucius said *renew the people* and left this ideogram as commentary: axe, tree, wood-pile.

Everywhere lie contradictions, opposing opinions, human costs for speaking up. Checking into our hotel, Harrison explains to Jeannine and Charlotte, "Liu Binyan, China's leading journalist and Communist gadfly, was booted from the Party in 1957 for outspoken criticisms of corruption. He was readmitted in 1979, then expelled again in 1987 and inexplicably given a visa to travel the West." Harrison squeezes his lips shut and stares at us, shaking his head. Such mixed signals have been coming out of China since it reopened this decade.

"It's a mammoth clam," Harrison says with a grimace,"that will open cautiously and close tightly, if threatened." Today, the deposed Mr. Liu teaches "Chinese Literature and Society in the 1980s" at UCLA, before heading on to Harvard and Paris. It seems odd to disembark in his homeland, as he arrives on our own campus.

"Finding the precise word for the voiceless heart's tone," Confucius wrote in *Ta Hsio,* or *The Great Digest,* "means not deceiving yourself, as in hating a bad smell or loving a lovely person, also called respecting your own nose.

"In this instance, the real man looks his heart in the eye, even when he is alone."

II

Meeting the Chinese at Dawn

But if we are ever to communicate with the orient, or cohabit a planet rapidly becoming more quickly circumnavigable, had we not better try to find the proportions, try perhaps to collect some of our own better writers (of the ages) to present to our oriental contemporaries, rather than offer them an unmixed export of grossness, barbarities, stove pipes and machine guns?
—EZRA POUND, 1938

Roberta Hill Whiteman

Joseph, Maxine, Earll Hong Kingston

A Writer's China

Imperial Palace

Jeannine Johnson at the Great Wall

Fruit pedlars

A WRITER'S CHINA

Robert Rees

The Great Wall Tourist Trade

Beijing Traffic

Waking Beijing

WE AWAKE BEFORE FOUR A.M. and leave the darkened hotel for a three-and-a-half-hour walk through the capital city. In addition to being strong-minded and quite clear about herself, Jeannine is strikingly tall, even by western standards—five-foot-ten and Scots red-haired, with heaps of auburn curls piled up in waves. She walks through a Beijing crowd like a masthead, a crowd of amazed Chinese in tow, catching a glimpse of the tallest woman they've ever seen on their streets, with the reddest hair in Red China. Some venture close enough to notice my blond eyebrows and innocently reach over to touch them. It feels like being on a strange planet with other humanoids not quite believing we're human.

So we limber up with Tai Chi Chuan in the park among the gathering elders and caged birds. Painted eyebrow thrushes in bamboo cages chirrup in the early sun. The children lollygag to school, the younger ones dressed in flaring reds and yellows. Their brightness contrasts with the basic Mao blue and khaki dun on the adults.

"Shsss," an eighty-year-old Tai Chi master laughs at losing his balance on "return to mountain." The sparrows in the sparse trees chatter the dawn. *Yielding, like ice about to melt,* Lao Tsu advises, *simple, like uncarved blocks of wood.*

Wearing white gauze masks, small women sweep the sidewalks with handmade whisk brooms. The cyclists come out one by one, then in pairs, then in coveys by six a.m. Flying Pigeon and Phoenix are the deluxe bicycle models, Unicorn and Butterfly the economy wheels. By seven, the young are busily pedaling their ways to work; by eight, it's gridlock at every intersection. Three and a half million Beijing bicycles ignore the street lights and flood both directions at once.

Men amble along the roadsides, rhythmically swaying covered thrush cages from each arm. "Birds feel like they flying," an old man tells us, jostling his cages. During the Red Guard craze, there were no birdsongs. Most flying things were eradicated a decade before by starving millions; birds in cages were considered bourgeois decadence. Now little more than a decade later, the young trot off to school noisily, soldiers saunter by, birders gather in the green parks. Everyone seems busy with purpose, direction, a sense of place. The sun rises dusky saffron over the low, old buildings of this ancient city.

Beijing works on a human scale of foot and bike traffic. It's absolutely nothing like Los Angeles, where machines rule the public domain. Pedestrians munch fried bean curd, catered on-the-go out of brown butcher paper. Acquaintances talk and smoke, then clatter off. Gasoline contraptions, the occasional scooter or three-wheel dumpster, remain oddities, except for the commuter-crammed buses. Even so, this is a modern city with its attendant complaints. "I hate those buses stinking of toothpaste, dirty socks and greasy hair!" a cyclist told reporters in Beijing, a few years back in *Chinese Profiles*.

Early morning Beijing is a city with purpose, Chinese practicality in motion. People's values remain humanly oriented, the needs personal—food, shelter, things-to-do, family, future. No poverty, drunkenness, or homelessness is evident on the streets. JJ hears one argument between a man and a woman at a bus stop. We witness one kitchen squabble, see two guys hunker to play cards on the walk, and discover a crowd of Tai Chi septuagenarians in the park, their bird cages hung on tree racks. Less than twenty years ago, the Red Guard terrorized this city, beating, jailing, and killing suspected opposition. Nearly all intellectuals and artists were "sent to the country" for reeducation. Writers "laid aside the pen" to swab public toilets, swill pigs, shovel trenches, and muse on factory assembly lines. Anyone suspected of Western bourgeois tendencies was punished; artists publically "confessed" their decadence and "reformed" their minds.

Today, a spring Yellow Wind drives the Gobi Desert across this city, a sandblast all the way from Afghanistan. The thick dust silts our lungs with every breath. Though state law forbids it, Beijingers notoriously hawk and spit in the streets. Add the insult of smoke from the soft coal briquets, used for cooking and heating (there are no trees left to burn, scant wild birds). The Chinese take to wearing face masks, and Westerners develop serious respiratory diseases here. When the internal combustion engine invades Beijing, this city will be uninhabitable.

"Help, I can't stand it," JJ says, emerging flustered from a public toilet. "There are five ground holes in there, with two-foot walls on the sides of each hole. Everyone squats down and pees together!" Maybe men do have some advantages, I think to myself.

"As the tallest female for five thousand miles around, I'm the target of staring squads, even in the bathroom!" The stench wafts a block down the street from common sewage pits, where workmen shovel "night honey" into open wheelbarrows and carry it off to the fields.

"It's something like growing up in Nebraska," I make a lame joke.

"Can you believe how they hack mucous everywhere?" JJ's voice rises to a shrill, then she checks her outburst and looks abashed. Along the streets, men lean over, hold one nostril, and blow snot out the other. She says more discretely under her breath, "Wherever we go, there are globs of slimy fluids!"

"Just walk around them," I mutter. "Treat them like cow paddies back home."

Low-tech housing predominates—the *pingfang* or tile-roofed one-story units in *hutang* corridors that look like tenement alleys. This ancient stonework is rebuilt from the rubble of countless invasions and revolutions, civil wars and industrial fiascos. Ubiquitously, coal dust powders everyone's lungs.

A wall of creature cages lines a restaurant exterior. Inside are live puppies, monkeys, snakes, strange critters like armadillos, cats, and unrecognizable beasts. Diners pick their animals, go inside, and half and hour later eat them.

As Jeannine and I return to the hotel, the first person we meet is our Beijing translator and escort, Henry Chen.

"Out for stroll?" he asks with a smile. "You get up early, friends, even for Beijingers."

"The time lag, you know," I fumble to explain, "it's late afternoon back home."

"Just watching the city come to life," JJ says with a wink. "Ken here wanted to try out his Tai Chi with the park bird-watchers. And I joined him to get a whiff of the steamed dumplings sold on the sidewalks."

"Well come join us for second breakfast," Chen offers graciously, "many things to do today, many peoples to meet." There is something instantly likeable about Xiao Chen, as Bob calls him, "younger" brother. Maybe it's the boyish grin, or his quickness—the keen way he takes charge—or simply his assumed name, Henry. I wonder where that tag comes from.

Henry Chen organizes a "small shop" party with our "free tourist dollars," and half a dozen capitalists troop out to shop 'til we drop. Stores carry handcrafts simply unknown in the States, but we can only buy in designated state "tourist shops." I start something of a stampede ordering a "chop" of black jade with my name and the ideograph of a bear, plus cinnabar ink pot. Allen Ginsberg showed me his chop a few years back, when he stamped his collected poems, so I had a design already in mind. No better country than China to locate a personal "sign" and consider one's lineage. Culture signals here with ancient meaning.

"The food is mildly spiced, just wonderful," JJ is pleased to report, "not like southern California Szechwan cooking, and there's loads of it along the streets."

"Watch out for the puppy-tender chicken," Ernie jokes, "that looks like duck. Your Sioux partner might get them mixed up, dog-sniffing around the streets."

One of our translators is a thirtyish UCLA graduate student in Comparative Literature, a trilingual poet, calligrapher, and scholar born in Korea. She says that her name, *Shu-mei Shih*, means "beautiful history book." Shu-mei has a gently round face, moon-like and alert, and a dragon-quick intelligence. Like a good Taoist, she always seems to be questioning and speaks in a melodic pointillism, her words darting across a subject, as her eyes light up.

"*Su Tung Po* is my favorite Taoist poet," Shu-mei tells me. "He's known as *Su Shih* of the Sung Dynasty—*I write as the clouds and water flow*, he said—and late in his life became a Buddhist."

"The Chinese make much of first impressions," our translator reflects, up and down the scale of her voice. Her voice carries a touch of warning in the Middle Kingdom. "There's an eighth-century play about men and women meeting. Since the women were sequestered, this was their only chance to make a match. Imagine that!—details of dress, gesture, expression, speech, and all sorts of subtle mannerisms would make or break a union." She looks at me with edged wonder. "Don't you think this is poignant?"

"Romantic destiny would be more than magazine stuff," I venture, then smile at her. "One arrow, one life, they say on the plains."

The People and the Pen

The Tao that can be told is not the everlasting Tao.
The name that can be named is not the everlasting name.
—LAO TSU

AT THE BEIJING WRITERS RECEPTION, artists counterface like politicians in overstuffed arm chairs, two parallel rows down a long smoky room. We sit stiffly, but go along with the prearranged structure. Awkward formality, the Chinese feel, is preferable to the chaos of change. History has taught them that someone is sure to take offence or lose face in the risks of disruption. Disastrously, thirty million Chinese starved during the 1950s Great Leap Forward. Their leaders have learned to move carefully, with small steps.

We long-legged Americans wait quietly, jet-lagging, trying to strike diplomatic poses. It's not easy for writers, not this bunch of individuals. We might be denounced by some of our own homeboy compatriots as "hooligans." Red Guard cant would have labeled us "capitalist roaders." I can see only Roberta next to me, Maxine across the way, Bob at the far end with the leaders, and Charles part way down the opposite line. The Chinese writers—all thirty-seven men and one lone woman—drink their ubiquitous tea, smoke and chat. The reception is clearly their show, and they try to appear at ease. With an affable lawyer's smile, the Minister of Culture, Wang Meng, sits directly opposite me. A rather blunt female translator perches on his left, and the Assistant Minister, Ying Ruocheng, sits to her left. The latter is a novelist, laconic coyote and sometime actor, who played the movie inquisitor in "The Last Emperor."

In historic session, the 37th Chinese Peoples' Congress has convened across town. Some of these diplomats have broken away to attend our soiree. Clearly politics, international exchange, a new liberalization, and some measure of cultural freedom buzz in the air, though in point of fact, it's hard to breathe in Beijing, given the coal smoke, Gobi dust, bus CO_2, and a male penchant for Raleigh's stinking weed. At least Beijingers ride bicycles.

We introduce ourselves individually as Americans, speaking our own minds, no voice-overs. By contrast, the Chinese leader, Feng Mu, gives abbreviated and awkward introductions for all thirty-seven of his comrades. The monologue tends to blur.

Our hosts seem to resemble the unearthed Xian clay effigies of the emperor's court retinue come to life. My mind wanders, and I wonder what impressions we implant. Our women strike me as formidable. Maxine is a small, powerfully impassive woman. She holds her ground in the fissures between Sino-American cultures, one still male chauvinist, the other materialist with a curse. Roberta is full-bodied and sweetly shy. She speaks for tribal concerns in a country that decimated native peoples by some ninety-seven percent. Alice asks hard and sensitive questions, fiery in a very feminine way. Jay Wright presents himself with calm dignity. Charles Wright, his Southern counterpart, seems a bit nervous with this public speaking. He sits somewhat gangly in his jeans and tennis shoes. A veteran of Vietnam, Larry Heinemann is even more painfully boyish, blitzkrieg novelist of Bravo Company trenches. With a cast on his arm, Barry Lopez sits quietly dazed. Bob Rees makes the bureaucratic gestures with finesse, keeps the show rolling, and plays group leader with a low profile. Harrison Salisbury settles into the head diplomat's role with a blend of Midwestern ease and elderly pomp. What stirs beneath the surface of all these impressions?

The contrasts between East and West draw my attention initially. Hammers, shovels, scissors, and picks work as primary instruments in rebuilding China, and so do words serve as practical tools of the body politic. Reading is widely popular. Press runs for books of serious poetry can be 100,000 to 200,000 copies, and people buy books inexpensively. The literary-cultural journal, *Word Vision,* an editor tells me, carries half a million distribution. The writer in China believes in a readership, serves the needs of the people, and enjoys certain prestige, a few even a state salary. Our host Chinese Writers Association with chapters in every city serves as a powerful cultural and political arm of the peoples' movement—not as a hack instrument of the state, but as a respected humanist voice. Words count in China.

In the United States, literary matters appear somewhat differently. In the designs of "high art," for the most part where I teach academically, style precedes content. How something is said, the formula goes, *is what it is.* Beyond the university canon, our writers-at-large indulge a circumstantial freedom to say what they please, in manners they freely choose. The marketplace is our policy maker. Dramatists need audiences, and publishers print books to sell, while serious writers divide over art-for-art's sake. The bottom line: it's hard to make a living as an American author, unless you teach, even though a few popular writers do sell mass paperbacks. Stephen King, Tony Hillerman, Judith Krantz got rich on popular fiction, and Ronald Reagan's favorite author, Louis L'Amour, wrote over ninety books that sold millions. That's the American writer's dream, while a majority make next to nothing with New York publishers or Hollywood studios. "Free" verse, free style, or freedom of choice may have freed many from a reading audience and sustaining trade.

Poetic matters are worse. American press runs for a promising book of verse range anywhere from five hundred to five thousand copies. The literary journals and "little" poetry magazines are scanned mostly by academics. Writers are certainly underpaid, hanging from the sleeves of colleges and universities. Hardly a poet earns a living on poetry alone.

Except for sensationalist fiction, New York drama, or Hollywood film, precious few writers have any sense of a following, a communal purpose, an ideological vision, or a traditional past. Television (alas) may be our most popular medium for "the people." When film companies buy a script, they tear it up, fire the author, and shoot their own made-up version. Writers play second fiddle to matinee idols, slick cops, and shapely nurses.

So we are "free," for better or worse, from the coercions, persuasions, and collectivities of socialist politics. Indeed we are "free" from a community-based aesthetics that would impose guidelines on our writing, reading, or viewing. We seem lonely, our "art" cries out, as colonized consumers, and our anti-intellectual history haunts us. Jamestown colonists, all men, were scratching a living from the new land, no time for *belles lettres.* The anti-elitist work ethic stands Puritan firm today.

Thus the contexts for writing in China and the United States appear fundamentally different. Baldly put, there's a crevass between Oriental content and Occidental form. The year before I was born, May 1942, the Communists were at war with Chiang Kai-shek's Nationalists *and* the Japanese invaders. Mao Zedong lectured his comrades at the Yenan Forum on Art and Literature and stressed the need for a "cultural army" to unite the people through the "rich and lively language of the masses." Mao dismissed high art "without savor or sap." He charged that a "crowd of students who could neither fetch nor carry for themselves" would never unify or rebuild China. Back in 1927, Mao fashioned his own hammer-and-sickle inside a red star flag. Though the intellectuals' "hands" might be "soiled and their feet smeared with cow dung," their petit-bourgeois voices remained suspect. "The masses do not appreciate your high-sounding talk," Mao hectored aesthetes. "The more you put on airs as veteran 'heroes,' and the harder you try to sell your ideas, the more the people refuse to be impressed."

Recent party doctrine is underlayered with ancient collective thinking and conditions the Chinese to consider foremost "what" they say as a body of people. Literature, popular in the broadest sense, is shaped toward an end, a purpose, a need in China. *How will these words affect our readers?* Chinese writers ask, and *What do the people need to know?* Didactic intent does not rule out formal grace.

Harrison insisted at breakfast that the Party, the leaders, in effect the "moral majority" lift heavy hands normatively in China. At the same time, a much desired, if limited, freedom of expression seems stirring at present. So what is determined *good* for the whole is deemed *right* by declaration, and so propagated. *One Family, One Child*, for example, now states policy for 1.2 billion people. The prescript is advertised on billboards, in slogans, at block rallies, and through penalty taxes. Women report their monthly periods to block captains, according to some reports. Since the 1949 revolution, the Chinese life span has doubled from thirty-five to seventy, and the population, from the 1960s to the 1980s, has swollen by some four hundred million. And yet, less than four percent of the people are Party members, and some eighty percent live in the country. That too is changing. Six hundred million peasants will soon be displaced by mechanized farming and relocated in the cities.

After telling us all this over "fried eggs," Harrison looks down at his greasy plate and scowls. Over-population and joblessness among a billion hungry mouths do not vanish in an ideological debate, but grow to biological imperative. In a culture of male dominance, couples quietly abort female foetuses, while others worry about a generation of pampered boys indulged by doting relatives, historically accustomed to large families. Harrison's ice-blue eyes hold the point.

From breakfast to our state sitting, my mind tries to pull these thoughts together. If all this critical difference seems the schism between writers in the two countries, open to exception (political, evangelical, or get-rich books), issues of publishing freedom cast old shadows. Here lie the literary yang and yin of the *I Ching*, some 4,500 years old in China, the sunny and shady sides of the worthsmith's hill.

And we sit here in the Great Hall to collaborate on convergent concerns and divergent contexts: how "the word" moves our readers, or how art works best in given contexts. Indeed, how does "freedom" (from or to?) mean different things to different peoples? How do writers reach across differing languages, cultures, histories, and ideologies to connect? Basically, we're here to discuss how we live this process called writing, from independence, to teaching, to serving the state, to speaking from and for "the people."

Roberta and I quietly play pass-the-pen (in the banquet rush she forgot hers) as we sit through droning speech after speech. "Like graduate school, eh Ken?" she whispers. Bobbi is large-boned and tall as myself, with dark ringlets and brown owlish eyes, skipping behind plastic-rimmed glasses. "My clan is Turtle," she says lowering her gaze. I ask my new Iroquois friend, by notepad, how she "got started writing blank verse," and she scribbles back, "Richard Hugo inspired me. My family wanted me to be a doctor. I got a B.A. in psychology as a compromise, writing in stolen moments."

"How did you get into poetry?" I scratch on the pad.

"A teacher in Minneapolis told me to study with Hugo in Montana." Now she's on a three-year fellowship leave from Wisconsin-Eau Claire to complete a Ph.D. in American Studies at the University of Minnesota. The only other Indian I know with a native doctorate is Paula Gunn Allen, my Pueblo colleague.

There will be considerable genuflecting this trip. The "administrators" stretch the metaphors thin, or they pound decorum into the ground. The favorite Chinese saying among comrades, "Old friends," means, "Didn't I meet you two years ago in Malibu? Four years ago at the Great Wall?" Some Americans say it feels like "coming home" to Beijing, but "like" turns on a precious few days, four years ago. For the moment, I'm unconvinced. Are we saying simply that it's good to be here among "like minds," moving toward friendship, a global "family" of man? JJ squints at the men, Maxine and Alice take them on. Ah, here's the rub: where *are* the women, old pals? "If only I were a man," says a woman in *Dream of the Red Chamber*, the foremost classical novel of China, "I could do something."

We bring three honest-to-God women writers, two poets and a novelist: Chinese-American, mixed-blood Oneida, and working-class New Yorker. Tillie Olson and Carolyn Forché dropped out at the last minute. So Maxine, then Roberta, then Alice ask more or less probing, if not inflammatory, questions about the absence of women today. Daughter of a stowaway to the New World, Maxine stresses there's "no such thing" as the Chinese and the American "sides" to things. She's the embodiment of their collaboration across the waters. "You men should be ashamed not to bring women writers to this forum," she challenges bluntly. "Where is the revolution of women's liberation?" There are still rumors of men beating women across China, selling them, trading them for pigs and cows, tossing female infants down wells.

Roberta accents her "people's" sense of themselves as Oneida natives. "We know who we are, in the face of historical disaster. We are rebuilding our cultures, mothering our people." Alice strikes to the social quick— asking about feminist organizations, women in the labor force, and men sharing family duties with the children. Following Maxine's lead, she asks again, "Where are your women writers in this conference?"

The Chinese old boys are caught with their pants on backwards. After finessing our feminist challenges as honest questions, Bob tries to rescue the discussion with a quip about too "solemn" exchanges among new friends. The Chinese old boys strike up steam-room jokes to steer away from these feminist cliffs.

Much of the verbal punning is lost on us, as is the collegial teasing, but one joke tells the tale, delivered by Zhong Jieying, magpie among the bunch. Zhong is an innocently mocking rhymster on the surface, who makes up extemporaneous lyrics, playing between English and Chinese tongues. "The multi-tonal *ma* says it all," Zhong tells us through the translator, Henry. "Mandarin has four tones, Cantonese nine. Up high *ma* means 'mother.' Rising middle to high means 'hemp.' Falling, then rising means 'horse.' High to low means 'scold'."

Henry pauses and looks impish, as Zhong continues. "Yet *ni hao ma* means 'Hello, how are you?' *Ma* indicates asking."

Zhong smirks, and Henry translates the joke deadpan, "Awkward

American at dinner party reverses word order, *ma ni hao,* asking maiden Chinese hostess, 'Mother, how are you?' She takes insult. He try again, 'Hemp, how are you?' Further insult. 'Horse, how are you?' man voice wavers. 'It's good to scold you,' he blurts in Chinese." Henry seems relieved to come to the end of the joke and smiles self-deprecatingly. The Chinese delegates roar and puff on their cigarettes.

The comic possibilities seem endless, hence the point: an anciently encoded, multi-tonal tongue, Chinese can be played on exquisitely by native speakers. It is next to impossible for an outsider to master, simply a blank wall to translate precisely. Puns layer the tonal variations and lead to endless tittering, if not insinuation. In a round-about way, the Chinese men answer our feminist broadsides, in effect saying, "Thank you, no thanks, ladies, we'll handle our own concerns here in China." Perhaps it's a parlor lesson in diplomacy.

Incorrigibly, Mr. Zhong tells the story of a Chinese-American student's "letter home" in broken verse that mangles the mother tongue. He then tosses off another pun, "About Face," on the title of Harrison's best seller, *The Long March.* This sparks the Assistant Minister of Culture to spin a joke on an American offering a "gift of love" to an unwilling Chinese maiden. "I don't want your gift" mistranslates as "I love you," and the fun is on.

After what seems an interminable battery of old-boy humor, followed by stiff pauses and cigarettes, we Westerners try to look amused and "at home." I offer a stale American Indian bromide. "What did the natives say at Plymouth Rock when they saw the Mayflower sails?"

"How long you think they'll stay?" Henry translates into Mandarin. That empties the room. Our tearoom fête grinds to a halt, with Colonel Sanders occupying Tiananmen Square.

I risk the rush-hour streets to check on some personalized signature chops, as a flood of humanity goes home from work. No individual exists apart from the others in China—theirs is a sociology of numbers, massive tribalization. And I stroll alone among them in my grey wool suit, red dress shirt, and Italian silk tie with a Navajo turquoise-and-silver tack. A few Yugoslavs from the hotel ogle, going the other direction.

Back at the hotel, my dinner companion is a staff reporter from *China Daily,* the country's leading English newspaper. He says writers can and do speak more freely (stressing the relative degree in "more"), but still the editors cut about thirty percent from what he writes. "It's not a bad average," he says, "even in the West."

Yu Wentao seems straightforward with me, speaks wryly of the speechmaking, and offers to translate my work into Chinese. He especially wants to see *Indi'n Humor*. Mr. Yu has been to the Colville Indian Reservation in Washington for one day and wants to know more about what the Chinese call "Indyaner Amerikan," as does the editor of a leading publishing house, also a novelist, sitting to my right. All this transpires over Beijing delicacies, sprinkled liberally with bell and nut peppers, and good Chinese beer. We've been warned not to drink the water. Most Chinese drink sweet soda, and their guests are offered white wine.

"If thirty-six of thirty-eight writers here are neither poets nor women," I ask, "what forms of writing do they follow?"

"Their own forms," says Yu Wentao, my reporter friend. He translates "Dear Abby" for his newspaper. From the gist of formal addresses so far, writers concentrate on what is being said, less than how to say it. *Why* and *what* take precedence over *self*-expression. This becomes a question not just of technique, but of primary intent and content.

Are writers here, I ask Mr. Yu, pressed to act as sociologists or folklorists or propagandists? Are they then "interpreters" of the "people" from a party line?

"Depends on the writer," he says, "but you can't forget the peoples' needs or government big brother. Art is not just beauty in China." From the bureaucratic boilerplate thus far, I fear that collective art may have its way of snuffing not only free expression, but lyric grace.

"Imagine Jesse Helms taking an aesthetic line of attack on communism," JJ muses later in our hotel room.

> *Tsai Yu was sleeping in day-time. Confucius said: Rotten wood cannot be carved; a wall of dung won't hold plaster, what's the use of chastising him?*
>
> *He said: When I started I used to hear words, and believe they would be acted on; now I listen to what men say and observe what they do.*
>
> —THE ANALECTS

Blue Dragon Spring

THIS IS THE CHINESE YEAR OF THE DRAGON, "First of the Animals of the Four Directions," an image of eastern rebirth. The Taoist quadrant system—Blue Dragon in the east, Scarlet Bird in the south, White Tiger in the west, Somber Warrior in the north—doubles with many Native American ideas of the "four winds," where tribal images in coded color flesh time out traditionally. Black Elk's "Great Vision" images the fall blue west with rainstorms and lightning, the wintry white north with healing herbs and migrating geese, the spring red east with daybreak star and medicine pipe, the summer yellow south with sacred hoop and flowering staff.

Spring swells in the buds on the trees. The earth lies hardpacked, a composite of clays and fine Gobi sands, time physicalized. In the countryside, the fields give off ocher and rust, almost Sierra Madre brickreds. The foothills leading up to the Great Wall remind me of the dry eastern Sierra Nevada slopes with scant rainfall. Sky is the color of dust, the stubble short and brown. The horizon kneels beneath an ash tarp, the dished earth chopped up for seeding, harrowed squares in brown patches.

The Chinese have begun a massive tree planting campaign to reforest a country defoliated over a millennium ago. Most of the country's timber was cut down, burned, and carved up. The remaining orchards hug the hardpan—elms, some poplars, pines, hardy fruit trees such as apple, quince, pear, persimmon, and a kind of locust tree, whose seedpods fly like miniature lace kites in the wind. There's no snowmelt to feed the streams, hence a vast and dessicated peneplain stretches all the way across the Gobi to Yugoslavia. The modest rain and snowfall have all run off, and the land is terribly dry, reminding me of childhood Great Plains in late March. Survival comes the hard way, low to the ground. China has over a billion people to feed, little arable land (less than 20 per cent of the land mass farmable, given the vast mountains and desert), and relatively moderate resources. The numbers are staggering—the population of the United States plus a *thousand million* more hungry mouths.

Everywhere people are busy building, rebuilding, digging, pedaling countless bicycles, or driving brisk lorries that do the basic work of China—carting, hauling, trucking, schlepping. Along the highway there may be three hundred men hand-trenching for a waterpipe system. Up the power line pole scale two repairmen. In the highway crowd, the buses and vans and motorized bikes and more pedal-powered two-wheelers bump along. Small suburban shops, ramshackle as any in the suburbs of Rome or London, line the roadside, while hundreds of unfinished highrise apartments girder the skies. This is not bigger, better, faster by American standards, but reconstructing on a human scale, the imprint of human hands, sweat, blood, and common frustration.

Chinese collectivity came by way of a terrible bloodletting, to be sure—at least three million landlords executed in the late 1940s and early 1950s. To repeat a crucial point, up to thirty million more starved in The Great Leap Forward, a dismal failure at collective production. Everyone stopped farming and read Mao's little red book. Soon there was no food, and people ate birds, mice, weeds, and sawdust. Grass soup was the national staple. "Even the worms were hungry," peasants said. Ripples of terror, aftershocks as it were, coursed down through the rampages of the Red Guard: Mao liquidating the "four pests," the sacrificing of dogs and cats during starvation, and abuses of "roaders" out of favor during any given reform. A revolution feeds on scapegoats. For forty years, the "five black categories" were landlords, rich peasants, counter-revolutionaries, rightists, and "bad elements." Anyone could be accused.

*

The Great Wall

"WELL, TERRORISM ISN'T ISOLATED TO CHINA," Bob points out on our bus ride to the Great Wall. "In Nazi Europe, or Afrikaner South Africa, or Muslim Bosnia, violence has been the *cost* of progress. Rationalized at the time as *manifest* destiny, the United States rolled over Native Americans with fascist resolve. Peace is the issue today—how to make and keep it, locally and globally." That includes Norman Cousins' agenda, which designates Bob as the boss of our cattle drive across China.

If You Haven't Climbed the Great Wall, a crimson billboard announces along the highway in Chinese and English, *You Haven't Lived*. It's an old Chinese proverb. "Love China, Repair Her Great Wall" has became the party slogan. The thing itself, *Chang Cheng*, is a magnificent stone snake that wends its way through mountains and across deserts across northern

China for 10,000 *li,* or about 6,000 kilometers. Qin Shi Huangdi, from whom the name China derives, built the Great Wall in the third century before Christ. Legend has it that the Tang emperor was entombed with 10,000 clay soldiers. Imagine something like a walled fortress, from L.A. across the Angeles Mountains and Mojave Desert, negotiating the Grand Canyon and Continental Divide into Denver, then trailing across the plains, snaking through the Alleghenies, and leveling out in Manhattan. Li Po wrote of war south of the Great Wall:

> *War last year at the Sang-kan's headwaters,*
> *war this year on the roads at Ts-ung River:*
>
> *we've washed weapons clean in T'iao-chih sea-swells,*
> *winter pastured horses in T'ien Mountain's snowy grasses.*
>
> *War in ten-thousand-mile campaigns*
> *leaves our Three Armies old and broken,*
>
> *but the Hsiung-nu have made slaughter their spring plowing.*
> *It never changes: nothing from ancient times but*
> > *whitened bones in fields of yellow sand.*
>
> *A Ch'in emperor built the Great Wall to wall Mongols out,*
> *and still, in the Han, we're torching beacon flames bright.*

As Barry says, the Great Wall is the only man-made form on earth discernible from the moon. Its foundation goes back to Confucius' day, when the many Chinas of warring lords tried to consolidate against the Mongolian "barbarians" to the north. The Shandong people are big and tough and make good policemen. So China walled the northerners out with millions of stones, hand architected by millions more men across the mountain passes and out across the desert. The Wall also served to protect the Silk Road to Persia and the Mediterranean markets.

The Gobi wind gusts sharply, and there's late winter bite in the spring cold. The wall humps solidly along the spines of the ridges, notched in classic patterns, wide enough for six horses or ten men abreast, and solid as Gilbraltar. Charles Wright carves a poem out of the scene:

> *North wind like a fine drill*
> > *sky Ming porcelain for a thousand miles*
> *The danger of what's-to-come is not in its distance*
> *Two inches can break the heart*

Whether or not it kept the hordes out, this Great Wall unified masses in a common labor, a stand against the outside. It was an ancient Star Wars concept that today seems outdated. Who's "other" anymore? BBC shortwave pipes into China. CBS television, Mercedes Benz buses, Western rock music, Kentucky Fried Chicken across from Mao's tomb: Computerland finances our first writers exchange. All this *modernization* updates and perhaps antiquates the Wall, more symbolic than defensive necessity. In fact, *we* are the "other," especially our out-spoken women writers. The Chinese government has invited and paid us to visit with our decadent poems, bold ideas, feminist firebrands, and bourgeois prose. This all seems funny when we get to talking, writers to writers, East to West. "Quite a stir you make," Henry refers to the Beijing meeting yesterday. "Many fireflies and crackers in the air."

Questions of intent, form, content, reader response, feminism, dialogue, truth and beauty bubble up like so much cultural soda. There may be some fixed opinions among American writers, a few paranoias, plenty of suspicions (endemic to artists), but few universals. "Have no twisty thoughts," Pound translated Confucius, and Frost answered, truly American, with the "straight crookedness" of a good walking stick. "Freedom," we want to know, "how free are you to express yourselves?" All the while we question our own freedom to say and do what we please.

"Henry," I tell my escort, "Americans don't know when to keep their mouths shut. We've got an obsession with confronting issues."

"OK, boss, no problem," he says in a clipped voice. "I just translate."

Our saving grace may be an open mind, balancing on the due mean or unwobbling pivot of "heart's-eye." This is the Chinese ideogram for composure. The Lakota say something similar of integrity, *çante ista* or "heart's eye." As long counseled in China—*wei wu wei*—look into your heart *not* going against nature.

My name-tag name is transcribed *Ken*, the moon shining up through a stop-and-go sign, on either side of *Lin* or Forest, two trees side-by-side, hence Ken Lin Ken: 肯林肯. Abraham Lincoln, the Great Emancipator, already got his personal Chinese chop, so mine must be improvised. Everything means something more than it appears in such an anciently cultivated culture.

Arriving among the Great Wall hawkers, this capitalist roader buys two fur hats, a hand crocheted tablecloth, five old coins to throw the *I Ching*, a

Mongolian Buddha, three chunks of iridescent glass, and a picture book.

Bobbi sits in a stone alcove on the Great Wall and composes lines in her scarred notebook:

WOLF SMOKE

I'm that nomad woman tossed from the lap of dawn,
faithful only to the yellow dust
driving itself to the sea.

Look at me, guard of a riddle, this Great Wall
where a wedge of five horsemen rides
on watch for us. Barbarians, you say.

Feel motion a magnet in your blood
when you signal from the tower,
lighting your fire of wolf dung.

Even while wolf smoke skitters across
the turquoise dome of our common home, the sky,
I'll still ricochet over my astonishing wasteland.

My orphan blood bears witness
to the crime of being kept out,
my crime of blasting through,

the crime for us to speak together of our love
for wind, humming as it does,
from the Gobi to the Sahara,

from the Aracama to the Great Plains.
On my tongue, it never tastes the same.
Yet that same wind

now ruffles our hair. On each strand it writes
the names of those we've loved,
the names of those we've lost.

Why must you prod those masons
hemmed inside ten feet of stone?
My longing to know you lights the wolf's red eyes

when it meets your fire this coming twilight.
Out here, cold rain means ravine,
but the sheen on mulberry leaves

often draws us into dancing.
Dark as roots, your eyes uncover mine and make
me hesitate, waiting for some splendor

to rise within this moment
where we yet may call a greeting
instead of bleeding for each other.

*

Tai Chi and Caged Thrushes
He who stands on tiptoe is not steady.
—LAO TSU

SUNRISE IN BEIHAI PARK, once part of the Imperial Palace, with lake water lapping, birds singing in cages, old men talking and smoking. Groups perform communal Tai Chi guided by white-gloved teachers, while other elders warm up with Chinese rock and roll imported from Taiwan, *laonian disike*, popularly known as "old folks' disco." Pods of people dot the park, from joggers, to fishermen, to many forms and levels of Tai Chi, to stationary Yoga postures, to ceremonial swordplay. In the evening at the opera, we see how these stylized movements shape ballet, mime, acrobatics, fencing, and classical comedy—a people's theater eclectically combining the high and low arts of China. Imagine that the Los Angeles Music Center and Venice carnival boardwalk met midway on the west side.

At first light we branch out—Ernie cassette-taping morning sounds for his kinetic sculpture, Earll and his son Joseph jogging around the lake, Bob and Barry with Henry interviewing the old men about their birds, Maxine and Bobbi shyly miming an old Tai Chi master, Jeannine with a large group doing aesthetic calisthentics (rub your nose ten times, slap your knees, etc.). I try out some basic Tai Chi forms by the lake, along with Yoga sun salutations. After twenty years of these exercises, I'm addicted to starting the day with meditations at the water's edge.

"What a wonderful way to wake up!" Maxine chirps, dropping her reserve. "We should *all* be doing this back home! Let's take this Tai Chi back for everybody, Ken, will you help me?"

A wizened little man with a Fu Manchu moustache catches 200 spiders each morning and brings them to the park to sell, seven for ten cents. The bottled spiders feed the caged birds. Collecting spiders, he can make more than a factory worker. The bird men, in turn, sell their thrushes for about forty yuan or ten dollars. So the live spiders in wrapped tubes of graph paper feed the caged birds, who in turn sing for the old men. During the revolution they had no birds, no Tai Chi in the park, no songs of freedom, no yuan.

"What a sad thing to be a single old man," the birdman says his thrush sings, "and *my* bird can imitate the sound of a cat." A young toymaker, who's taught himself English from radio lessons each day, wants "funny money," or tourist currency, to buy a colored TV. "Change money?" comes the familiar street greeting. I have none. He tags along anyway, curious about these morning Americans mingling with the old people, birds, and exercisers.

With ten of us heading back, the taxi drivers are fearful of getting tickets for more than four passengers in a cab, now that the city is awake and the patrols are out. Bob and I volunteer to walk around a couple of hours and meet at 9 a.m. near the Forbidden City's south gate.

The back streets of Beijing bustle with people getting up. Brushing teeth on the front step is a state-mandated reform (dental packages are left in our hotel room). People are greeting, going to work, "sweeping the dirt" (no paving, so they broom the hardpan), eating, and reading the newspapers posted on billboard public areas. Bob and I stroll to the old dragon Bell Tower, talking of our pasts, plans, and delights in this city and country.

"The hands-on feel of these streets, packed clay and all, remind me of my boyhood in the west," Bob reminisces. "You know, we grew up much the same, Ken. Our fathers went crazy with booze. Our mothers were deep down frustrated with male obstinacy. Working-class hard-pan, that was some beginning, the horizon always beckoning. Did you ever dream of coming to China?"

"I never thought I'd get out of Nebraska, Bob. It still seems like I'm leaving home for Oz."

Bob and I sample life on the streets—photographing, taking notes, talking—testing a Beijing worker's breakfast of twisted frybread in a long bun, something like a screw donut.

"Not bad," Bob muses, "nothing like Bagelmania, but tasty."

Later we stop in a workers' small cafe, sort of a soupline, and order another frybread roll and soybean milk gruel.

"This tastes sweet, like mild coconut milk," Bob says reflectively. Raised a Mormon near cowboys and Indians in Arizona and Colorado, his family ravaged by alcoholism, Bob has a serious air about him. He's genial, kindly in the best western sense—morally genteel. We've been UCLA professors since 1969, and I know his value as a colleague and friend.

The streets are chaos now, more bike gridlock. A motorbike roars down the lane and almost snuffs a cyclist. Carts of leeks, bags of ginger, roasting sweet potatoes line the lanes. Everyone's industriously going about the day's business.

I locate a third sampling of street fare. My sidewalk chef cracks an egg and smears it on a thin tortilla, something like Hopi piki bread. He tosses in chopped onions, the ubiquitous frybread corded as ballast, and some hot sauce, then rolls the whole gizmo into a tasty crepe.

"It beats hotel breakfast," Bob says wryly.

For centuries, *Dog Meat Monk* has been the beloved trickster "Buddha" of China. His specialty was canine gourmet. After the 1949 revolution, indeed, when a billion people were starving, most of the dogs, cats, rodents, and birds disappeared in China. The people either ate what they found, or died.

*

The Forbidden City
I admire Confucius. He's the first man who was not divinely inspired.
—VOLTAIRE

WE RETURN TO THE HOTEL and set out on a tour of The Forbidden City. The classically ornate Imperial Palace was closed for centuries to all but royalty and its eunuch guard. The palatial grand colors—rust-red, saffron, with trimmings of kelp green and Fra Angelico blues—meld and rise brightly off the beams, fusing form in dizzying reflection. And the people seem to love being inside this "forbidden" palace, now a political and cultural relic in Communist China. The museums are exquisite and endless: we check out ceramics, metallurgy, sculpture, and scroll painting of the Ming Dynasty (1368-1644 A.D.). On the lookout for secret alcoves, JJ discovers a corridor with life-size figures in stone. The statue torsos recall Tai Chi motions—flexed knees, some leaning forward, a triple curvature in the more lively pieces—but over all the calm gaiety of Chinese classicism, the Confucian smile.

Maddy Rees has brought a beat-up football, and the courtyard expanse invites a few lobs across the ghostly paths of Chinese emperors. Before long, Barry and I team up with Maddy and Bobby in a game of touch football, a pasttime I left back in college. The boys are in far better shape than the old men, and Chinese tourists stare open-mouthed at this Western horseplay. Between middle-age jet lag and Beijing air pollution, our noses soon sting and lungs burn, so the game is over in ten minutes.

On to the Heavenly City: We stand at a spot, open to the air and sky, where voices resonate into the wind across a twenty-six-yard diameter. Acoustically designed to perfection, sound bounces around the four marble horizontal panels like a ping-pong ball. Larry Heinemann tells me of the power of an Upper Penninsula Quinalt sweat lodge he's been attending for several years.

"Nothing helped the flash-backs, you know." He pauses and sinks into himself. "The numbness always came in February, the month I came home from Vietnam. It's what physicians call delayed stress, cuz, used to be 'battle fatigue' in our dads' wars. My life felt hopeless every February, until I spent some time with the Quinalt Indians. They have ceremonies for warriors coming home—ground their men back in the culture, then retrain them to go out again as people, not killers." Larry's eyes carry what vets call the *thousand-meter stare*, a crystalline blue not to be forgotten.

I soon learned that when Larry liked you, he used familiar terms of address, even bloodlines in our case. So as we spoke, he would punctuate his sentences with "cuz" and "cousin Ken," walking down the street.

"I'm writing a book on delayed stress among Vietnam vets, then no more war stories." He smiles to himself. "Maybe a novel about Chicago baseball. You know, cuz, the wind blows so hard in Chicago," Larry adds, "it comes straight down at you."

By afternoon I need rest. My eyes are doubling, contacts sticking, gout prickling my thumbs like joint fever. Four hours' sleep a night has taken its toll, so I nap, read, and write. Then Barry Lopez and I head over to check on the chops. They've reversed L to J on mine, so I'm "Jincoln," the bear.

"I know some of your writer friends back east," Barry says. "Howard Norman and Bill Merwin and Peter Matthiessen. We go walking together, talk about everything from writing, to war, to women."

"Well say hi for me," I toss in, "or *hello and howdy*, as Larry would say." Traveling all the time, Barry is working on the landscape of "hope" at the moment. He cobbles a life together, trying to make a living outside of institutions on an Oregon farm. In another month, Barry is off to the Galapagos with fellow "walkers," then Antarctica. Pilgrim poets, peripatetic writers.

"I'm worried about an offer to take an American Studies chair at Notre Dame, my alma mater," he says, wrinkling his forehead. "Do you think I could get along with academics, let alone all those students? That committee stuff, the promotion ladder and grading, scare me. I can deal with wolves and bears just fine, but head-tripping…" His voice trails off.

"Some of us don't have a choice, Barry," I confess. "Do it if you want to sink down in one place." I force a grin and add, "If you have to work for a living. I'm not sure professing is for everyone, lots of toadies and theory mongers at your throat. I'd figure twice about academia, if you have choices. It might be hard to give up all that freedom to come and go when the spirit moves you."

The National Book Award for *Arctic Dreams*, recent attention for *Of Wolves and Men*, and now a Guggenheim have led to a popularity Barry didn't always enjoy. He's flattered by the academic offer, a bit overwhelmed, and certainly confused about leaving his Oregon farm and committing to South Bend winters. Mid-life brings us flat up against these decisions. Everything has consequences, reverberations—a lesson Barry has learned in the wilderness, now coming home.

*

"Trashcan" Buddhas
If the root is confused, nothing will be governed well.
—THE GREAT DIGEST

BOB AND HENRY PINHOLE A COUPLE OF US, Barry and myself, for five o'clock dinner with a group of Chinese writers interested in "cultural exchange." We walk Beijing streets for fifteen minutes and enter the restaurant through a delivery back alley, almost mafia-style, strolling through elegantly sculpted stone boulders along an architected lake (no wonder the Chinese so like Disneyland). Barry is nervous, mumbling about jet fatigue, and I feel the meeting start stiffly. Bob is all small talk and smiles, doing his best to break the ice.

We warm up with tea and Tsingtao, listen to our hosts pitch the offer, gauge their proposal for cultural exchange. We Americans are invited to study Chinese arts in the interests of "world peace" and a "modest" monetary exchange.

Henry winks at me and whispers, "Up-front feeler for mutual profit."

After more tea and talk, mostly listening, we begin to eat frog legs, sea urchins, tiny corn, tasty fish dishes, sauced beef and chicken, mostly gourmet fares we've not been getting in the hotel.

We've come to "make wells together," Henry translates the offer over chopsticks. He tries to find the right bi-lingual words on both sides to match the good will mixed with caution. Most of the time, I think Henry is blade-serious in his translations, some of the time he's pulling my leg.

The playright, Zhong Jieying, sizes me up over nibbles, trading quips through Henry. He remains intent on the food. Finally, in desperation to get a conversation going, I mention my research on Indian tricksters and wonder out-loud about Chinese comedy. "How does humor work in your plays?" I ask Mr. Zhong directly.

He chuckles, hesitates, pops a frog leg in his mouth, and deflects the question. "Art is to surprise people," he says through Henry, who purses his lips and speaks carefully. "If not that, art is to make people happy." Zhong tosses down another frog leg. "Failing that, art makes them sad." Again, munching reflectively, he pauses. "And if not that, it makes them think."

Zhong Jieying rattles off these prescripts like a street vendor and continues to snatch at the food with chopsticks. It's an odd mix of art talk and unmasked appetite. On the walk over, Henry said that no one gets to eat like this, until foreigners come to town.

"Does Chinese humor depend on verbal play, puns and such?" I ask.

There's a time lag, as Henry rephrases the question. Zhong responds in a dry joke about a bald old man with two wives. "It's a joke for intellectuals," Zhong says, "not workers."

The nub is lost on me, though I nod and smile. "Compliment to bald spot," Henry says soberly, "sign your wisdom." He chews a frog leg reflectively

"Compensation for being an old guy, Henry? Ask Mr. Zhong where he learned to laugh about things that puzzle us," I respond more boldly.

"Learned humor through labor," Zhong explains, via Henry, looking straight into my eyes, "shoveling pig shit with workers." He lets that sink in, munches some more. "Ah, yes, I was compelled to it. Workers have belief in their lives," Zhong thinks back, sucking on a sea urchin, "this fellow feeling grounds art."

"And how does someone learn to be a Chinese writer?" I ask.

"Ten years hard labor," Henry shoots back, not losing a beat.

We scat around subjects: pride in the Yosemite Sequoia trees, fake antique Buddhas at the Great Wall, how to train writers. Zhong has just written a smash hit, *Buddies Get Rich,* sequel to a play about slack workers, *Buddies Make Troubles.* These were take-offs on the new state incentives for decentralization and self-initiative, after Mao tried to purge the "tails of capitalism" in small enterprise. "Get rich by working!" went the new slogans. "To get rich is glorious!" Deng Xiaoping broadcast.

All our chat comes to rest in my western pocket, around a black market bronze buddha from the Great Wall. Henry sips a Tsingtao, grins broadly, and reports. "Mister Zhong current play, *Buddies Get Rich,* feature two hooligans selling 'Trashcan Buddhas' to American tourist at Great Wall."

Prairie homeboys call this a *gotcha.*

III

Xian, China's Oldest City

Like people whistling past a graveyard in the night, Chinese leaders are uncertainly feeling their way, and hoping that everything will work out all right. . . . How many Chinese are stirred by the propaganda campaign to promote a list of socialist virtues, which include the Five Things to Stress (decorum, good manners, hygiene, discipline, and morals), the Four Things to Beautify (ideology, language, behavior, and the environment), and the Three Loves (for the motherland, for socialism, and for the Chinese Communist Party)?
—ORVILLE SCHELL, *TO GET RICH IS GLORIOUS*

Barry Lopez, Joseph and Earll Kingston

Edie and Larry Heinemann

A WRITER'S CHINA

Xian Billboard Worker

Red Vase

Workers with Cart

Xian Street

Two Children in Xian

Anti-Smoking Chalkboard

Nurses at Street Table

A WRITER'S CHINA

The Squared Circle

THE PLANE TO XIAN is a lumbering Russian boxcar that will leave three hours late with us and a full load of Chinese. The natives fly for less than half our fare. Buddies, get rich—comrades, gouge the tourists. The Great Wall will be a while coming down. Looking at the leather stretched another way: each American writer is given foreign exchange certificates, or tourist money, equal to three years' salary for a Chinese worker.

"It makes me feel guilty and a little giddy," says Shu-mei, embarrassed by our Beijing luxuries. "The hotel room each night costs twice the monthly salary of the lobby attendant. On duty all night, he sleeps across two chairs pulled together." Her voice rises to a pitch of self-reproach, each word in bell-like syllables. "At the hospital I was treated for a skin rash in the *foreigners'* section, with comfortable chairs and small courtesies. Beijing locals stood in the halls for hours."

I'm a bit abashed, after feeling so heady over finally being in China. Tough love grounding isn't something I expect so soon. As we wait for the plane, Shu-mei continues, "At the train stations, we are ushered into spacious waiting rooms with couches and TV. The people sleep by the thousands on the floors. And on the Yangtze River boat we are reserved two-person berth cabins facing the river. The fifth-class Chinese sleep on mats in the walkways and eat spiced rice in their own bowls." Her face darkens and eyes flash. "We gorge on meats, fish, and beer, the rice always brought last as complementary afterthought."

A Chinese-American raised in Korea, now a graduate student in Comparative Literature, Shu-mei distrusts tourist luxuries from a government that still works its own people mercilessly and terrorized all intellectuals only ten years ago. Her clear-spoken English steps delicately among native Mandarin, childhood Korean, and adoptive American with a mockingbird's rise and fall. Shu-mei's tones carry a hint of self-parody, a whipsaw pointillism among three tongues. More than the rest of us, she senses all at once the fissures between East and West, and the desperate need to *connect*. We are all acting out, without fully knowing, some millennial stage play of dialects and persuasions, centuries in the meeting.

So in a Marxist country, no surprise, attendant hierarchies and inequities trouble those who bother to look. Communists, the local reasoning goes, can't have pure equality. Development is still in the socialist phases, and leaders must be more than fit to lead the masses. This stratifies society, just as in capitalist countries, where our Reagan tax revolution frees the rich to hoard more riches. The message these days, capitalist or communist: get all you can get. *Buddies get rich* floats in polluted skies and rivers. No doubt about it: Absolute power corrupts absolutely, from philosopher-kings in Plato's Athens, to Renaissance enlightened despotism, to representative oligarchy in our American elite. Mao was at least candid saying that *truth comes from the barrel of a gun.*

"Big Pot, Medium Pot, Small Pot," Shu-mei says with disdain. "The Chinese say this of communist gradations after the revolution. Mao's *small pot* meant more care in cooking less meat." For pointing out such, our traveling counterpart in the States, Liu Binyan, was thrown out of the party twice—now into the Big Pot of American capitalism at UCLA and Harvard.

"This century, the Chinese look out for themselves," Shu-mei says, "their way to deal with trauma and civil violence." *Protect yourself; go home safely,* the street signs say. There is no mention of pedestrian caution.

The breakup of warring feudal factions and collapse of Western imperialism cleared the way for Japanese invasion in the 1930s, the Red Army's long march and revolution in the 1940s, finally Chiang Kai-shek's exodus. China "reorganized" only to undergo the Cultural Revolution and Red Guard mayhem of 1966-1976. Those alive today struggled on nothing to survive. "Protect yourself; go home richly," Shu-mei says wryly.

The Chinese seem publicly cold at times. Their insensitivity to animals bothers some, though outsiders are quick to forget starving hungers. "Birds, rats, dogs, or even worms have meant protein during famine," Shu-mei says. "Still, the lack of public affection is shocking. People cannot openly display love."

Male armor is layered thick here, whereas the women hold hands almost longingly when they first meet. Innuendo or slip of the tongue can turn an entire conversation. The men are steeled from their suffering, possibly repressed through survival. The need and the fear to touch must create immense conflict within, a kind of Victorian sensuality, even fantacized sex. The slit of a skirt or curved silhouette is beckoning, a man's walk or the hair on his arm. Our Western displays of intimacy either intrigue or embarrass them.

"Between Chinese men and women there's little open affection," Shu-mei says with half-closed eyes, "less sensuous talk, lots of mystery. Chinese men do not speak of their wives publicly. It would be considered indiscreet or self-centered."

This privacy carries into the streets, where I notice less jostling for space than in a Western marketplace, ten million human cubicles all bustling through the streets, interacting, but not touching, like a school of busy fish. Beijing is different from the harried confusion of American shopping malls, freeways, or crowded walkways. The Chinese seem more accustomed to numbers, while Americans prize private space and fear crowds.

Standing around in the airport, Larry Heinemann and I discover that we're in fact distant cousins, through my father and his mother's Fulton lines. For sure, we're both blue-collar in a Midwest immigrant heritage. I played high school football and wrestled with guys like this, Teutonic farm stock, salt-of-the-earth old boys. True to his Chicago birthplace, Larry is big-shouldered and beefy. My daughter would say a *hunk*. He has those blizzard-blue eyes that give Larry a startling ascetic look, despite his musculature and folksy ways. We start to trade notes about writing.

"Reach down into your own voice," Larry says he tells students, "not someone else's, surely not the professor's. You've got to have something of your own to do and say, like any other respectable trade, a carpenter, a plumber, a tailor." His father drove a city bus through Chicago, and so did Larry when he returned from Vietnam. "Joseph Conrad saw men in action and wrote what he saw," he says with intensity, "what *works* worked best for him." This writer speaks with a booming Chicago sprawl, a kind of carny barker's pitch, part-comic, part-dead-serious. Larry wears a Nootka sandcast silver buckle of a killer whale with a cricket in its mouth. He says it was a gift from the Olympic penninsula Indian healers, who took him through cleansing sweats and returning warrior rituals. Larry notices Charles Wright's belt buckle, a bearpaw with Hopi rain and thunder images. "Ho, brother Charles, you're wearing a silver buckle, too!" The diffident Virginian sidles up to us.

"When I was eleven camping in the Smokies," Charles says softly, "on Mount LeConte in Tennessee, I sleepwalked to the edge of a thousand-foot cliff. I ran right into a black bear that woke me up and saved my life." He regards us with quizzical, owlish glances through horn-rimmed glasses. "I never told anyone about that bear for years, then one day sat down and wrote a poem about it." He looks away abashed and gets quiet. Charles has a Fifties look and dress, refusing the yuppie Eighties and its sleek, mod style. He's more of a down-home country boy, lanky and thoughtful, who found his stride in the late Fifties. He caught a measure of bohemian spunk and classic art in the poetry circles at the Iowa Writers' Workshop, then bore down into that posture for a lifetime, come hell or high water.

"Natives have long seen Old Man Bear as a healer and a warrior," I add to his story, "even a teacher. A bear digs for herbs and roots, growls down enemies, and walks on two legs like a man. He's my Lakota guardian, too—through a name I share with my Sioux brother, Mark, *Mato Yamni.* It means Three Bears."

"Well, I was connected with this cousin bear," Larry jokes of our family strings, "before he could pee straight down."

Barry Lopez catches the last few words and tosses off in passing, "What do you get when you cross a Mafioso with a deconstructionist?" We look blank as he holds for the punchline. "An offer you can't understand." Barry is about my height, but lean and dark-browed, with a hungry, even haunted look. He speaks in low, measured tones, as though underwater, fearful of actually *being* overheard. His wife, Sandy, is a fine book designer, an accomplished artist herself. The two live on a farm in Finn Rock, Oregon, when Barry isn't trekking somewhere. A camper and naturalist, he's a walker, a pilgrim of wilderness values, fierce in defending natural landscapes. He seems like many pacifists and idealists of the Sixties, who found environmental defense a lifetime extension of radical politics, counter-cultural alternatives, and street protest.

Barry, Larry, and I set off the metal detectors boarding the plane. My pocket harmonica, Larry's belaying pins, and Barry's hunting jacket full of gadgets overload the X-ray machine. We settle into the belly of the flying whale, a Soviet Ilyushin rising thousands of feet above northern China. Harrison and Charlotte sit in front of us, the senior statesman none too pleased with our delays, or my newly acquired red fox Mongol hat from the Great Wall. In 1973 Charlotte published her own *China Diary* with practical travel tips. Take a shortwave radio, she advised, and good walking shoes. "When the country, the people, the language—everything is strange to you, there is nothing so comforting as the Voice of America or the nursery jingle that starts the BBC daily broadcasts."

Civil Aviation Adminstration of China, or "CAAC," is a state-run airline with global renown for its "chaotic management, filthy planes, and surly service," according to Orville Schell. We hear some Swedes renaming it "China Airlines Always Canceled." Hopefully, our flight will fare better than KAL 007, a few years ago near the Russian border.

I look up Charles' bear poem, "Two Stories," in *Fifty Years of American Poetry*, and read it to Jeannine on the Soviet plane ride to Xian:

> *Deeper in sleep than the shrubs,*
> *I stepped out, it appears,*
> *Onto the smooth lip of the rock cape of the cliff,*
> *When my left hand, and then my right hand,*
> *Stopped me as they were stopped*
> *By the breathing side of a bear which woke me*
> *And there we were,*
> > *the child and the black bear and the cliff-drop,*
> *And this is the way it went—*
> > *I stepped back, and I turned around,*
> *And I walked down through the rhododendron*
> *And never looked back,*
> > *truly awake in the throbbing world,*
> *And I ducked through the low flap*
> *Of the tent, so quietly, and I went to sleep*
> *And never told anyone*

*

"Magic" Chen, Translator and Walking Poet

IN OUR XIAN HOTEL ROOM, Channel One broadcasts an English lesson through color TV clips from a British sit com.

"You're not old . . . hardly middle-aged," a man reassures a woman, and she answers dryly, "Thank *you*."

"This is irony to some, not to others," the moderator says to his two Chinese students, debating the woman's tone.

"Does she mean it," one asks, "or doesn't she?" Long Chinese pause.

"You're both right," the moderator says buoyantly, "she *thanks* him and she snubs him with the same word!" This seems to delight the Chinese speakers learning English. And "sarcasm" also has its object lesson from British TV: "The King invited *me* to tea," a black man wryly says. Four-tonal Chinese speakers are learning English humor, everything from irony to whimsy, out of public television, Walt Disney, and Colonel Sanders ads. The boob tube is our cultural conduit to China. "Dallas" and "Dynasty" are broadcast as global American windows of the 1980s.

Xiao Chen and I go to check out a reception banquet. As we walk back, munching frybread for breakfast, Henry tells me one of his poems, the way Frost used to "talk" his verse.

"It about shoes," he says slyly. "I got pair shoes weigh me down, and I walk like old man. Two shoes pretty when new, but now bit scuffed. I like walk barefoot a while."

"You know what the poem about?" he quizzes, and I don't. "The shoes, my newborn twins—only *legal* way to have more than one child in China." He looks at me as though any single man, claiming to be a poet, would get the point. There's a lyrical, playful tilt to the way Henry speaks, often ending on an up-tone question. He seems to have a mind alive to everything, liking and knowing how to manuver people, entertaining possibilities in the world, interested *in it*, as Marianne Moore says we can be interested *in* things of poetic merit, both the genuine and the raw.

"Poet guy has freedoms that others don't get," Chen tells me. "Poet can have mistress on side, for example, ordinary people can't." Again he looks at me knowingly. "Extramarital sex over most China. *Moral majority* in compound try to curb it, but public humiliation does not work so well anymore. Divorce difficult, but possible. Young do date and carouse. But they have no private space, so crowded our land—no rooms or own cars like in your country—no place for intimacy. Holding hands in public seen as daring, you know."

The Italian communist, Alberto Moravia, considers such repression in *The Red Book and the Great Wall*, "the drastic and manifold nature of

Chinese 'austerity,' which indiscriminately condemns Shakespeare and miniskirts, Chinese classics and dance-music records, Dostoevsky and silk stockings. It is a totalitarian austerity based on the very simple idea that the counterrevolution can incubate anywhere, even in a tube of lipstick." Our own Puritan ancestors suspected just as much from pilgrims who might drop over the pallisade walls and consort with Indians. John Rolfe's tryst with Pocahontas scared more than a few xenophobic pilgrims.

There's play in all this serious talk. Tonal puns fill the Chinese lexicon, surely, but little scatology, or smut, or satire. Humor seems a national pasttime.

"Zhong *ve-ry* funny," Henry agrees, "peoples' favorite playwright. *Buddies Get Rich* give street-life humor for thinking workers. Funny from common point of view," Xiao Chen adds. "Popular satire on 'free' enterprise, an-ti-qui-ty, and Buddha icons at Great Wall." Here are my "trashcan" Buddhas again, à la Beckett.

Henry postscripts his comments with a Chinese joke about male-dominant humor:

"Describe bedsheet to me, mother asks child. What is it?"

"I don't know, child answers."

"It's under the bedspread."

"The blanket? child wonders."

"No, under that."

"Daddy."

"Still under that."

"Mommy."

Bob has dubbed Henry "Xiao" Chen, as a familiar term of address for a younger man. Henry walks on the balls of his feet, upbeat, leaning forward and upward, as though about to take flight at any moment. He dresses in clothes simple and well-fitted, slacks and white shirt, open at the collar. By contrast, our translator is far from drab. Maoist youth learned to be quick, taking the yoke of protective coloration and conformity under Red Guard mayhem. So "Xiao" Chen, on his way up, seems a commonly tailored cross between a Boston Common student and a Beijing street entrepeneur.

I give Henry a Laker t-shirt with Ervin Johnson's grinning face— the sign of a playmaker, someone who knows the ropes. "The Magic

Man plays the streets, pulls off the impossible, and all with unmatchable humor," I tell him of Magic Johnson, the Laker miracle man. So he's "Magic" Chen to me and says he would like to come to the States for graduate work in American Studies. A ticket to LA alone would cost two years' salary.

"How would Magic support himself abroad?" I ask.

"Would be hard, but I can do. Like to write thesis on John Berryman, crazy-funny poet, or Allen Ginsberger, literary legend in China. Ginsberger free to be, say, and write what he choose. He can be lovable homosexual, no sweat, drug guy, fallen Jew."

"So an aging Allen Ginsberg is *enfant terrible* to the Chinese," I think outloud, "dissident, decadent, *beat*. You know he's an American establishment icon now, ironically enough, the respectable 'degenerate.' Every dog has his day eventually, they say, especially when Harper & Row prints your collected works."

Get-rich liberalism is circling the globe. "If I can put a Maxim's in Peking," Pierre Cardin boasted in 1983, "I can put a Maxim's on the moon." The next year Cardin opened a "Minim's" fast-food downstairs from Maxim's de Beijing. Pierre said up-front, "I am aiming at the biggest market in the world—China," as the American tobacco industry targeted four hundred million Chinese women new to the workforce. Only five years before, when China "opened doors" again to the West, the *Peking Daily* published modernizing objections from Mao's old guard: "Instead of devoting themselves to work, these young people prefer to wear pornographic, bell-bottom trousers, spend hours getting their hair permed, and excite themselves doing foreign dances." The old slogan, "A hoe in the field and a pillow at home," is being replaced by rocking hipsters "going out to look for heat and noise" or *qu kan renao*.

"Deng Xiaoping visit States in 1979. Ronald Reagan come to China in April 1984 and sign trade agreements," Henry recalls. "First American writers arrive then too. Year before, five to ten thousand public executions take place." He looks off into the smog-choked skies.

"Condoms given to married couple free of charge," Xiao Chen says with a sour face. "Beyond policy of 'one couple, one child,' abortions strongly encouraged, reinforced by privilege and penalty incentives." Today elite Chinese women "Westernize" with lipstick, eye shadow, and eyelid surgery, adding a second epicanthus fold for "rounder" eyes.

"During 1920s and 30s, many said that moon shine brighter and rounder outside China," Henry tells me. "They think *modernism* is future. This exactly what revolution react against, *yang* or 'foreign' privilege that exploit native populism."

So, Western "heat and noise" have returned to China looking for commerce, labor, and markets. There's newly discovered oil in the South China Sea (equivalent to the North Sea fields, "China's Houston," Atlantic Richfield thinks). Coal has always been buried in Shanxi (several billion tons for Occidental Petroleum). A dozen nuclear power plants have sprung up (some twenty billion dollars construction).

"And aesthetics?" I ask Henry. "What do Party hacks think of poetry?"

"Mao write poetry, sure, but he called art and literature *cogs and screws* of revolution. Not sure what that mean today, with 'Kentucky' in Tiananmen and all."

"How many drive-ins and drilling ventures does this add up to?"

"*If* things don't go too far, lots more disco and Denny's," Magic footnotes the new openness. "Who know how far? People want bigger chicken in Chinese pots."

"They've come a long way from imperialist Opium Wars," I add, "when the British imported drugs for silk, tea, and silver."

"Long road back to Mao's reform in *simplicity and bitter struggle*," Henry notes. "Iron-rice-bowls in state-promise wages and *wubao* or 'five guarantees'—food, clothing, medicine, housing, burial." Magic closes his mouth and gives me an end-of-the-discussion stare.

Henry thinks some more and tacks on a postscript with utmost seriousness. "Poetry not understand by all people, never translate right. Chinese say *Shi Wu Da Gu,* 'poetry can only be sensed.'" He hands me reprinted lines of *feng qi wu,* a melody from the Song dynasty:

> it is dangerous here
> at the upper-story guard railing
> the far horizon is a pinnacle of pain
> my home so many days beyond
> how calm and gentle is the wind
> the sun's dying light
> casts shadows over the spring grasses

and the mountains darken
who in the world understands
how I feel leaning against this rail

I try to calm myself
or forget drinking like the others
we ought to sing carousing I know
but the wine tastes stale
when my friends call me to join them
I live like a scarecrow in my baggy clothes
but I don't regret it at all
it is worth looking haggard
for a woman you love

*

Old Soldiers

Confucius said: a meal of uncut rice to eat, water to drink,
bent arm for a pillow, I can be happy this way. Riches and
prizes got by injustice are so many drifting clouds.
—THE ANALECTS

THE XIAN PEOPLES' HOTEL, built for Russian advisors and technocrats in 1953, looks like a Tsarist helmet dumped from an antique spaceship. A glittering lobby chandelier is being roped into place the day we depart, the place getting a mausoleum facelift. I read that Mao's chief advisor during the Long March was a German Marxist trained in Moscow, Otto Braun, but in 1959 Khrushchev yanked Soviet advisors and nixed all aid to the Chinese. The old border disputes and differences of opinion couldn't be simply bridged by Leninist ideology. Today, the two countries parry for talks of reunion.

During the sixth century, Xian was the largest city in the world, two million citizens. The countryside was blessed with richer soil than Beijing. Winter wheat, a cash crop, contours the new green of the land today. Rice and sugar cane grow in low-lying fields. The locals make a lethal white lightning from sorghum called *maotai* that tastes like rancid tequila. I'll bet maotai would strip rust off a gun barrel.

At misty sunrise, I go out alone to do Tai Chi in the park with an eighty-year old who can still kick higher than his head. His complex motions and forms turn him into a birdlike dawn image, a model of rebirth in old age: *wei wu wei,* knowing the "right" natural way, by way of *no* wrong moves. The old man slides low to the ground, flicks his wrists like a sparrow plucking a worm, curves his arms with the grace of a crane's arched neck, comes across the body's grain in natural flight. Martial arts wrestlers tussle and tumble on the grass to our right. The birds whistle away in cages behind, and across the road, I see a Chinese man photographing us with a telephoto lens. Exchanging the high sign, the old man gives me a radiant smile when I leave.

At breakfast some Russians enter the dining room, now lighted with running neon over a small front stage. Ernie Whiteman, Arapaho artist from Wyoming, talks sculpting with me, his "Rusty Cat" assemblage made from scrap highway auto parts. "I'd like to back them with a Chinese sound track," he says with the air of a sound engineer preparing an installation. "I want it all natural, but off-beat. Found objects fascinate me—old Zen precisions leaking through the accidents of natural art. I sit and stare at a door ajar for hours, to open my imagination to the world." Like a mountain cougar about to pounce, Ernie is a new breed of college-educated Indian, crossing cultures.

We make weak complaints about the "see-through coffee" and "brambled eggs," as Maxine joins us. She's all salt-and-pepper, with a glance of inquisitive intelligence.

"What do you do for a living?" Maxine asks Ernie.

"I'm an enterprising artist," he says without blinking. "I wanted to start a Minneapolis used car lot called 'Honest Injun' Cars. Someday I'll make telescopic teepee poles, then maybe portable sweat lodges and menstrual huts."

Ernie adds with a straight face, "I may become an Indi'n evangelist." The month-old coffee and eggs taste better with some laughs thrown in.

Maxine starts telling the mythical story behind her just completed novel, *Tripmaster Monkey.* "Long ago, you see, a Chinese monk rode to India with his monkey and came back on a white horse with Hindu sutras. Those are meditations for right living, deposited at the Greater

Goose Pagoda, right here in Xian." Ernie's bushy eyebrows dart up. "The first set was blank, so he went back with his monkey to get the *real* ones, which the Indian scribes gladly gave him: 'Oh, you wanted those, OK, here you go.' When the Chinese monk came back the second time to Xian, delivered the sutras, and got down to the scrolls, he and his monkey found that the blank ones were the *real* ones."

"You mean the written ones were fake?" Ernie bites.

"Well, they weren't as *real,* anyway, as the blank ones."

"Is monkey some native trickster?" he asks.

"Oooh yeees," Maxine says elongating the vowels, eyes as wide as her round mouth. "He pours out the sacred wine at the altar, and pisses in the cups, and the monks drink it!"

"So monkey tricks the monks?"

"Yes, yes! Just like that!"

"And brings culture to China?"

"Yes, the sutras on a white horse, back from India ..."

"But the wrong ones, the written ones."

"I guess so..." She leaves the story hanging, as we cruise off to join the departing writers.

Boarding the bus for the Summer Palace, Henry tells me a local parable. "Father with three sons plans to move mountain with succeeding grandsons. Wise man comes along and says it foolish to think so: simply do nothing. *Wei wu wei,* leave mountain be. Mao, cagey, reverse Confucius paradigm, people must rebuild China moving mountains with sons and daughters. So, Mao combine Lao Tsu, riddles and reverse stuff, with Confucius, old practical center. Mao ban all past, but apply classics to Chinese socialism."

With his *little red book* sayings, Mao simply replaced classical signatures with his own slogans and revolutionized China along Marxist lines with revised folk wisdoms. Vast and vastly diverse, China has fifty-six indigenous ethnic groups, ruled historically by Han, Manchu, Mongol, Hui, and Tibetan dynasties. Collective will is the fulcrum to the peoples' movement here—over a billion people moving all directions, more or less together.

"After Cultural Revolution come *scar literature,*" Henry says, "writers write sufferings. Then come *reflection literature,* kind of take stock, then renewed *modern literature,* and now *crisis of belief.* Government reverse itself so often, Marxism shoot full of paradox. Now we have *liberal* trends toward *free* enterprise, just like U-ni-ted States." Henry seems infatuated with the parallel, leaning toward the West. Like so many swarms of mosquitoes, literary fads and political slogans come and go, but the people remain eager for modernization.

"During Cultural Revolution, intellectual and teacher all named bad and 'sent to country' for *laogai* or 'reform through labor,'" Henry says again, "just as Mao campaign against 'four pests': mosquitoes, flies, rats, and birds. Fifth pest is 'rightist' or 'capitalist roader.' Western decadent must collect one hundred flies each day, intellectuals extra twenty. If guy not make quota, bottle every day, double ante next day. Beatings after that."

Little more than a decade after the Cultural Revolution, we bus to the imperial watering hole at the foot of a mountain where Chiang Kai-shek jumped out the window in his pajamas, sans false teeth and glasses in 1937.

"He ran halfway up the hillside, where warlord soldiers caught him hiding in a cave," Harrison tells us, when I ask naively about Chaing's scruples. "The Maoists eventually made a deal, pressured by the Russians, to reinstate Chiang if he'd stop hounding the left. In return the old boy arrested his arrestors, executed one, and the other is still in jail on the 'free' island of nationalist China." He ponders that moment in history.

"You can't trust a one of 'em," Harrison says pensively, frowning, "they're all thieves and crooks. This country has been raided, for centuries, warred over and betrayed endlessly, by its own people."

Harrison smiles at the placid lake. "The emperors came here to winter, take the waters, and cavort with their concubines."

Halfway up the mountain, the blossoming cherry trees fleck the hillside. *Their eyes mid many wrinkles, their eyes,* W. B. Yeats wrote of Chinese ascetics climbing a mountain, *Their ancient, glittering eyes are gay.* How "gay" are old men's eyes today, who take up birding in the parks to deal with retirement? By the turn of the century, a third of our respective populations in China and the U.S. will be over sixty-five.

"Women and men are different," an old fellow tells Bob. "They have their work at home, we have our birds." The men press hard all their lives. They live so busily that time on their hands, late in life, forces a life crisis. *A young man in the dark am I, / But a wild old man in the light,* Yeats chanted, *That can make a cat laugh.*

*

Terra Cotta Treasures

THE XIAN TERRA COTTA WARRIORS, sculpted in 1087, seem to be walking out of the earth from which they were made, an emergent image of the new China from the old. *As though we blink they might march away,* the sign says.

"Legend has it," Harrison adds, "that the Tang emperor spared his servants' lives. He had these fired clay replicas buried, perhaps 10,000 of them, when he was entombed. The men and horses could live on after him, rather than being sacrificed at his death." Like Harrison himself, their faces appear wise and kindly, despite warrior fierceness, with crinkly smiles at the corners of their mouths, twinkles in their eyes—a powerful blend of disciplined strength and humor, all facing forward together. The effigies seem to hear ancient melodies inside burnished clay, like Yeats's mythic gods and Celtic heroes.

Bob has been scribbling a poem on the bus ride. He hands his red notebook over the seat:

SPRING COMES TO THE MING TOMBS

The persimmons are gone,
those soft suns with
astringent skins and sweet
slippery meat that held
summer past first frost.

The trees are still bare,
though sparrows and finches—
singers of early green—
keep chorus there.

Along the road
peasants sell Chinese pears,
sallow skinned from cellars
dark as tombs.

Beyond the vermilion walls
acacias scatter buds,
and the forsythia blossoms
in tiny yellow butterflies.

Here where royalty once rode
in golden coaches, stone
horses and elephants keep vigil.

In their winter caves
the emperors and empresses
sleep on.

Dust shawls China, and the landscape tastes of grit-born history. The people walk, work with their hands, plant, breathe the earth, break the rocks, and bear the soil in their skin tones—earthen mixtures of amber, sienna, adobe, and auburn.

We drive to the dig of a 6,000-year-old village where archeologists have reconstructed neolithic Chinese homes. One is a mud-covered wigwam, seemingly a cross between a sunken Mandan earth hut and a conical plains teepee, the approximate vintage of Yuki Indian archaeology in Round Valley, California.

"Here, Ken, from China to you," Maxine smiles, and through the bus window, presents me with a local bottle of Tequ *maotai,* the regional snakebite. "This will run your lawn mower through brambles," Max says knowingly.

By the time the tour reaches the Greater Goose pagoda, we're touristed out. I settle for offerings at the foot of the Buddha, where a paid monk gongs the bell.

"Common joke," Henry says, "these *holy men* really salaried bureaucrats." The gong still sounds enlightening to me. Inside the pagoda, Charles shows me a peach pit carved as the happy Buddha, then leaves it as a gift, and I lay down prairie sage. The day seems to be dissolving into mist.

"My monkey novel ends in this temple," Maxine says shyly. She shows me an offering page, where Wittman Ah Sing, down on his luck in the Tenderloin skidrow of San Francisco, remembers Jack Kerouac:

Soldiers, sailors,
the panhandlers and drifters,

(no) zoot suitors, the hoodlums,
the young men who washed dishes in cafeterias from coast to coast,
the hitchhikers, the hustlers, the drunks,
the battered lonely young Negroes,
the twinkling little Chinese,
the dark Puerto Ricans (and braceros and pachucos)
and the varieties of dungareed Young Americans . . . .

Well, no such red and purple whore or resplendent homosexual. Might as well expect a taxi door to open and out step a geisha in autumn kimono, her face painted white with tippy red lips and smudge-moth eyebrows, white tabi feet winking her out of sight on an assignation in the floating demimonde.

Shit. The 'twinkling little Chinese' must be none other than himself. 'Twinkling'?! 'Little'?! Shit. Bumkicked again. If King Kerouac, King of the Beats, were walking here tonight, he'd see Wittman and think, 'Twinkling little Chinese.' Refute 'little.' Gainsay 'twinkling.' A man does not twinkle. A man with balls is not little. As a matter of fact, Kerouac didn't get 'Chinese' right either. Big football player white all-American jock Kerouac. Jock Kerouac. I call into question your naming of me. I trust your sight no more. You tell people by their jobs. And by their nation. And the wrong nation at that. If Ah Sing were to run into Kerouac—grab him by the lapels of his lumberjack shirt. Pull him up on his toes. Listen here, you twinkling little Canuck. What do you know, Kerouac? What do you know? You don't know shit. I'm the American here. I'm the American walking here. Fuck Kerouac and his American road anyway. Et tu, Kerouac. Aiya, even you. Just for that, I showed you, I grew to six feet. May still be growing.

*

Bicycle Brigade to Stele Forest

I RENT A FLYING PIGEON BIKE and pedal about Xian all day. Bicycling is akin to driving a moped in Italy, the school of sardines method, all together, don't bump. Xian teems with street life. Men play cards and a kind of block dominoes by the roadside. Women wash clothes at public faucets. Grampas carry infants about, and young men hawk their wares. On street corners loudspeakers (for political broadcasts a decade back) crackle out the latest pop rock-and-roll. Everywhere bicycles, like the dust, regulate the street rhythms, and sidecart motorbikes create havoc. Blasting its horn insistently, an occasional bus or unlikely car pushes through the bikes and pedestrians. Clots of humanity part by instinct.

The level of disrepair resembles Mexico or southern Italy, except that buildings look natural, with bricks tumbling off a wall into the street, or the lintel of an entryway mortared together. Everything has been touched, broken, repaired, and re-touched ten thousand times, as with the people themselves—an ancient humanity of survivors, among the oldest civilizations, that goes back continuously five thousand or more years. China is still ongoing, remaking itself, continuing its Confucian, Buddhist, Islamic and polygot heritage under the guise of Maoist communism. The point is survival, on whatever terms possible.

The walls of Xian are solidly bricked at right angles, and the streets intersect sensibly, so a cyclist can pedal around with ease. It's a classical design—the squared city—dating back to the second century, a Tai Chi center since then.

The Forest of Stele, begun in the second century, is said to be the world's oldest dictionary. Some of the stones rise from the backs of giant turtles. They're inscribed with calligraphy that marshals itself in descending vertical columns—hundreds of thousands all vertically disciplined and elegant in their own gestures, like the terra cotta warriors. Ezra Pound thought he'd found the cornerstone of culture and right reason in Confucian China: "great plan needeth great architect," he translated a line from the classic *Shih-ching* anthology. Or from *Ta Hsio,* called *The Great Digest,* Pound translated: "the true word is in the middle inside and will show on the outside. Therefore the man of real breeding who carries the cultural and moral heritage must look his heart in the eye when alone." This new poetics was fired by Ernest Fenollosa's Chinese ideogram studies at the century's turn, when Victorian-encrusted literature needed scouring. Thus, "concrete" images, sculpted lines, "cut" verse, and "speakable" diction, Fenollosa contended, all track to the immediacy of the "Chinese written character," and Pound printed the claim. Today, Chinese writers look back to 1920s modernist writing as a turn toward their own heritage.

KENNETH LINCOLN

The old stone chiselings strike to the heart of language. Confucian sense, Pound reasoned, could right a lopsided Western aesthetics gone sour. "The very soil of Chinese life seems entangled in the roots of its speech," Fenollosa felt. "At the base of the pyramid lie *things*, but stunned, as it were." The imagist phrase, steeped in real speech, turns poetry back into real things, "pregnant, charged, and luminous from within." The Chinese verb for "is" gives us a concrete image, "to snatch from the moon with the hand." Rather than "the dead white plaster of the copula," the critic reasoned that Chinese verbs, like those in Shakespeare, can be seen, felt, touched. Brightness shows up as "sun-and-moon," literally "begetter" and "measurer." The color "red" blends cherry, rose, sunset, iron-rust, and flamingo. "East" entangles the horizon sun in a tree's branches. As mentioned, I got a quick lesson in the concrete images of calligraphy when my namecard, Ken Lin Ken, was translated as the moon looking up through a tangle as an image of willed desire, then two trees joined as a forest, repeated with the moon-in-desire image. How languages and poetries cross, even the losses that Frost called poetry, fascinate me.

This kind of reinvigorated organic logic signaled a new poetics across the Western waters. The poet would be a word sculptor, Pound preached, the book "a ball of light in one's hand." So Ezra translated Dante, the pre-Renaissance master via Confucius, "Knowledge of a definite thing comes from a knowledge of things defined" ("Confucius and Mencius"). Over two thousand years, this "concrete" premise has stood in the Forest of Stele. Reborn modernists urged Western classicists to "make it new" again.

"Feels like going to church," I tell Charles, "all these inscribed stones, a living cemetery of words." I've asked for a pressing of the Cold Mountain poem, and the workman plasters a white gauze over the stone, squigees its wet surface into the indentations, and swabs the oversized sheet with a black-ink paintbrush.

"If we took this much care over poems. . . ," Charles ponders, adjusting his glasses and softening his forehead. "Think about three thousand years of poetic tradition, back to Homer in the same language. Brings you to your knees."

Children fly brightly fluttering kites in the park. At lunch Maxine tells of the old kite maker who sold her one. "For the life of me," she stands amazed, "I couldn't get it to fly." China seems to turn on this kite flying. "I would run up and down the grass with this wounded bird, gasping and plunging to the ground. All the children cried, *Oooohh*. Yet the old man's kite seemed to have wind *in* it. He'd fluff his tissue paper, tug on the string, and up the kite would go like an ascending angel. The children sighed, *Ahhhaaah*."

Our plane is fogged in at a distant airport, so we pile into the buses, after trekking three hours to wait in the Xian terminal. Back in the hotel, we are told to be up at 3 a.m. and leave at 4:40 a.m. on a seventeen-hour train to Chengdu. All planes are grounded. Xiao Chen called the Minister of Railways in Beijing, who put on a special sleeper car for us. There was bureaucratic resistance, until Chen warned of journalistic repercussions. "You know how these writers can be," Magic told the Minister, and yes, the bureaucrat *knew* how writers could be. So we steam (on a coal-burning train) toward our four-day conference in Chengdu, a day late.

The writers debate for an hour after dinner about the coming conference. Will we talk shop or politics? style or content? Can we raise sensitive issues such as feminism or Tibet? What about religious freedoms or human rights or ideological contradictions? Can we have differences of opinion, outright dialogue, even disputes?

"All of the above," Harrison assures us, "say whatever you're thinking, whatever is on your mind. The Chinese are forthright. They want an honest discussion. They may avoid your question, but they'll respect your right to ask. The point is to open up talk. That's how we did it with the Russians in 1957 and here in China four years ago. We've come this far to talk."

So talk we will. I throw the *I Ching* and it forecasts "struggle." Water over mountain: *give way when necessary, appoint feudal princes.*

*

Sleeper Car Across China
He who knows that enough is enough will always have enough.
—LAO TSU

OUT THE MORNING WINDOW, I see a young farm girl come up the train station stairs, hesitate and hold up her box of blue eggs in the sepia light. I gesture no thanks, and she disappears. A man rides a bike through the rain with an umbrella held forty-five degrees forward. I still can't help noticing the activity everywhere. People are waking up, doing exercises, jogging, pulling carts, walking everywhere with picks and shovels, pulling and bearing and backpacking loads. At intervals by the train tracks, there seem to be burial mounds with headstones and tattered prayer flags, perhaps for workers who died building the railroad. Convicts and soldiers were the bulk of the labor force, interred where they fell.

The light dawns now, with slender alders damp in the morning rain. The winter wheat fields are the color of soft moss. The dawn train toilet stinks in a sweetly fetid way that takes me back to childhood barnyards. Again, I throw the *I Ching*. The teaching forecasts a beginning, heaven over heaven—six dragons pull a warrior's chariot across the sky. There will be good fortune, the prophecy says; keep the "head" low.

Breakfast requires walking through six cars of sleeping Chinese travelers, as Shu-mei warned, stacked three tiers high. Wash cloths dangle on lines over the windows, bowls of soup perch on ledges, blackened eggs dimple protective corners. The people look up curiously, some smile, all seem accepting of our intrusion, or maybe just inured to disruptions.

The train enters the foothills, and the river courses muddy, a kind of dirty magenta from mountain rain runoff. Mists shroud the ridges. The peaks thrust out of the land, and we labor up a grade. The river gathers speed, as the train slows down, then enters one of many endless tunnels. Higher up reigns that in-between time, winter to spring, when the stuff of the past lies strewn about and roots stir down under. Trees are ghostly silhouetted against the hillsides—waterfalls spew foamy horsetails, clay soils thrust upward, a no-green land for mountain goats and monkeys. Soon the buds will burst, leaves unwrinkle, and the land will be dotted with new-green life. The dragons awake.

Men plow with oxen up here, their women follow scattering seeds, the ravens waiting patiently to feed. The river bends to flow west, as we descend the grade. Trees have been sacked of their lower branches for firewood, so topknots sprout at the crests, shadowing the land like wisps of hair on old men. Mustard flower or "rape" sprouts pale yellow, plum and cherry trees blossom white, winter wheat spikes green, as the river flows east, west, then east again. Charles writes away on the moving train:

> Halfway to Chengdu; past noon.
> Against the brown riprap and scree grass
> Two peach trees in blossom,
>   speechless from daybreak till now.

Finally, we arrive at Chengdu and board a bus for Leshan. I scribble tumbled notes through the fogged window: rice paddies and water buffalo, pigs quartered on racks, man brushing his teeth, woman with bowl of breakfast noodle soup, cane and scallions in bundles, bikes, trucks, buses, all kinds of pedal-powered vehicles, newly-tiled collective housing, torrents of TV antennas, tires, machine parts, gunnysacks, donkey carts, stands of cigarettes, woks, cafes, pool rooms, brick, gravel, charcoal depot, building and rebuilding, beekeepers and boxes, sugar cane carts, cedar logs, chest on a bike, mattresses on a bike, pool table on a bike, geese in a basket on a bike, one hundred rice hats in two piles on a bike, an old woman with a cane and six geese crossing her yard, sacks, baskets, boxes, crates, barrels, cartons, bushels, cases of pop, bicycle repair shops. Everything in China is on this road, including us. We come as a group of individuals, loosely connected, and hope we're not stonewalled by party line.

How much do I know my traveling companions so far? The men poets keep a bit distant: Jay Wright, pleasant yet hesitant to advance, a black Socratic in combat. Charles Wright, listening for Buddha's silence and the echo of Flaubert's *le mot juste*, fastidious and congenial, a man of southern gentility.

The women are fascinating: Maxine Hong Kingston, wide-eyed and tightly strung, insistent on her interethnic feminist platforms. Alice Fulton is targeted that we "discuss" feminism, what her students call the "f-word." She speaks in a voice that entices and cuts through surfaces, dedicated to the shaped phrase, as are the other poets, but willing to risk the weird coinage or the offbeat idea.

In the middle distance rise voices of conscience: Roberta Whiteman, working academic mother, a powerful Iroquois woman. Her Oneida lines go back through clan mothers who directed warriors in the days when Washington, Franklin, and Jefferson allied with the Iroquois Six Nations.

Bobbi speaks from a tribal humanist base, a poet of "We-the-people." And Bob Rees, the organizational genius behind this foray, dedicated to literature and inspired by the arts, a humanist morally grounded.

Our tribal dog soldiers are formidable: Barry Lopez, evangelical of the natural world, quick-witted, a professional coyote. Larry Heinemann, Vietnam vet and hearty Chicago native, fingering a Chinese "chigar," chugging *maotai*, telling a tale. A likeable man who's humped through war with a heart still open.

The group leader is senior historian of the Long March, Harrison Salisbury, still going strong at eighty. He's an old-school journalist, first a war reporter in 1942, eventually a powerful columnist and editor, honored twice by Pulitzer nominations. *The Long March* was serialized in China for an estimated five million readers. The Chinese publishers on this trip are handling him with silk gloves. Tall and direct as a Minnesota farm boy with snowbank-blue eyes and a kindly social manner—Harrison holds his head up, humane and dignified, with silvering, straight-back hair.

"A young group of writers," one of the Chinese guides says to him.

"Yes, quite lively," Harrison reflects, lifting a bushy grey eyebrow.

IV

In Conference:
making wells together

Confucius said: the wise are not flustered, the humane are not broody, the bold are not anxious.
—THE ANALECTS

Shu-mei Shih

Jay Wright and Charles Wright

A WRITER'S CHINA

Rich Is Glorious!"

Struggle is seeded in the daily social order. "You human right guys," Henry whispers to me, "speak against freedom losses. Yes, loss clearly lead to big power abuse. Old guy repress dissent and manipulate young to kill, steal, and bully. Lies fuel our wars. Misuse language and power. Wash brains, yes, all round barn, everywhere." He pauses to take a sip of cold green tea from a jar. "So civil rights loss lead to war itself, get it? Old greedy sacrifice social tolerance for self-gain. Women know this more terrible—lover, husband, son, brother, father killed then suffer their loss. Beloved women left behind, they grieve." Henry is genuinely caught up in his own narrative, in striking contrast to the belabored translative process taking place in the room. I fear that he will insult my Chinese colleagues, mumbling away at my elbow, but the interpretive time lapse allows for a dead space that fills up with chatter. Everyone talks through most of the speeches. The noise seems alright, even desirable to fill the public vacuum, while a tiresome second tongue is relayed across continents and histories.

Professor Chen Liao sits to my right, a senior literary critic who wears thick glasses and an old-fashioned Chinese cap. He bears himself with a certain pomp that makes me think of classical persimmon paintings and Victorian dons. When Professor Chen speaks into the microphone, he recalls that in the 1950s, the Silk Curtain walled off socialism from capitalism. Western literature was officially dismissed as "decadent." Since the Gang of Four's fall, American literature has been reassessed as "multipolar and pluralistic." It is, indeed, a "heterogenous" mix of cultures, which the Chinese view as an "undying curiosity for new things." Chinese literature, meanwhile, has grown "kaleidoscopic," Professor Chen says, and "root-seeking." He sees vitality and flexibility on both sides, while "revolutionary realism" still separates his "countrymen from American letters."

Henry sits still, like a toad turning into stone, saying nothing.

In short, the Chinese professor wheels his big Marxist machine to a stop, literature remains "social culture" in both countries, even if more liberally in China now, while the West continues to skeeze around art-for-art's-sake. He comes to a neat parallel caesura: Americans explore "inner worlds," Professor Chen feels, as the Chinese survey "outer worlds" of their respective peoples.

"Obvious difference between Chinese social reform and States writer freedom," Henry whispers to my right. "Serve inverse interests, both sides. You guys expose to communal thought here in our country, we to individual freedom when you here. Think that about." Henry resumes the toad pose, and Professor Chen adds one small postscript. "China has never won a Nobel Prize in Literature." Perhaps the alliance in the air today will lead to better translations, mutual recognitions. China will take its place in the sun in the twenty-first century.

By the time Professor Chen has ended, and been tailed by the translators, he and I have each peeled two respective oranges and added the skins to a common pile. Henry, eyes almost closed, seems to be dozing. The professor and I nod deferentially, he blinking in a kindly senior way. Feeling at a loss for words, I say *Shi de* or "yes," one of the few phrases I carry from King-Kok's coaching. With a start, Henry stands up and walks to the front, replacing the former translator at the head microphone.

Yixi Danzeng, a young Tibetan novelist, speaks next of the reconstructions in his country, now open with "sunshine" to tourism. Today Yixi, pronounced "Ishi" like the last California Yana (whose White-extracted "name" meant simply "man") is our token Tibetan. The Han dynasty, then the Maoists, were never too cordial toward these western frontier Buddhists. Yixi seems something of a diplomatic regular guy. This handsome artist was first recognized for painting Mao in Lhasa, now for writing *The Survivor*. His smiling portrayal of the 1981 "peaceful liberation of Tibet" doesn't quite square with reports of Tibetan resistance to Chinese domination. Religious freedoms, native rights, women's liberation, and territorial sovereignty, it occurs to me, place Tibet in an analogous situation to Native American peoples under the United States.

"Do you believe this guy?" Shu-mei sidles in next to me, taking Henry's metal chair.

"What do you mean?" I reply innocently.

"Pretty boy, toady hack. Don't trust him as far as you can spittle." She winks and leans over to take notes.

The third Chinese writer to draw literary lines is Liu Shahe, a classical poet experimenting with modernist free forms, vice-president of the Chinese Writers Association, Sichuan Branch. Almost sixty, Liu is thin, with wispy hair spraying all directions. Like the thrushes in the park, Liu's larynx wobbles when he speaks. He's published fourteen books, poems, stories, essays, and translations. Liu Shahe finds "something in common in all kinds of poetry," a garden of "air" propped up by three pillars: the "soul of emotion," the "wisdom of intellect," and the "imagery of the mind." Ezra Pound traced similar poetic terms from sound, sight, and thought. Liu's own writing records, he says with tenderness, "the pain and the humor of the people." For twenty-two years he was ordered silent, so he burned his poems and sat weeping, running his fingers through the ashes. *A Record of the Traces of the Tooth of a Saw* sets down his prose memoir as a carpenter, once a classical poet, who went through nightmarish tortures during the Cultural Revolution. He was locked in a closet for three years.

I find a poem of his, written Autumn 1966, in a little pamphlet that Shu-mei hands over, *Poets from the People's Republic of China:*

> To my Lover
>
> *Looking back at the road I had passed*
> *I was silently shocked*
> *Why so winding and zigzagging*
> *Winding and zigzagging to waste my life*
> *If I had made a straight cut*
> *Wouldn't I have saved much precious time*
>
> *Now I understand*
> *Each step was an approach to you*
> *Without those zigzags*
> *We would have been strangers all our lives*
> *One second late, there will be no meeting*
> *Just as two stars pass each other in the Milky Way.*

Mr. Liu says that he has "attained inner peace climbing history's mountain," that he's "gleaned some humor from the twists of forced labor." Not conquest, but the climb interests him, as in the Zen "befriending" of Everest some years ago, though the West saw Hilary "conquer" the mountain. His wife is a Buddhist reader who "doesn't like writing," and his children "prefer rock music" to his poetry. Still there are in China "young creative artists who have a vision of the future." Spring is "always with us," Liu reassures us and himself, as his birdsong voice rises and falls tonally. Poetry is the "handmaiden of

China's revolution," he borrows from Mao, and there are "no insuperable obstacles." As for newfound freedoms, "we like to speak with different voices." Liu Shahe clearly believes in a Chinese renaissance as part of the great rebirthings this century.

"Not bad speech for old man, eh Doc Ken?" Henry is back, and Shu-mei has taken his place up front. "You like talk Mr. Shahe, boss, you guys later."

"Yes, please Henry, set it up, will you?"

Now it's our turn to speak. Maxine Hong Kingston takes the microphone, perched like a mongoose ready to collar a cobra. Ten days ago, Max finished seven years' work on a novel, *Tripmaster Monkey*, she tells the crowd, based partly on the classical Chinese text translated by Arthur Waley, *Monkey, A Journey of the West*. "It's a fiction with improvisational jazz riffs," Maxine says. "The fabled Monkey King reawakens as a war protestor in the 1960s, a Berkeley Chinese-American street kid, and is converted to non-violence during the free speech movement. It's kind of funny," she says with a wrinkled nose, "and kind of serious, all at once."

"I see myself as *jointly* Chinese-and-American," Maxine explains common sensically, "a Han person of global majority, minority represented in America. I speak up for the International P.E.N. society's watch over minority rights in both West and East. Whether Native American or Tibetan, we defend the freedom to write what one believes and sees."

Our American women clearly have an agenda. The shortest of our troupe, all of four-feet-ten-inches, Max may stand tallest in guts and heart. "In 1925, my father made a one-way trip to New York City, nailed inside a cargo crate. He became a professional gambler and Chinese laundry man in the New World." She pauses to consider that cross, then drops her tone and says quietly, "My mother was a doctor who ran a cave hospital during the Japanese invasion of Canton. In 1939, she bribed her way onto a ship bound for San Francisco." So Maxine was born in the Bay area, grew up Californian with Chinese parents, and crossed over into the New World. "Both my parents sang Tang songs and quoted classical poems," she adds, "during my California childhood." In the late Sixties, Maxine reimagined herself in a new land as *warrior woman*. Her dream memoir by that title spun my graduate-school head around, as I spent summers with Berkeley in-laws.

Chinese cousins welcomed Maxine to her mother's village in 1984. Her platform of returning to China protests the repression of P.E.N. designates, specifically the suppression of women writers. She leans on the point that only twelve per cent of the entire Chinese Writers Association is female. Max sets her small feet squarely toward the issues and will not budge. She also campaigns for fair payment to Chinese artists for their work, salaries at least equivalent to farmers or government officials. She champions the new literature of "roots" and poetry written in minority Chinese languages. Maxine's agenda is crisp, her courage up-front, her candor unbending. Clearly there are personal and political issues at stake here, questions of human rights, not to mention gender, culture, home, and tongue.

"Isn't she a bright light in this room?" Shu-mei says and applauds, taking Henry's seat again.

"A beacon, yes," I agree, "a bonfire."

"Men and women, Ken, are not equal in China. You know that?" Shu-mei searches my face.

"So I've heard. The war back home isn't over yet either, seventy cents on a man's working dollar. I've learned this much raising a daughter. Her economic future concerns me deeply."

Shu-mei looks at me searchingly, then out across the murmuring audience.

Barry Lopez takes the floor to speak of "landscape and personality," how the "naturalist" today tries to record the "truthful drama of place." He talks in measured cadences, pauses to reflect, and softens the tone of the proceedings. "Hope can be triggered by saliencies of landscape," Barry reasons, just as the "grotesque, or even death" figures physically in natural scenery. The land itself is still our ground of being, for better or worse, as "the roots of culture in nature and among animals" set the textures of human life. Here in the "Middle Kingdom," Barry is listening for "words that will serve" this rehumanizing through attention to the biosphere, watching for the "significant topography of cultural travel."

"Hmmm," Shu-mei ponders, exiting quizzically. Henry comes back from the "talk show," he says, grinning.

Larry Heinemann stands up, several hundred pounds of a Chicago bus driver's son, whose mother came from a farm. "My grandfather was a storyteller," he begins. "I write about family, work and war, ordinary people surviving. We've had our own wars at home, you know. The benchmark of Vietnam separates those Americans who fought and those who didn't." He pauses, and I wonder whether that includes or excludes war protestors, my own stance in the Sixties. "Our own *scar stories*, then, in some way parallel Chinese literature, following the Cultural Revolution." Larry wrote of the Vietnam trenches and "grunt humps" in *Close Quarters* in 1977, then the coming home agony, *Paco's Story* in 1986. His second novel just won the National Book Award. "Our century is filled with the global difficulties of coming home from war," he says with pain in his booming voice, softened for the moment. "And it doesn't end with the ceasefire. Delayed stress is just another term for what they called *combat fatigue* after World War Two or *shell shock* following World War One. A war ghost trails many of us, a corpse that will not leave our house, a nail in my head."

"Did America abandon the Vietnam war because it couldn't hate enough?" Larry ponders. "The deliberate and mean-spirited repeat of such ill-thinking seems heartbreaking in Central America or the Middle East today." This veteran writes as honestly as he can from the foreign trenches, or home gutters, about "what war is"—without euphemism, politeness, or decorative taste. His is a good example of American straight talk and self-criticism. Larry believes that honesty moves people and betters their means of dealing with reality. His candor is hardwon. "Since 1975, three hundred novels and twenty-five films have dealt with Vietnam," he says with finality and a clenched jaw. "The extraordinary firestorm of protest against the Vietnamese war," he thinks, "inhibits the hawks today. God bless you all."

As I scan the horseshoe table and see every other writer representing China and alternately America, it strikes me again that these people, to a man and woman, know how wars fester from the loss of public freedoms, as Henry says: censorship, discrimination, sexism, racism, despoiling rivers, cutting forests, killing animals wantonly. As we turn away from care for "others," terrorist acts at home erode any check against abuses in our own backyard. Eventually people will step on anyone's back to get more of anything, redwoods, rivers, oil, tobacco, slaves, gold, bison, whales, or pandas.

"When stake raise and right of *others* lower," Henry mutters at my shoulder, "war come home. Not *them* we should fear," he says with mixed tones, "own moral slip. Believe me. Small, everyday concession grease machine that roll over *us* and *them*." This child during Red Guard mayhem knows the local violence of his own land.

Li Ziyun, a stolidly elder woman and literary critic, answers Maxine on the issue of Chinese feminism. "Here men and women share the same work and social responsibilities," she tracks the party line. "They even dressed the same ten years ago. Not until 1979 were 'feminine' concerns, earlier seen in the revolution as 'bourgeois,' raised among writers," she says icily. "The work of Chinese women writers today addresses social inequalities, questions male preroga-tives, challenges the double standard." No questions of home rule here, no fuss in the kitchen. The Beijing female translator is about as stony as Li Ziyun herself. I think of Nancy Reagan and Lynn Cheney, anti-feminist dragon ladies back home.

The only official female delegate, Madame Li speaks impassively without hint of self-drama. "If women in the provinces are practicing female infanticide through state directives," she intones, her only hint of national censure, "the future of China hangs in the balance." Reports indicate that a million female births are done away with each year. Maxine worries there may be little progress from the days when women's feet were bound. With one-couple-one-child laws for two generations now, a dramatic population decline could be in the mak-ing. Demographers fear the collapse of an entire people.

"Our women do have more energy than comparable men writers," Madame Li piques her colleagues, "their personal 'stars' shine more brightly."

"Big fine deal," Henry mutters. Shu-mei is back at the front table, listening with an odd smile.

The seeds of feminism are just stirring. In the Peoples' Congress last week, a woman lawyer stood up and challenged a "senile" man's right to a seat of power. Three dissenting votes were the first *contested* poll on assembly record in the Peoples' Congress.

"The last ten years of 'sound and fury,'" Madame Li surveys, "were filled with middle-aged, silenced writers who rushed into the vacuum with *scar literature*. Then younger writers experimented with *modernist nihilism*. Now *cooler* writers of all ages are adapting psychological realism to Chinese social concerns." This proves a solution to her. "*Root-seeking* peaked in 1986," Li feels, and none too soon. "What lies ahead?" she ends her speech tonelessly.

Bob passes a folded sheet of paper across the table. It opens to a poem he has been writing about Liu Shahe:

> *His speech makes measured*
> *music in the old Sichuan dialect.*
> *He quotes Confucius, Walt*
> *Whitman and Li Po then*
> *tells the American writer*
> *her name sounds like pearls*
> *dropping in a dish—*
> *Hong-ting-ting.*
>
> *During the long darkness Liu*
> *shaped hard wood with plane and saw,*
> *fashioned cabinets tight as tombs.*
> *As witness to his children,*
> *he wrote poems in the night.*
> *When the Red Guards came he*
> *burned the scraps of paper,*
> *then threw the ashes on the wind.*
>
> *These days he stays home,*
> *writes old style poems—*
> "traces of the saw tooth's edge—
> cipher of awl and auger"—
> *and complains about young poets*
> *writing crazy verse.*
> "My children no longer read my
> poems," *he says.* "They just
> rock and roll . . .
>
> Rolling Stones."

Henry taps me on the shoulder. He's found a woman doctor in the hotel who will administer acupuncture for gout in my hands. We leave as unobtrusively as possible and go to a room where the doctor examines me, listens to my complaint, and says she will "try." It's that

A WRITER'S CHINA

simple—a 3,000-year-old folk science, the ages-old wisdom of holistic systems, still practiced by *barefoot doctors* across China. I feel the eight silver needles penetrate close to the bone, piercing to the swollen pain.

"You think of Turtle, son of Dragon," the doctor's translator tells me reassuringly, "symbol of longevity and durability."

"One of our writers, Roberta Whiteman, belongs to the Oneida turtle clan," I say through the medical translator. "The Iroquois tell old stories about floating on the back of *turtle island.*"

"Ah, tur-tle is-land!" the translator beams. She translates and the woman doctor smiles and adjusts the silver needles. "Strong back, stronger heart," the translator says softly. The ache in my hands eases as culture and science intermix in this acupuncture session. Late afternoon slides into nightfall.

*

Three-Way Dialogues: No Twisty Thoughts
To talk little is nature's way.
High winds do not last all morning.
—LAO TSU

TAI CHI AT PRE-DAWN ON THE HOTEL VERANDAH. Below the hill, rice paddies and muddy river lie quiet, punctuated by an intermittent frogsong. Water striders stir the surface on the bonsai pond. Carp drift through the murky green, as the old stones seem to rise underwater. Potted flowers dot the borders with coral and crimson. In this reflective morning, oddly enough, the *I Ching* reads "Strife," heaven over water. Be cautiously firm, give ground—the "leather belt will be awarded in the end."

Our writers' morning session opens rapid-fire with Jin Yun, a playwright, explaining how Arthur Miller's *Death of a Salesman* influenced the bitterness in his *Lord Doggie's Nirvana.* Foreign "spare parts" for TVs are being reassembled in China (he adds an oblique metaphor) but this must not be done cheaply.

Zhou Keqin, the novelist, speaks of the millennnia-old "earth literature" today in China; no "true urban writing" has yet surfaced. There are in fact, he notes, no real cities as yet, but "towns" where country people have relocated, only recently. Small farm life is the norm, though today's Chinese may be crowded into "towns" of sixteen million. The country has some seventy million TVs, multiplied by five viewers each, which gives Chinese television an audience of 350 million and growing. This helps to explain why "book sales are down" to twenty-five percent of what they were a decade ago. Yet "Kung Fu fiction" has reached a mass pulp high, and the popular songs from Hong Kong and Taiwan flood young ears. Chinese conservatives are "wary" of this Western pollution.

"Sex, drug, rocker-roll," Henry mutters under his breath. "Same as U.S."

"Why do the young gravitate to pop tunes over folk songs?" Liu Shahe wants us to ask. We should neither bewail the "closing" of minds, nor genuflect to "great" traditions, he says, but strike in good Marxist fashion to the "cultural roots" of the problem. "Ask why," and answer functionally. Liu's head weaves and bobs with the four tones of his classical Chinese, a wraithlike presence with pale skin, fine thin bones, and fluttering eyelids. His own books of poetry "sold 50,000 only seven years ago, and but 3,000 this year." The poet wants reasons, other than his own aging.

"Too bad, poetry," Henry seconds, "kids wants TV, baseball, skate-board." With that he walks back to the translator table, and Shu-mei slides in beside me.

"Drunk old Li Po drowned, reaching for the moon's reflection in the lake," she says quietly, "maybe kids know better, eh? Du Fu wrote against war, too, probably a *rightwing roader* in Mao's eyes."

"What, against war?" I ask.

"Conscription, for example, twelve hundred years ago, the Army Wagon Ballad." Shu-mei stares me down quoting the lines. *"But have you not seen / On the Black Lake's shore / The old white bones no one has gathered, / Where new ghosts cry out, old ghosts remain bitter, / Rain-soaked from dark clouds in deadly squabble?"*

The old war correspondent, Harrison is tuning in BBC each morn-ing on short-wave. He stands up to announce, smiling broadly, "Bertolucci's film, *The Last Emperor*, has just won nine Oscars, includ-ing best picture." The Chinese applaud for several minutes.

A cicada strikes up outside the window, musically scratching its dry wings. Henry and Shu-mei exit with the other translators. The crickets begin to scritch in the room's shadows, and we break for tea and biscuits.

After we reconvene, Charles Wright talks of discovering the lyric poem, by way of Pound's Li Po translations in *Cathay* and the *Cantos*. "These poems are impersonal as spiderwebs," he says with approval. He's "never happy" with his own work because things "never get said properly," though he's "very happy" teaching. There's something lanky in this tall man's voice, a Tennessee angularity that spreads his vowels into melodic cadences. I notice his short poem from *China Trace* among the writer bios:

> REPLY TO CHI K'ANG
> *There is no light for us at the end of the light.*
> *No one redeems the grass our shadows lie on.*
>
> *Each night, in its handful of sleep, the mimosa blooms.*
> *Each night the future forgives.*
> *Inside us, albino roots are starting to take hold.*

"Poetry is a fading art," Charles feels, "a condition of disappearances, and as such, public attention is irrelevant." His black-rimmed glasses sit steadily on the firm bridge of his nose, and he blinks after he speaks. A man of the perfect cadence, the measured thought, composed and poised through natural speech—he's also something of a country spiritualist, though loathe to confess it. All "real poems," Charles insists, "gravitate toward Dante's chagrin for the soul's salvation" in the *Commedia*, "ultimately unapproachable." Another *China Trace* note catches my eye:

> REUNION
> *Already one day has detached itself from all the rest up ahead.*
> *It has my photograph in its soft pocket.*
> *It wants to carry my breath into the past in its bag of wind.*
>
> *I write poems to untie myself, to do penance and disappear*
> *Through the upper right-hand corner of things, to say grace.*

"Emily Dickinson is the only poet I really think I know," he admits, "along with radio country music, the 'white soul' of mountain people in my Tennessee youth." Charles considers the measure of that statement, then continues. "In that respect, a writer must engage the local first, or go nowhere." Charles' own work, he admits, "fades, vanishes, asks more than it is or can be." He confesses to a "good ear and a bad memory," prone to melodious aphorisms of Wallace Stevens' *Adagia*. The Tennessee poet strings out some examples from his notebook: "I live between the adjective and the noun." Apolitically political: "It either adds or it takes away: nothing is ever neutral in poems." Stoically: "Renunciation is stronger than participation." Cryptically: "All tactile things are doors to the infinite." Style and form fixate him, as they combine musically. "If you can't sing," he borrows from an old folk saying, "you've got to get out of the choir." An aphorism: "The way out," he muses, "is the way in." Finally: "All poems are transations." Charles feels that "One has to learn to leave things alone. It's best to keep unwritten as much as possible. Poetry is just the shadow of the dog. It helps us to know the dog is around, but it's not the dog. The dog is elsewhere, and constantly on the move."

The poet looks down, then sideways. "Discontent is my source," he adds, "and poems come to me as lyric prayers, wistfully underlayered." Charles ends his presentation with lines just written, borrowing from the Lakota concept of a moving prime mover, *Takuskanskan*, "What-moves-moves."

> *Sky color of old steam*
> > *the power that moves what moves*
> *Moves as the Buddha moves unmoving*
> > *great river goes eastward*

Work goes on outside the window where the cicadas are in full chorus. A tractor passes and smudges the air, as a Chinese writer loudly slurps his tea.

Bobbi Whiteman traces her writing to the shadow of her Mohawk physician grandmother, Lily Rose Monica Hill, adopted by a Quaker. "My grandmother was a woman who could carry the village on her back," Bobbi says, peering out through her thick glasses, her large shoulders sloping toward the page. Lily bore her father, Charles Hill, Oneida farmer and musician, hard drinker and lethal smoker. In a sweetly resonant voice, this poet asks us to understand her life. "My mother died when I was nine, as her father's mother had died when he was seven. My extended family of brothers and sisters came to include people, animals, plants, rocks, stars, trees. Another's ways," she says, "give us our own. And mine is a dream culture that trod on pathways of the heart and mind, where the earth is united by the rivers of our words." She adds her lines to Charles' work:

I stand drunk in this glitter, under the sky's grey shelter.
The city maple, not half so bitter, hurls itself

in two directions, until both tips darken and disappear,
as I darken my reflection in the smoking mirror

of my home. How faint the sound of dry leaves,
like the clattering keys of another morning, another world.

Like all artists, Roberta gropes toward reality and reaches through her voice toward grace.

Truth waits in the creek, cutting the winter brown hills:
it sings of its needles of ice, sings because of the scars.

The room hushes, even the cicadas and crickets quiet down, as the Chinese translation comes through Shu-mei.

Jay Wright, in turn, identifies with modernist "exiles" of the Irish Renaissance. He turns to the reassurance of *tone* in the face of racial bias, intellectual arrogance, his own passion, and general ignorance. Raised in New Mexico, now living in Vermont, Jay says that he "meets facts with disdain, spirit with detachment." The black poet speaks in a voice soft and musical, like a warm summer wind through mountain aspen. Once an army soldier, Jay is a working-class Afro-American who wrote his way into the country's poetry circles, no less than Langston Hughes or Rita Dove—shy and proud, making for a fiercely inverted intelligence, at times, a stonewalling quietness. Jazz is his passion, the bass his instrument, resonance his forte. Jay chants softly from "Areito" in *Dimensions of History:*

This is my mitote,
batoco,
areito,
my bareitote.
This is my bareitote,
areito, batoco,
my a-ba-mitote.

Corre, corrido, navideño.

Friday the thirteenth
and snow in the birch.

Love's days all begin
with that kind of coldness.
We had come down
to the fog and the bite of the sea,
another of love's soft nibbles
                on the skin.
The axe had chipped in the trees.
High up, the squabble of birds
through the evergreens
became the painful sound of palms.

And the woman sang:
"I've got love all around me
My own treasure's found me
My savior
is a boy in bloom."

Jay sings a black Homeric blues, an odyssey from Albuquerque to LA and Guadalajara, from New York to Mississippi and Vera Cruz. The line that stays with me, *Why had I chosen the cold?* centers his work.

    Color, dolori, passa
    A strength in a weary land
    A shelter in the time of a storm.

The Chinese seem puzzled by this tall ethnic poet-scholar. He doesn't fit their expectations of a fire-breathing radical. Instead Jay lectures on "polysemous" meanings in his work and "the act of becoming aware, active, and transformed through a poet's life in words." This poet speaks in a quietly precise manner, even didactically about American literature and culture. He does not want our works or ideas to be ideologically caged and "misrepresented." This man claims to be a "realist of verse, a purist of forms and definitions," and as such, he is an anomaly to this Chinese audience—an anchronism to their Maoist purges and anti-modernist stances. Jay sits down as unobtrusively as he stood up, without reading more of his work.

"Shoulder chip, boss?" Henry observes at my elbow.

"Probably has his reasons, Xiao Chen. Jay certainly doesn't want to be taken as our token ethnic poet. Not to say that I blame him—it would be no party being the only white guy in this gathering."

The Chinese novelist, Zong Pu, shifts focus to a "literature of localities." Her own work has been part of the "root-seeking movement" this past decade. Zong objects to "overly vulgar diction," searching for the "purity and beauty of language." Concerning gender splits in China, she feels that "men and women are better at different things." Her impassive expression declares this to be point of fact, as the heating pipes in the room groan and knock.

"Creativity expresses itself in different ways, in different fields," Ms. Zong co-opts differences. "Literature is not something abstract," she concludes, "it is concerned with cultural traditions, backgrounds, customs, habits of living, courtesies, daily behaviors, marriage, funerals, life and death, medicine, fortune-telling, astrology, phrenology."

Muttering "party hacker," Henry has left and walked up front. Shu-mei sits down with a sigh.

Alice Fulton follows decorously, as a work whistle blows outside the window. She takes Zong Pu's dismissals of gender differences head-on. "All obsessions are a form of religion," she announces with pursed lips. "Poets question bedrock assumptions of marginality, especially the patriarchal worldview that permeates much of the culture." Zong sits stiffly, and Harrison leaves the room on this note. "His over hers, the father over mother, man above woman: the implications of pronouns, historical privilege, and patriarchal subtexts insidiously charge a culture with warps of the heart." In no uncertain words, a tongue sharp to the point, Alice calls for feminist reappraisals. She lays down a bold challenge to Chinese patriarchy, not to say American paternalism.

I glance at the end of Alice's poem to her mother, "The Perpetual Light," from *Dance Script With Electric Ballerina:*

> And the dead . . . let's hope
> they're different, too.
> That they no longer wait with heavy patience
> for our arrival at some ever-open gate,
>
> but hotfoot it through the universe
> like supple disco stars: their glamor sifting
> into our rare, breathtaking dreams, our rarer prayers
> mere twinges in their unimaginable limbs.

Henry chants a Berryman line under his breath, *All the girls, with their vivacious littles / visited him in dream: he was interested in their tops &*

bottoms / *& even in their middles.* I keep my mouth shut, hoping Henry's Berryman riff doesn't get out of hand.

In a high, thin voice, Liu Shahe stands up to speak of "social responsibility," "classical language and poetry," and the 1920s "new literature" he learned in college. He saw a "modernist watershed in China." His short stories, essays, and some poetry were first published when he was sixteen, later silenced during the Cultural Revolution. "My descendants need to know how *unreasonable* the purges were— that a writer must *work* to survive repression—that he must write *faithfully* when he could hide his poems." In 1979, Liu "regained his literary position and wrote to protest the darkness." He also began to publish cultural criticism and translations, introducing Taiwanese poets to the mainland, trying to reconcile Chinese factions.

"*Try Dr God, clown ball,*" Henry chants Berryman's dream song, "*low come you in blue sad darkie moan / worsing than yours, too.*" I lower my head to get him to keep quiet. All this talk, and counter-translation, seems to be getting to Henry. Or maybe he's just genetically a trickster. Henry jockeys between tongues and tries to sort the true voices from the fakes.

Barry Lopez starts talking again, this time of "making new friends on the road," then oddly switches to note "grace and disorder in every nation." With a fondness for the microphone, he addresses disturbing social issues. Barry admits, as an American, to our "younger experience in civilization than the Chinese." Still, simply put, we today are "a group of men and women who write, but therein face the kinds of darkness all writers know, drawing on common blood and tears to speak to the truth."

"Sound nice," Henry says in a clipped voice, "but Berryman better. *Give it to Henry harder.*" Henry walks to the tea shelf and pours another cup. "*My mother has you shotgun,*" then looks up. "*Sir Bone: is stuff, / de worl', wif feeding girl.*"

Our statements and discussions seem a kind of cumbersome ball game, up and down the translative court. There are no winners or losers, but everyone a bi-hemispheric player. I think of the wild monkeys and lions in the forested hills above us, the mountain Buddha up the river over the next ridge. The meeting drones on through the late afternoon, and I follow Bob into the latrine.

"Pretty heady in there, don't you think?" I ask him.

126

"Like a nuclear plant. I love it," Bob says, "this is what we came for."

As we stand, doing our business in the restroom, firecrackers start popping outside. We look out to see a burial service taking place on the opposite hillside, draped with white mourning streamers. White signifies death, more daily present here than anywhere we've been. With so many people and little urban space for cemeteries, cremation is legally imperative.

In the evening, we read and perform our works together. The Chinese know their lines by heart, tongue twisters, popular quips, local color, ribald humor, materials passed on through folk cultures. He Shiguang, the novelist, recites his prose deadpan: "From far off it looks like a pagoda. From up close it looks like a pagoda. The more and more I look at it, it looks like a pagoda. I must finally conclude that it is a pagoda."

The jokes are idiomatic, culturally specific, and the Chinese roar approval. The word for "joke" means literally "smile talk" in Chinese. Jin Yun, the playwright, performs the role of a beggar, who breaks his bowl on the ground, a wonderfully exaggerated "character" part. Joking of Dogmeat Buddha, modern translations and mistranslations, Jin says, in a lowered voice, that one of his characters tells an audience that he "never eats dogs alive, only writes plays." A listener replies, "I do eat dog meat."

Against this, the rest of us offer assorted lines, and Larry reads the firestorm opening of *Paco's Story:*

. . . out into God's Everlasting Cosmos. Out where it's hot enough to shrivel your eyeballs to the shape and consistency of raisins; out where it's cold enough to freeze your breath to resemble slab plastic.

And we're pushing up daisies for half a handful of millennnia (we're all pushing up daisies, James), until we're powder finer than talc, finer than fine, as smooth and hollow as an old salt lick—but that blood-curdling scream is rattling all over God's ever-loving Creation like a BB in a boxcar, only louder.

Charles ends the evening with "Snow" from *China Trace:*

If we, as we are, are dust, and dust, as it will, rises,
Then we will rise, and recongregate
In the wind, in the cloud, and be their issue,

Things in a fall in a world of fall, and slip
Through the spiked branches and snapped joints of the evergreens,
White ants, white ants and the little ribs.

The Great Buddha: Unwobbling Pivot

You have seen the blossoms in the leaves;
tell me, how long will they stay?
—HAN-SHAN, COLD MOUNTAIN

TIME IS A GALLOPING WHITE HORSE, the Chinese say, *seen through a crack in a fence.* So much to say and see, so few words and time. A grain of rice, a glance out the window.

The official conference seems to pick up speed as we go along, in spite of the interminable introductions, speeches, and time-warp of translations. We endure endless banquets. Head colds sweep through our group like spring blizzards of wet, mussy congestion.

We visit the Great Buddha at Leshan, a happy-bellied fella carved from a sandstone mountainside. The red porous rock, also the hue of the Beijing Imperial Palace, reminds me of Dakota pipestone—the sacred stone for medicine pipes, ancestral "body of the people," the Lakota say. Wherever the earth is red, it seems, people worship and find home, from Adam meaning "red earth" in Hebrew, to Oklahoma meaning "red earth people" in Choctaw, to brickred Tuscan fields in Siena, to red symbolizing "beautiful" in Russia, "good" in Lakota, and "happiness" in China. Perhaps it has something to do with common blood. "Under the skin we are all colored," says the New Mexico poet, Sabine Ulibarri, "the color of blood."

Henry jostles along next to me on the bus through Chengdu valley. Looking over the back of a seat, Lu Wenfu, the head Chinese delegate, agrees that nuclear "fusion" might serve as the energy source of the future. It would solve China's critical needs to modernize, to minimize coal and internal combustion pollution, as well as bring all peoples and nations together. Fusion is a fetching image of cultural interaction, too, so we start with the writers.

"Last night," Henry recalls, "we ate quail eggs shaped as peace dove." He looks pensively out the bus window, then back at Lu Wenfu.

"Distrust," I tell Mr. Lu over the bus seat, "rots post-modernism. It's not just ennui among poets. Political paranoia seems to run rampant around the world. Even here in dialogue, arguments between communism and capitalism would snag us all in one last burst of cynical self-interest."

"You from hunger, Mr. Bone," Henry quotes his poet mentor. Lu Wenfu looks at our translator as though he were mad.

Ernie hears from Harrison that we're "shooting 'em up" in Panama these days. "This Rambo stuff is gunboat diplomacy, a way of diverting attention from the national debt."

"My daughter's future," I agree.

"And pirating self-gain," Ernie adds.

"Let me see, junk bonds, takeovers, the new tax scam on the middle class," I uncork my frustrations, "salting away more riches for the rich." A kvetching peck of us amble up Buddha's mountain, pilgrims at the flood plain confluences of three rivers. "If the water reaches Buddha's toes," they say here, "get out."

"Let's not forget the sleaze factor in the late Reagan days," Ernie says with an impish look. "Enough pork-barrel politics to make Harding cringe."

"Yeah, under the sod."

"A country where a grade B actor," Alice adds, "can be tomorrow's President."

My mind drifts from grousing to the countryside. Men with iron tools labor along the roadway. One man swings a huge sledge on a long bamboo handle that flexes and whips and snaps, as he heaves his whole body into the arc. The workers set up a musical score of sledge on spike, hammer on stone, and pick on earth. Axes ring out against hardwood, chisels clang on limestone and lava.

"In one generation," Ernie says, peering at the mountain, "these people will leap a century of Western mechanics, I betcha. They'll enter the global market with state-of-the-art technology." He glances over with a quizzical look. "Given a fifth of the world population and pragmatics to rival Ben Franklin, all China needs is technical know-how. They can dominate world production."

"America will sell that, no doubt," Harrison seconds, "and create a partnership to offset Russian expansion, even Third World factionalism."

"We could learn a more tribal behavior from these people," Ernie thinks, "in return for our lessons in self-help." His large Arapaho frame, dark curly hair and shaggy eyebrows accent the point. I muse how *free* enterprise might flourish on communal ground. A capital-based collective sense could rise up between political differences.

"The world could return where humanity began so long ago in the East," Harrison offers. "It would be a new sunrise for an old world."

"To the Chinese," Ernie agrees, "West is 'east.' New guys, we represent the dawn and live in the sun's young house."

"Don't forget this year's icon is blue dragon in spring," Harrison adds with a smile.

Tomorrow is a new moon. The cherry and plum trees blossom like popcorn. The *I Ching* comes up "Youth," spring under the mountain—the fresh source of old stone. The lesson is *How to bring out the best in the young.*

Along the hike, Ernie and I find *Tian Shen Qiu* or "healthy balls" for sale from a trail pedlar. They were once walnuts, now several sizes of marble stone balls, or in some cases shiny metal ones. We roll the "healthy balls" in our palms to loosen arthritic finger joints. Musicians, elders, and artists have long limbered up their hands this way. The exercise seems to draw the gout crystals from my sockets.

The largest Buddha in China seems to be sleeping quietly above the muddy river. He's ten stories high and close-lidded, with elephant ears, listening to some inner voice. Monks' caves pocket the cliff walls to the side, and a stairwell winds down from his copper-stained earthen head. A gentle power infuses the earth here, a sense of composure and delight in the shrubs that grow out of the cliff-wall image.

Children cluster and follow us on the way back from the Buddha. "Hello," they chirp like little birds, "Hello" and "Hello." They want their pictures taken. One boy seems to call, "Hello, money," and I shake my head no. It's the first panhandling I've heard. He's insistent, but so am I. Edie Heinemann finally explains that he's saying, "Morning," his special English, apart from the others. "Hello, morning," his own foreign words of address.

"This is the only country," Ernie remarks, "where I've seen no beggars and not many street hawkers." Still, China's new incentive thinking brings tourist solicitation, billboards, the public eye everywhere.

"A bit of capitalist spirit might not hurt China," Harrison suggests.

"Too much will corrupt her," Barry fears. "Cars will smother Beijing with smog."

"Imagine a Cal Worthington used car salesman in Chengdu." Ernie picks up the conversation. "Can you see a Jimmy Swaggart monk or Tammy Bakker evangelist around the Great Buddha?"

At best, it strikes me, Chinese and Americans seem to share a forthrightness, a sense of industry and fair play, an honesty, if not integrity—both

Christian and Confucian—that allies the peoples more than some think.

"The Chinese like to do things and get them done," Harrison keeps insisting, beyond his own political skepticism. "They are immensely practical-minded, back to Confucius."

"And reflective, to boot," Bob says, "Buddha means *I am awake.*"

"Awake to what?" Harrison says, "that's the question."

At lunch I'm late (packing again) and "the custom for late-guest" Henry says for the others, "is to drink three full toasts with others at the table." Down go three big glasses of Chengdu beer. We chatter away, sip soup, dribble Chinese noodles from chop sticks, nibble the dozen or so delicacies (par for noon banquet). More beer, more chatter. Then one of three Leshan writers suggests that we switch to our left hands with the chopsticks.

Liu Shahe laughs quietly across the round table. The frail old poet with wispy eyelashes has pupils that seem pained by daylight. During the Cultural Revolution, he was forced into hard labor that would have broken an able-bodied man. Liu survived. My bus mate Lu Wenfu says that whenever this bird-poet speaks, everyone wants to laugh. Perhaps Liu's humor carried him through the pain.

Mao once ate the ashes of Buddhist sutras, burned by his parents as an offering. His starving people came to eat sawdust and weeds during the Great Leap Forward when grass soup was the day's recipe.

"I burned my precious poems in the 1970s," Mr. Liu repeats, "and sat for hours sifting the ashes. Now my children prefer pop music to poetry."

Liu and I get into conversation, via Henry's quick-spirited translation.

"He's curious about Lincoln lineage," Henry says with a smile. "Ancestor worship big deal in China."

"My grandfather was a nobleman," one of the Chengdu writers, a bit tipsy, interrupts.

"No, a groom for the gentry," corrects a second.

So we all join and drink several toasts to Uncle Abe, gentry, and grooms.

"Mister Liu is such a fine poet," I offer, "he must have a songbird for an ancestor." There's a pause in our talk.

"No," he reflects softly, "sorry to say he was a frog."

Then one of the Chengdu troika tells of the frog who became a beautiful maiden and was transported to the moon, where we sing to her, froglike.

"Some say," Henry translates, "moon was married woman given

two pills—one for never grow old, other for immortal life. Instead of give one pill to husband and take one pill herself, she swallow both. Now moon lonely, young forever. Other story say husband mistreat moon wife, why she flee into sky."

"Americans must know her," Mr. Liu offers, "since they have been up there on moon." Henry tells me that he is a leading member of the Chinese UFO society. *Chariots of the Gods* got Liu interested in Mayans.

At this lunch, the common agreement seems to be that poets, all of us at heart, love to drink and dream. "Accord to Chinese custom," Henry insists, "produce one hundred poems at maltei drinking binge." We're well beyond the mark by now.

Mr. Liu has been suffering a "stomach ailment," so he rises to leave and comes around to shake my hand. I'm deeply flattered, and in my fluster to rise, I knock over a soup bowl.

"Ahhh," the Chengdu three sing out, "custom in China is you must drink three full toasts again." So bottoms up, and over the top we go, inebriate poems and all.

The bus ride back to Chengdu presents another six-hour bump and grind through the countryside, our police-ticketed driver standing on his horn the whole way.

"Not worry," Henry says, "county cheese send flunky ahead to fix citation he receive for speeding us to conference."

I've never been so happy to find a poet's latrine, as three hours later when we pull into the Su Dong Pa memorial, Taoist poet of the eleventh century Sung dynasty.

"The translator has done his best, though his best may not be good enough," reads the preface to *Selected Poems of Du Fu*, sold locally. Du Fu, a wanderer, wrote poems on the people's suffering from a thatched Chengdu cottage.

"Du Fu is also known as Shih Tsu," Shu-mei says. "He wrote in the *shih* form, five or seven characters per line, regular verses with Taoist wrinkles."

"And these are linked syllabic verses?" I ask.

"Yes, highly formal," Shu-mei says. "*Tsu* means 'words,' cognate with Lao Tsu, 'old scholar' man. *Shih* is the general term for poetry." Shu-mei beams and adds, "Like my name, Shu-mei Shih, too! Shih Tsu is known for his variations in short and long lines."

The poet's home a millennium ago is now a national shrine—gardens upon gardens of strolling grounds, lava and limestone sculptures, reflecting pools and canals, bamboo, bonsais, cedar, and flowering fruit trees. Mao Zedong visited the poet's hutch in 1957. Commemoration of the Chairman's visit all but dwarfs Du Fu—stately trees, waterways, cicadas, and singing birds.

"Try imagine," Henry muses, "Ronald Reagan visit John Berryman grave."

Li Po teased his friend Du Fu:

> *Here on Fan-k'o Mountain peak, my pal Du Fu*
> *tilts his big farmer's hat under a noon sun.*
>
> *How is it you've grown so thin since we last met?*
> *Must be all those poems you've been agonizing over.*

"You know, Liu Shahe has a point," I tell Shu-mei and a translator from the Beijing Institute, Liu Xinmin. "Most of my students would rather wear Walkman headphones and listen to Sting than rhyme a couplet. For them, MTV beats blank verse. I'm not sure they even get the 'free' verse of American speech."

"It's no better in China these days," Liu tells me. "Teachers are underpaid, and students disillusioned with bureaucracy. I make one hundred RMB, about twenty-five dollars a month, as a twelve-month-a-year Assistant Professor in Comparative Literature." He adds, "Hotel attendants make about four hundred RMB, or a hundred dollars a month." Shu-mei hangs her head in dismay.

Nevertheless, this classical poet's home serves as a shrine for a father and his two poet sons of the eighth century. *I write as the clouds and streams flow,* Shu-mei shows me the inscription on the doorpost entrance. *Takuskanskan,* I am reminded, is that formless power-that-moves-what-moves in Lakota culture back home. "Watercourse way," Alan Watts said of the Tao. The *I Ching,* Lao Tsu, Shih Tsu, and my own sense of Native America crisscross histories.

"All his life, Shih Tsu was outspoken," Maxine says, joining us around a calligraphy table. "Spent most of his time in exile."

We are served tea in a reserved room with scrolls on the walls and spittoons for the tea leaves, rising loose-leaf to the surface of covered porcelain cups. Everywhere bus drivers, truckers, laborers, commuters, or bikers gather, we find small jars of tea. Shu-mei brush-inks two rice paper mementos, I jot a few verse lines, and we all sign.

Petals, Three Gorges

"The fragrance of the magnolia
lasts forever"

Two crossing stems
firm, falling

grace notes suspended
pink magnolias
in C minor

heroic mode
lyric courage

one stroke
no mistake
embrace tiger
return to mountains

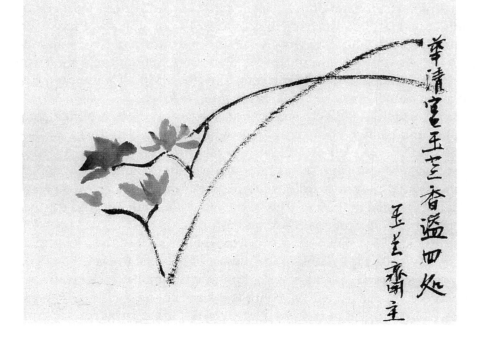

華清宮玉兰香溢四处

玉兰斋主

Strokes
"The Flowers are Fragrant
and the emotion is—"

Dark petalled lotus
angular stems
triplet of pink
tongue-tipped stamen
the slender stylus
bent

breath on breath
risen white roots
pressed rice paper

dark characters
true.

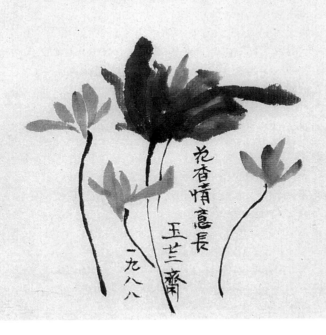

Modern Masters

He was wrongly labeled as a 'rightist' in 1957 and was made silent since then, and did physical labour for over twenty years. He took up his pen once again after the downfall of the Gang of Four in 1976.
—Introduction to Deng Youmei's *Snuff Bottles*

Bob is writing a piece on a birdkeeper whose treasured songbirds are killed during the Cultural Revolution. The birdkeeper retreats to museums and libraries where artistic birds are hidden in scrolls or paintings, even inscribed under the Forbidden City eaves.

Bob wants to interview Deng Youmei about birdkeepers, so we set up a four-way dialogue across the bus seats with Shu-mei, the translator, turned around in her seat. She conducts the English-Chinese triad bouncing through the Chengdu valley. The sky is brushed in grey cotton, the countryside verdant jade with new crops.

The bus lurches and chugs for six hours through the richest loam valley in China, as we hear Deng's thoughts on songbirds, the old men in the parks, Tai Chi (which he took up after reading that jogging could be injurious), and the art of the short story.

"And what happened to you during the Red Guard?" Bob finally asks Deng. An hour of talk has exhausted Shu-mei, now replaced by Liu Xinmin, translator from Beijing.

"The world had gone crazy," Deng begins anew, his face falling impassive. "I was curious if it would get crazier. All was over sooner than I thought. The state goons came one day and saw my garden. They forced me to eat the flowers, then a head of cabbage. "'W h i c h do you like best?' the Red Guard quizzed, so I chose the cabbage. 'Then why do you waste time growing decadent flowers?' they shouted and beat me. Had I chosen flowers, they would have destroyed the cabbages and beaten me as well.

"Always the contrary and its complement," Deng says, cupping his hands Tai Chi fashion. "At various times, the Guard would interrogate and beat me to the edge of death. Then they would suggest that life was terribly painful—perhaps the electrified cord or kitchen knife would help me end it."

We pass a bicycling woman with several dozen live geese stuffed up to their necks in two wicker baskets.

"All artists and intellectuals," Deng says with a drawn face, "were forced into hard labor during the 1970s purge." At fifty-seven today, he looks to be a man of forty, despite the tortures. "The school children would be marched out before us at sunrise, bowing naked from our waists down. The kids were prodded to spit on us and revile our intellectual decadence." He looks down into his hands.

"The Guard gave my wife the choice of loyalty to the Communist Party, or marriage to a decadent. She was forced to divorce. I did not see my two children for twelve years. My wife remarried before I was released from prison."

As an intellectual, Deng was in the eye of the storm, he feels, a politicized lightning rod only for being a writer. "I did not want my loved ones to suffer because of me. I did not grieve for myself when the children were spitting, but rather for them. A generation of Chinese young were taught to hate intellectuals, and so to reject their own minds."

"What allows a man to do such evil to another?" Bob asks incredulously.

"A very deep question," Deng says wringing his hands and looking down a long time. "There is something dark in human nature, such as yin and yang, bad and good. It cannot be eradicated. It must be lived with, it must be tamed as best we can."

"Will such a reactionary time ever return to China?" Bob wonders.

"It may, it may, I am afraid," Deng answers with a gaunt face.

Perhaps this eruption was an aftershock of the catastrophic revolution from 1946 to 1949, when landlords were bludgeoned to death by enraged peasants. The people had been servants indentured to their own land, and centuries of repression erupted in the bloodbath. Harrison says they didn't waste bullets on executions, but used clubs, axes, old swords, and knives. So, these "sons" of native revolutionary sons would have been ripe for anti-elitist "heroism" twenty years later. The next generation, raised on their fathers' war stories and the emotional charge of massive reprisals, might crave their own terrorism. In the name of Mao and the motherland, the Gang of Five turned them loose without check. Red Guard teen-age gangs, armed and ideologically terrorist, unleashed their rage on artists and intellectuals, anyone suspected of Western sympathy.

"Are we exempt in America?" Ernie turns to ask Bob, as Deng sinks back into his bus seat.

"You've been in the trenches," he tosses back, "what do you think?"

"Well, there was Cortés the conquistador, certainly a bloody executioner. And Cotton Mather the evangelist was witch hunter and Indian killer." Ernie screws up his face like a sour walnut. "Andy Jackson removed the Five Civilized Tribes at gunpoint. More recently we've had Walker Williams, the Nicaraguan freedom fighter, and all those CIA insurgents."

Bob smiles wryly. "Yeah, I grew up out west too. I know about Custer the Indian killer. Come to think of it, he's only a cut above Joe McCarthy, the Commie baiter. I guess we've ginned up our share of misguided idealists."

"A frontier history of genocide and landgrabbing," Ernie tacks on with a grimace, "from boomtown to gold-rush. We've got our own White Boys' Guard."

"Not to mention slavery or poverty with thirty million citizens today," Bob reflects. "We could use a dose of collective mobilization in the good old U.S. of A. More TVs, cars, commercials, and guns won't improve our standard of living."

"Remember what Lao Tsu advised," Deng Youmei says, looking out the bus window. *"Conduct your triumph as a funeral."*

By late afternoon we reach Chengdu. The main boulevard is lined with three to seven-story apartment buildings, new high rises for offices, and billboards advertising the "modern" China: cars, propane tanks, TVs, sugar, liquors, electrical tools, skiing, furniture, lathes, office equipment, soft drinks, xerox machines, pandas in the zoo, washers and dryers, stoves, etc. Modernization, machines, advertising, and consumer frenzy are flooding China. The country is leaping from the late Medieval period of the "feudal" countryside into the urban twenty-first century.

Our castoff plumbing pipes tourism into China. Our hotel toilet bowls are all "American Standard." My head cold is in full gale, and the old auguries stay on target. *I Ching* comes up *Po* or "Overthrow." Tuesday signaled "Beginning" for the opening conference, Wednesday "Struggle," and Thursday "Youth."

Lao Tsu advises, "No fight: no blame." See eternity in a grain of rice, a glance out the window.

Lu Wenfu

"During the 'cultural revolution,' he put aside his pen until
he resumed his literary writing ten years later."
—OFFICIAL BLURB ON LU WENFU

HENRY AND I TALK on the bus to the Chengdu waterworks, a thousand-year-old engineering miracle to tame the river. Before I know it, Lu Wenfu's bemused round face appears moonlike through the notch beween the seats. Lu has the shyly alert glance of a grey meercat.

"*Guan Ying* is Chinese female Buddha," Lu says through Henry's translation, "equivalent to lotus or white elephant. Original male Buddha from India, you know, undergo sex change in China. He become woman before go on to Japan. *Guan Ying* preach sermon on mounted three days. In end no listeners know what she say. She ask small stone, and it know whole teach."

"Tao, Confucius, Buddha," Lu reflects, "form bedrock Chinese thought. What transpire since 1946, these cannot be root out China. Sutras far more complex than Christianity," he contends, stretching his arms to indicate the literal size of the books.

There's considerable play in these busride talks, modest undercurrents. Lu defines two forms of Chinese humor, for example: "folk pratfalls, obvious exaggerate or buffoons; then subtle more, kind of philosophical layer, like water currents under ripple surface. When Chinese humor successful," Lu thinks, "one tempted to laugh, then suffer, result in 'quizzical smile.'"

"I've seen this in the Buddha's lips," I remember, "the curl at the edges of a face that will suffer, endure, all that it sees."

"Yes, all is!" Lu says with delight. "Low-lid eyes may be open or close." The meditative irresolution, the equipoise in *waking up,* forms an opening for the spirit.

"Buddha see all, and nothing," Lu adds. "Big ears watch when eyes close." He half-shuts his eyes and smiles to himself.

"Once," Lu confesses, "I drink so much wine with writer friends that fall off bicycle going home at night. I just lie on back by road look up sky. Man come and try help me up."

"'This not your business,' I protest. 'I enjoy heaven by road! Leave alone.'"

With down-home hosts we dine royally on several dozen mildly spiced dishes and dumplings, "eight secrets" desert rice, and tumblers of local kiwi wine. "The real riches of China are not jade or pearls," a Chinese proverb says, "but the *five grains*—rice, soybeans, wheat, barley, and millet."

Like cherry blossoms blinking into spring, our dining gets quite "lively," as Harrison remarked a few weeks back, noisy and a touch outrageous. "Toast, cuz," Larry salutes me. We drain the kiwi wine, and all turn their glasses over. The Chinese women salute one another as intellectuals "equal" with the men, holding their own on this outing. Four of one hundred and ten Beijing writers are paid a salary. Women number one in ten of the organization.

The apricot gingko bonsai in the courtyard have an unkempt elegance, unwired, unweeded, sparingly pruned. Their new leaves look like tiny green scarves covering the branches. It's an ideal setting to take Henry's picture.

"The female gingkos were banned from Manhattan's Central Park," Barry says, "because of stinking fruit on the ground."

"Would your Buddhist grandmother approve of our drinking feast?" I ask Lu, as we board the bus. He hesitates, holds his expression, shakes his head slightly. I apologize, "Then we must ask her forgiveness."

"It was not nearly wild enough," he says impishly.

*

Wrap-up
Yield and overcome;
Bend and be straight;
Empty out and be full.
—LAO TSU

NEW MOON TODAY and the last of our formal discussions. We are bussed, endlessly, to a drab office building. Three flights upstairs awaits a conference hall decorated with pink, silver, gold, red, and green patterned tinsel, along with blinking Christmas tree lights. Two potted ferns grace a horseshoe of tables set with blue and purple flowering plants. Sunlight floods through a bank of windows, all along the southern wall. A brace of sky hooks scrapes the outside patio shrubbery, *tschuss, tschuss*, rattling against the greenery. The swinging shadows add a strange counterpoint to conference summations.

"Sighted any UFOs?" I tease Liu Shahe, the moon-frog poet who watched me spill the soup.

He points across the street and says, sheepishly with pride, "This is home—telescope on roof." Liu sits on the board of the Sichuan UFO Research Institute, quite serious about flying saucers.

"Ladies and Gentlemen, Comrades and Friends," Zhong Pu opens the session, talking about Hawthorne's "Rappaccini's Daughter." This elder woman sees a Chinese parallel in the father who kills his daughter, walling her in his garden. Alice and Maxine have been trying to make the point for a month. Dong's first short story in 1979, "Who Am I," led to a collection about women, *Warmth of the Light Shining from Abroad*, and her work has been translated and published in *The Antioch Review*. Lu Wenfu, meanwhile, wrote a "short" story of only eight hundred characters, "External Influence and Literary Disturbance," about Western free forms on fire in China's backyard. Feminism seems one of those brushfires. There was "no need to put it out," he explains. "From 618 to 907 A.D., the short story served as a Buddhist form." Now, as we all can see, "The floodgates to the West stand open, and three choices face the Chinese: *follow me* with anti-traditional froth on the water's surface; make *cooler uses* of this hot material in deeper Chinese currents; or *close the gate* and join the alarmists." Lu cautions, "Don't sneer at the third group—they harbor real fears of Westernizing. Avoid the over-caution of the second group, in reaction to the excited first party. Mao said *if you don't strike, the enemy won't fall*. If you do strike," Lu warns, "the enemy still may not fall. The point is to know the difference between *rats* and *furry rabbits*," he advises.

"Both rodents," Henry says cryptically, stealing a line again from Berryman, *"Where did it all go wrong? | There ought to be law against Henry."*

I shush him with the punchline,"—*Mr. Bones: there is.*"

Sun Jingxuan, poet and guest of honor, fears "transparency in the new writing." *Your enemy is your mouth*, goes an old folk saying. "Folk songs exist side by side with the classics of China," Mr. Sun reminds us, "the great national tradition that resists external influence. *Journey to the West, Romance of the Three Kingdoms,* and *Dream of the Red Chamber* sink bedrock texts into Chinese folklore. Each nation survives in a global forest of cultures," he thinks, "each native to itself. So the more a writer belongs to one nation, the more he belongs to the world."

"Which one nation, in China?" Henry wonders. "Mao Gang, or my nation? *However things hurt, men hurt worse,*" he tosses in.

"Shhh, Henry," I try to quiet him.

"Need dialogue here," Henry says, "or end up with *thinky death,* Mr. Bones say."

Charles defers to "Buddha's silence, the aesthetics of exclusion," while Jay says "there is no chronometer or odometer to measure our journey." The male poets are typically succinct, short-winded, quiet. I chart this point highest on my life's journey up the mountain, though my head cold feels as though someone sluiced the Fu River through my sinuses. Having just taken four yellow tablets of Ganmaoling Pian, brought by a thoughtful interpreter, I may be "staying forever." It seems prudent to fall back on Confucius' ideogramatic advice toward style in thanking the Chinese: *(1) get the point across, (2) stop.*

"Good point, boss," Henry seconds. "Talk go on long time. Lady Macbeth say, *More matter less art.*"

Madame Chen feels that "we learn in our deconstructive fissures about common concerns—war, roots, family, and love. We can find parallels, if not overlappings, and certainly we counter influence one another."

Henry makes a wry face, but keeps silent. Barry adds the testimony of an Eastern Cree in James Bay territory, when asked if he would tell the whole truth, facing massive flooding of his village. "I can tell you only what I know."

"Want hear all that, guys?" Henry whispers.

Alice appeals to our "mutual faith in language," certainly the "treasure that we all hold in common." Words are special to her, the odder the better. Her poems put spin on words and things. "We must each try to speak," she encourages, "and not fall into silence." Maxine feels we have been "showered with gifts." She fears, along with Alice, that her "feminist harshness has been taken wrong. Men and women should learn to hug each other affectionately," she pleads in a concilatory tone, "without any male pull-away, no fear of misinterpretation." Maxine pauses for the punchline. "But *buddies, pals, and guys* are not women," she concludes, "so there's a lot more inventing to do in our languages."

Yixi thanks us for some new Americanisms: "OK" and "Let's eat" and "What's up, dude?" which Bob's boys have taught him. Yixi invites us to Tibet, "the highest mountains, rivers, lakes, and skies in the world. I wish long life for us all and hope for a reunion in another forty years time." Bobbi reads a poem, "Patterns," translated by Zong Pu simultaneously:

> For a moment, we are together,
> where salt-stunted trees glory in the sun, where verbena
> and jasmine light the wind with clean tomorrows.
> I felt us there, felt myself and not-myself there.
> We lived those promises ridiculed in solemn days.
> We lived with a hunger only solitude can afford.

Bobbi thanks the Chinese for the Beijing saucer of sweets, the ubiquitous banquets, and these kind words today. Larry recalls many hearty toasts. "I wish you all every good thing in my heart. A headcold is a small price to pay for these festive exchanges."

Liu Shahe with his musician's wrists, a gold ring on his left index finger, goes around the room eulogizing each writer: Larry's "brave heart," Bobbi's "Iroquois gentility," and Maxine's "microcosmic grace." Her Chinese name, *Tingting*, sounds like "pearls dropping into a dish," Liu says with a smile. He toasts Alice's "femininist courage" and Barry's "defense of natural ecosystems." Finally, Liu salutes Jay's "quiet depth," Charles' "poetic mistiness," my "Abraham Lincoln kinship," and Bob's "golden silence."

Zhou Keqin invites us to his hometown: "The Chinese people welcome you once more with strong liquor and warm hearts. When you come again, doors will be open."

Bob, our American-style Bodhisattva, would like us to live up to the idiom that silence is golden. "This experience is especially rich," he feels, "the real fruits may come long after this initial seeding." Bob lets that point register. "Internal differences," he thinks, paraphrasing Emily Dickinson, "are where the meanings are." Bob was moved by Deng Youmei's talk of children reviling him, feeling "not humiliation for yourself, but for a generation of young people schooled in insensitivity and brutality."

Deng Youmei answers that he's had no sleep, no easy summary, not enough words to express how he feels about our meetings. "Hearts are encased in hard, outer shells from sufferings," he knows. "For the last ten years, it has been impossible for such an exchange on this level. It took decades of effort to move toward this atmosphere of dialogue, yet still it's not possible globally. If the politicians could talk as writers do," he thinks, "the world would be a better place." This was Norman Cousins' initial motive, going back to the Russian-American talks at Dartmouth in 1957.

Finally, Lu Wenfu speaks of "the writer's lonely creation where our hearts wish the world to get better and better, as it does not change." Yet his confidence has risen, "given such people working to make peace as an international brigade of writers.

"Welcome to my hometown," he says with an open smile, "come fish and swim in the ponds there." Lu Wenfu officially closes the conference "with great success."

*

Dark Rich Loam
Ruling the country is like pan-frying a small fish.
—LAO TSU

I CHING CASTS "WATER OVER HEAVEN," which means waiting. The traveler pauses in the mud by the river, in sand, in blood. There will be rain and a great reception later.

We take an overnight train to an old village mountain outpost, Chongqing, meaning "double good luck," settled for seven centuries. In the mid-1930s, Chiang Kai-shek pursued the red army from this river outpost, and during World War II, Chongqing served as the capitol of China, a refugee city heavily bombed by the Japanese in 1939. The Yangtze joins the Jia Ling River here, and night bombers could easily follow the silver thread of the big river inland. Fourteen million people inhabit the heavily industrialized riverport.

All ten writers and their family members and translators check into the Yuzhou Guesthouse high on the crest of a hill. "If it was good enough for Kissinger," Bob says wryly,"it's good enough for us." So

WISH YOU HAVE A GOOD TIME

KENNETH LINCOLN

A WRITER'S CHINA

KENNETH LINCOLN

KENNETH LINCOLN

KENNETH LINCOLN

goes the folklore of travelers.

At dawn, rice paddies and terraced hillsides patch the Yangtze banks. Factories line the opposite side of the river, as the sun rises persimmon red and casts a saffron sash across the river. Bustling commerce and work speckles the fields and roads below.

For the first time I hear birds all around, sparrows and thrushes on the mountaintop. Blossoms and spring-leafing branches shadow-lace flying magpies with white-banded black wings. A rooster in the distance crows all afternoon. My head cold seems to be depressurizing. Herbal Chinese medicines work gradually, but thoroughly, with no side effects.

We're all processing several weeks of travel, where pods of friendships have configurated: the fellows, the wives, the poets, the point men, the musical and unmusical, the talkers and the thinkers, the worriers and the adventurers. We join, conjoin, and differentiate in endless circles of inclination and circumstance. Who sits at whose table can mean the difference between heavy *maotai* toasting with Chinese moonshine, or quiet courtesy, or fretting, or bemused tolerance of travel complaints. But we're interconnecting in the mysterious ways that humans reach out, evade, resist, or accept each other.

"There are friendships, yes, threading through little pods of us," Jeannine says over a Tsingtao beer. "And there are natural suspicions. You know how people are. The gender line is a clear demarcation, politics another."

"Things aren't really that different among writers and their mates," I agree. "We attach and disconnect. We gossip and flatter, put up with and reject each other in all too human ways."

"Well, hearing you all tune your strings at once can be grating, you know, Doctor K. I'd rather go shopping, or just walk the streets. These platitudes drone on and on."

"I'm sorry, that's the nature of the beast on this journey. Somewhere in all these words are broken keys to the Middle Kingdom." It must be tough, I think to myself, to be regarded as the junior league tag-along. Neither mother, wife, nor writer, JJ sometimes feels taken for granted as the single dad's tootsie. If they only knew. . . She's kept my little raft afloat for three years now, helping me raise a pugnacious teen-age daughter. Truth be known, Jeannine could pace many of the talents here, including mine.

The trip is not all sweetness and light. "Let's can that ukulele for a time," I hear someone bark on the train. Joseph Kingston is our strolling minstrel, the young Honolulu crooner, nice to have as background bus music, sometimes a bit much when nerves are stretching thin.

"Artists don't come with pocket-size egos," JJ is quick to add.

"We have some real differences. I hear some kvetch about hogging the microphone, or ethnic coopting, or the fastidious germ fears. Yet people seem to bond in their strangeness. We're in this together," I hold out, "American-style, each his own, oops, or her own. We're still partners across small differences."

JJ drains her Chinese beer. "That remains to be seen."

The Chinese keep asking, "How do you feel about being in China?" The United Nations translator, Lynette, interviews Larry and me at the banquet for an essay to be published in *China Reconstructs*. How do I feel?—ten thousand ways, mostly elated, blessed, challenged, chagrined, overfed, overtoasted, tipsy, ready for more. The Chinese writers—in particular, Deng Youmei, Lu Wenfu, and Liu Shahe—have survived hell to feast our meeting. We're deeply honored by their generosity and interest in the West.

At the Chengdu farewell party in a local nightclub, Larry toasts everyone with sorghum moonshine. He ambles over to give me a huge bear hug: "I'm so glad to find you, cuz. 'Cuz, well, you're a good guy." Later, even more *maotai* flowing, he plants a wet smooch on my cheek. Just before throwing up, Larry plops a slobbery smack on my ear.

"Blood is thicker than wine," I quote my grandmother's adage. "But tonight, cuz, it feels like sludge."

Larry and I toast each other with greased lightning liquors, "To thicker blood."

The tour bus will chug to the city's center for shopping and sightseeing. It's a nice afternoon for a stroll on my own, so I start up the hill, following the calligraphy signs, poppies, and cosmos in bloom. Birdsongs draw me to the Chongqing Chinese Traditional Academy of Painting, where artists in 1939 retreated while the Japanese bombed the city. Inside the academy, a short man dressed in black welcomes me with a simple hand gesture, as a young woman helps him prepare a large reception table.

"*Ni hao.*"

"Do you speak English?" I ask.

"Ahh," he pauses, turns to his left, and a small man, compact and slender, turns. He's dressed in the smartly tailored, traditional blue Mao suit, glowing against his brown skin. The man is about sixty years old, I guess, well-kempt, humbly elegant, with dancing, bright black eyes. "Wel-come. Come in." He waves his arms, "Lo-ok a-round." His words break crisply in the half-light of the large entry room, hung with traditional paintings. There's a lilt in his voice, a slight birdsong fillip.

I glance to the right, where my eye catches an ink-brush painting of a bamboo branch, two orange-breasted birds in flight, calligraphy at the top. The artist's chop signature stands in cinnabar at the bottom left column.

"Ahh," I let out breath, and my arm rises through the simple arc of the stroke.

"That mine," he beams.

"It's extraordinary, beautiful." The painting sweeps from the lower left-hand corner, overlapping joints up the side, to the excited calligraphy above, then separates, and rejoins, and breaks again across the top and out of the canvas. There are two flying birds—one tipped on wing toward the branch's joint, the other as though arrested in-flight, breast against its partner.

"And the calligraphy?" I ask.

"It's a po-em," he says simply. "It says—*Clear sky / thous-ands and thous-ands of miles / I want to fly / free-ly with wind.*"

"And the tree?"

"A ba-na-na. Here, you see, wind." His hand makes a forceful twist, a thrust for strong winds.

"A storm?"

"Yes. Past—" His arms indicate struggle and tension.

"The birds—?"

"Two swal-lows. Very free. They fly. Here."

"Yes, the storm, past—its shape left in the banana branch. And now the birds fly freely."

"Yes, so," he glows.

"So for artists after the Cultural Revolution," I hazard, "now free—"

"Free, free." He's pleased to connect through the canvas. I see that the painting sells for a thousand RMB, about $200. I swallow, look longingly, ask if there are less expensive works.

"Yes, yes," he gestures me into the next room. Many smaller, unframed or unscrolled originals lie on a table.

"More of your work?" I ask.

"Yes, yes." He presents his card: Chiang Wei-Liang. "My pen name, Ta Shan, means 'Moun-tain. . .Over There'."

"Other Mountain?"

"Yes, *over* there."

I think of Yeats' Ribh on Meru, the poem "There," where *all the barrel hoops are knit*. The world's dragon-snake, Oroboros, encircles itself and swallows its own tail. *There all the gyres converge in one, / There all the planets drop in the Sun.* Then I spot a delicate two-stroked orchid with strict, simple lines, plain frame, and soft burst of heliotrope. "Ahhh."

"That mine too," he says, pointing out the chop mark, *Other Mountain*.

"And the poem on this one?"

"It say," he squints, thinks: "*Lit-tle flow-er / lit-tle flow-er / let me pick you / and take you home, please.*"

I look at a dozen or so other paintings, none with the same elegance, then at the far end across the table and upside down, a larger canvas with seven unfolding coral hibiscuses. "Ahh, that I like."

"It mine too," he says with deepening pride. "Free style, I like," Ta Shan says several times, letting his forearm hang, then sweep gracefully through the air. The colorful hibiscus have a kind of homely grace, as they splay above cricket-like leaves. As sometimes happens with an artist, it feels that I'm seeing through his eyes, into his sense of delighted play with traditional forms in motion.

"The po-em say: *Wai-ting. And wai-ting.*"

"Yes." I pause to do some rough calculation, realize I could be in $300 or so, and keep walking into a third gallery room. I glance at half a dozen fine pieces, but no bells ring, then I turn to the fourth wall, and there's another "Other Mountain" piece for 1500 RMB, a white lotus.

"Pure," Ta Shan says, "it strong."

"Lotus?"

"Yes, yes! Lo-tus."

"I've read that Buddha lectured on beauty, simply by holding up a white lotus."

"Ah, it is so."

"And this—" I point to two water buffalo, "very powerful."

"Yes. A friend of mine. Very good."

The heads of the buffalo, almost abstract, rise above submerged bodies in water. "The poem?"

"It say: *Wa-ter buff-a-lo swim-ming.* My friend do this."

I'm struck by the connections made through these paintings, rising above dialect, age, politics, and history.

"Not so good here—" he points to a shadow behind part of the calligraphy. The flaw enhances the painting, but clearly is defective from the master's eye. The scrolled piece sells for 400 RMB.

I tell Ta Shan, "I'm a writer with nine others, who have just come from Leshan, where the Buddha stands by the river. We were in conference with ten Chinese writers. Do you know the poet, Liu Shahe?" He nods his awareness of Liu. "Deng Youmei and Lu Wenfu?"

"Yes, yes," his head shakes that he knows these names.

"Zhong Lu?"

"Yes, yes, very important writers." He pauses: "And you, important writer?"

I hold my index finger and thumb close together. "Not so much, little guy."

He smiles and laughs. "Since you lit-tle writ-er, I give discount—" He calculates about the water buffalo, "Two hun-dred fif-ty, half price. My friend, I know, so I can give discount."

"And the flying birds, the swallows?"

He walks with me toward the front room. "I like you writ-er art-ist. I give an-oth-er discount." He figures in his head, turns to the assistant, says something, turns back. "Eight hun-dred."

"Yes, *sheh-sheh.*"

Ta Shan explains that one hundred and twenty students study here from over the world, with seventy-two teachers. Mostly they paint at home in studios. He formerly worked in the "mus-e-um" and four years ago came to direct this institute. He is a Chongqing native, his parents living here when refugees fled from the Japanese. Ta Shan reminds me of my deceased father-in-law's gentle strength, Chinese-style—a wispy moustache, slightly cataracted brown eyes that dance, a soft lilt in his voice. *Their eyes mid many wrinkles, their eyes, / Their ancient, glittering eyes, are gay,* Yeats immortalizes the old masters.

Ta Shan's heroes lived in the Qing Dynasty, 1644-1911, "Bah-tah-san-ren" and "She-pe-zu," he says phonetically. "I like cal-lig-ra-phy, po-et-ry, pain-ting all to-geth-er," he chuckles. "Move-ment," his hands sweeps the air again.

A busload of American tourists pulls up, and I leave with my packaged paintings.

Warm mountaintop mists moisten the air. The birds sing away, too fleeting to be eradicated among the four Red Guard pests.

> *Clap hands, applaud the swirling petals—*
> *chin in hand, I conduct the singing birds.*
> *Who comes to applaud me on my life's music?*
> *Sometimes, a woodcutter passes by.*
>   —HAN-SHAN, COLD MOUNTAIN

Buddha pause, reflective time: breathing, eyes half-closed, thin line of light, heartbeat, birdsong. The night air drifts in like a cool mountain dove. Banana and palm trees thrive in this warmer river climate.

"Why do they paint in the old forms today?" I hear someone snipe in the guesthouse hall.

"To sell paintings. . ."

Is that why Western poets write in measured verse, musicians compose in sonata form, or painters might be interested in representation? Aside from the necessity of making a living, perhaps the traditional forms still inform an artistic vision. Must art always be "new" in the West? *Let be be finale of seem*, Stevens says. Ancient lines offer a horizon note, a ground sense, a harmony that the Chinese painter honors. As Ta Shen said, China is free of terror only ten years past. Sprinkled with blossoms and cicadas in Chongqing, what mud-green frog sings your future?

*

China in So Many Words
Do not tinkle like jade
Or rattle like stone chimes.
—LAO TSU

WHAT OF CHINA, TO THIS POINT?

Annie Dillard, here four years ago with another writers' group, saw "clear pools of the heart" in Chinese faces (*Encounters with Chinese Writers*). It seems to me more like facing the Great Stone Buddha in Leshan, or trading with a street pedlar at Mao's tomb: Chinese honesty and openness are markedly transparent, but that's only the quizzical surface. Stephen Greenblatt, another visitor who taught Shakespeare, calls party-line intimacy a "calculated and illusory frankness." These were killing fields, most of this century. Beneath cordial welcome lie depths so ancient and cross-grained as to render American good will naive. So this palimpsest of Chinese character is many-layered—historical complexity, racial pluralism, religious mix, geological magnificence, cultural enigma. The layers should check assumptions, too quickly drawn, about knowing the Chinese character, literary or otherwise. Momentarily drawn impressions are about all I can set down. As in the standard English vocabulary, with some five thousand individual "characters" basic to a literate vocabulary, the Chinese "sign" themselves idiosyncratically, elegantly (from sixty thousand characters in the lexicon), distinctly "other" to each other.

So, too, each American stumps for special interest groups: ecology, ethnicity, language, morality, miscegenation (the dominant Hans have long feared blood-mixing). Yet what each of us "protects," protects exposure beyond special interest, mutes dialogue across differences. Here among a billion voices, we preach to no choir but our own bouncing translated echoes. We divide up, not just by gender, age, and politics, but as poets, novelists, essayists, critics, or journalists. On both national sides, the poets seem rightly exacting, from Liu Shahe to Jay Wright, precise and suspicious of misusing of language and knowledge. From Harrison Salisbury to Liu Binyan, the journalists want to know how the story runs. Larry Heinemann to Deng Youmai, the novelists search for characters, and the essayists want concepts, Barry Lopez to Yixi Danzang, the Tibetan reconstructionist. The critics crave systems, from my orange-peeling tablemate in Leshan, Chen Liao, to Bob Rees, my old UCLA friend. A deafening kind of reticence threatens to mute the exchanges. Suspicion clouds a poet coming forward. Skepticism, tinged with resistance to party line, checks an essayist from talking freely. Company talk, diplomacy to ideology, muffles everyone.

The novelists, both Chinese and American, seem more forward and most trusting. They move directly into the foray to tell and gather stories.

They are not so much hesitant of misused words, as fearful of not hearing or catching the undertow of the narrative line. They feel even for the riptide of feminism and male chauvinism shearing against each other. This open sense of difference comes for perhaps the first public time in modern China.

We all ride the current of this trip for dear life. We glimpse "forbidden" cities, as it were, where a fifth of the world has been shrouded for half a century. Indeed, how much more do we know about China since Marco Polo?

V

Ancient Yellow River

Here we fizzle, a pack of poor scholars,
beleagured by extremes of hunger and cold.
We're out of work, our only kick is poetry:
scribble, scribble, we wear our brains thin.
Who wants to read the works of such men?
With that you can pocket your sighs and tears.
We could chisel our poems on dry biscuits
and the footloose dogs wouldn't stop to chew.
                    —HAN-SHAN, COLD MOUNTAIN

Deng Youmei

Yangtze River Batwing Boat

Yangtze Port

WU WANG, HEAVEN OVER THUNDER, the *I Ching* advises. "Sincerity" is the opposite of recklessness. Hold heaven's innocent simplicity firmly in the center, the sages record, and "there will be no error."

Blue Coaster buses, horns blazing among the Chongqing ox and donkey wagons, pull-carts, babies, bicycles, and old people walking. Public vans carry river rafts of fuel coal gas, strapped on top (Molotov cocktails the size of migrating whales). Frog-mouthed green trashcans line the city walks and belch back the trash.

Baskets show up everywhere in China—double burden baskets of dirt, perhaps seventy pounds a load, suspended at either end of a pole across a man's shoulders. A woman stands in the market with a string bag of eggs and lima beans. Everything is carried by hand. The weight of work is in bodies, hung from arms, rooted in hearts. The streets teem like an outdoor shopping mall, and again I'm compelled to list things: knife sharpener, tailor with ironing board and scissors, food vendors and hot soup stands, fry breads of all kinds, bicycle repairs, mechanic parts, sugar cane, more baskets in all sizes and weaves, clothing, shoe repairman, barber. All these trades take place under umbrellas, or squatting on the sidewalk, or walking.

Harrison tells me that our hilltop "Guest House" was built for diplomats and visiting dignitaries, Henry Kissinger, Richard Nixon, Mao Zedong, Chou Enlai. One *guest* palace per city was set aside as a party conference center. Now the party is a bit embarrassed at such catering holes, so they're converting them into tourist facilities for Japanese, American, or Russian tourists. We get charged quadruple the Chinese equivalent.

"Yesterday," Harrison says, "I visited a motorcycle factory. Twelve years ago when it was a munitions plant, ten thousand workers divied up anti-tank equipment, mortars, machine guns, and grenades to slaughter each other. Trying to seize power during the Red Guard mayhem, each side was self-righteously for 'Mao.' The losses in Chongqing were a hundred to two hundred *thousand* lives. Can you believe? As usual, intellectuals and artists, teachers and writers were harassed and humiliated and beaten. Worse than that, many were incarcerated, forced into labor, or killed." Harrison's Minnesota-blue eyes go cold with the thought, and he turns away.

A chorus of work music rises over China, above the raucous voices, birdsongs, engine growls, and bus horns. The *tchink, tchink, tchink* of hammer on stone richochets across the Yangtze, as workers on both sides hew stones to build roads. Work is being done everywhere, if wildly disordered. People rebuild their cities, modernize, push and load and shovel and blast China by hand, by sheer numbers and will.

We get a three-week glimpse of this, among the first outsiders now filtering into the Middle Kingdom. Personal moments focus the dizzying travel—those short moments with the artist, Ta Shan, the glance that snagged on his paintings, among the hundreds of others in the gallery. Confucius smiles cryptically, Buddha winks.

*

The Yangtze by Boat
But I alone drift on, not knowing where I am.
—Lao Tsu

We board a riverboat and begin to navigate the treacherous upper reaches of the Yangtze. Small metal sloops with red triangles are anchored near the shifting gravel bars to indicate the channel currents. The engines chug, thrusting us downstream, as the large steamer surges rhythmically in the current. The steam whistle bellows *whaaaaa*, warning the sampans, fishing boats, barges, trawlers, and other cruisers away. It sounds like *Om*.

Everyone is writing now. I see Maxine talking quietly with Chinese women in the stern. Larry leans over the railing to watch a sampan make its way across the river. Harrison is tuning in BBC radio. We go through China our own ways, shopping, nosing up alleys, singing or sneezing, grumbling or exclaiming. JJ is still laid up with the flu-cold that has slimed everyone. We are alternately meditative, satirical, fearful, expectant—but each traveler gets down to pen in hand over blank-lined pages. Writers, a breed apart. Poets, novelists, essayists, dramatists, speechmakers, naturalists, journalists—words are the compass of our frontiers, the belaying pins of our mountains—riprap trails of tones laid over the earth's shifting surfaces. Barry stands at the prow with binoculars. Larry admits that he doesn't know what to write about here: "The flood of things blitzes me. I really don't know what to say or think. All I've been wondering about is how the Chinese *work*."

"Yeah," he agrees with himself, "hard work, building this country with bare hands, the bottom up. Work is work, as Studs Terkel will tell you, any day of the week. Not much different than the pioneer west, eh cuz? Maybe that's what I'll write about," Larry muses.

Harrison shows us the dust jacket blurb on a novel, written forty years ago by our Chongqing host: "A story about a U.S. CIA prison-camp in Chongqing."

"Who does the torturing," Harrison wonders, "who is the tortured?" Then he reflects to himself, "Times have changed, but whips are still raised."

The sun has gone under a dense fog now. We seem to be steering into a small storm. The *plink, tchink, clink* of metal on stone rings sharply over the brisk wind. The river narrows to a gravel bar on the right. The water sloshes into the bank, and a stiff head wind rattles the swinging boat shutters.

A sampan is tied to the east bank, where half a dozen men in blue and blood-red shirts hammer at stones: an arm falls from above, then silence, then sound reaches us across the water. Everything changes in perspective on the river. We get little of the congestion and density of China's countryside, flooded roads, or parched streets, with trucks and buses and bikes rattling around. Here we sense the pace of distance, the quiet of suspended metal on stone. A river wind flaps the shutters.

Rivers form the arteries of a country; the lifeblood of commerce has flowed for millennnia up and down this one. The moist breeze is relief from pervasive dust that coats China with verdigris film—a droning limestone-and-clay shroud over the work, the incessant traffic, the dryness, the pollutants. On the west bank, eight men pull a sampan barge upriver against the current.

Men and women, paid for piece-work, run up and down the river-banks with double baskets, carts, bags, and barrows, hauling China to land. Or do they *want* to run back for another burden, heavier than their own bodies?

"Tough workers here, wiry, tenacious, both the women and the men," Larry notices. Pagodas spire from hilltops along the shore, ris-ing to heaven like elongated pine cones.

The blossoming *payola* trees speckle the hillsides among tidy plots and fields that tumble down to the sandbars. The river rises ten meters or more during monsoon rains (one marker indicates a twenty-seven meter flood level, a hundred feet). On the west bank, sacks of cement flume down a chute to be loaded on a waiting barge, while on the east bank are stacked thousands of firewood cords.

"China's precious timber is being replanted along the steep banks," Barry says. "Yeah, my surname, the first syllable, *Lin*," I remind him, "has two trees that signify a forest."

"Something of an elegy in this country," Barry adds. "The forests have been decimated for a thousand years. Through state incentives, reforestation is slowly reseeding the greenbelt. *Plant a tree for China's future*, they say."

Twelve men row a sampan off our port bow.

Charlotte Salisbury, knitting on the deck, tells me disdainfully, "I saw bloodied geese being unloaded from a Chongqing truck, just tossed to the ground, lying still, their legs broken."

"The Chinese are not especially sensitive to animals in the slaughteryard," I agree, "but then again, you ought to see a calf branding back home. We had them every spring, not a pretty sight. Or a pig bleeding, or cattle sledging."

Agricultural killing seems much the same the world over; animals bred for slaughter are just that. Some of my UCLA students seem to think that meat is born wrapped in cellophane. In a country where the Red Guard killed tens of thousands along the streets of a single city, where perhaps two hundred thousand humans died in an isolated mountain river "outpost" such as Chongqing, the fate of a truckload of geese may not seem crucial.

"Thirty million people starved to death during the Great Leap Forward," I recall Harrison's statistics.

"This is the point I am making," Charlotte insists. "A life is a life: orchid to street mongrel, honeybee to tree toad." She seems genuinely exasperated.

"We ate frog testicle soup in Chengdu," I kid her, "at least Ernie and I did. UFO delicacies have circled the lazy Susan more than a few rounds."

"Well, they're no better to each other than to those geese," Charlotte grumbles.

"My understanding is a far cry from Harrison's. I haven't been here long enough to judge. I simply don't know China's complicated history of warlords, kingdoms, and courtly corruptions." Still, it strikes me that the Chinese can't be any more self-interested than Westerners with our *great world wars* and bottom feeders of *free* enterprise.

Charlotte looks at me with an elder "you've-got-lots-to-learn" disdain, then smiles and says softly to herself. "Ah, to be forty again."

"It's no accident that English circles the world," I trail a lame horse. "Coca Cola rots teeth in every country on the globe. You've seen what I have—Marlboros and Kents sold on the Chinese streets everywhere. Lord save us, the American tobacco industry has targeted Chinese women for its next cancer crop. Some four hundred million women are new to the workforce and now *free* to smoke."

"Why do you think Jesse Helms packs his Bible and NRA squirrel gun," Charlotte looks at me quizzically, "to keep getting elected to the Senate from North Carolina?"

"Yeah, anti-smoking pressures are getting too stiff to support the market at home."

"Hmmm," she says, and goes back to her knitting. "You sound like my husband on a grumpy day."

"Harrison does his homework," I'm pleased to say, taking the remark as a back-handed compliment. America peddles economic self-interest in the name of democracy. We sell tractors and tools under the guise of Peace Corps idealism, then export half the world's military weapons.

"As peace-keepers, we've invaded Vietnam, Cambodia, Grenada, Panama, Iraq, and Lord-knows-where-next in the name of freedom."

"What does a man your age know of freedom?" she charges sternly. "The police shot Chinese prostitutes in the back of the head, left their bodies by the roadsides, then charged their families for the spent cartridges."

"Well, yes, you're. . .right," I stumble over that point. I gaze over the Yangtze and hector the river, "The dispossession of American Indians tells us about our own capacity for violating human rights. Why has the U.S. still not signed the United Nations treaty on genocide?"

"Lord only knows," Charlotte says, throwing a stitch, "but He's not talking."

Charlotte's right, I do feel grumpy. My head cold seems to be guttering back into the recesses of my head, while JJ is stuck in the cabin sick-bed. The jade mucous clutches at my sinuses like velcro moss. It's as though I'd dunked my skull in wet kelp.

And yet, there's a measure of quiet floating down this yellow river. Adrift on the Yangtze, no telephones, TVs, cars, meals to cook, shopping, fathering, teaching, or driving to work. Saffron-robed sun tips over the west bank. Umbrella pines puff green against the golden sky. The bats come out in coveys, the new moon slivered against the dark. Venus hangs amber above the yellow river.

We see an egret feeding, a river hawk fishing, and swallows carving the clouds today. This part of China seems at peace, *native* in the old and best sense, "born" of itself. Life here is stable as the ancient river gorge, even if passers-by move in shifting currents.

Maxine's son Joseph and I play ukelele and harmonica blues after dark on the deck. *I used to live the life of a millionaire, / Spent all my money, I didn't care, / Showin' my friends a real good time, / Bootleg liquor, champagne, wine...* Green-and-red-lighted buoys lead us down the channel. *No-o-body knows you when you're down and out . . . .*

*

The Three Gorges
O-mei Mountain moon swollen in autumn. Tonight sky light floods the P'ing-ch'iang River swirls

as I leave Ch'ing-ch'i for Three Gorges. I remember you in everything I can't see and pass downstream of Yü-chou.
—LI PO, 8TH CENTURY

AT MIDNIGHT WE GO ASHORE TO A MARKET TOWN, Wanxian: steel planking, rusting barges, stale urine smells, crowds flowing up the rubble banks. JJ, Henry, and I steeply climb a broken-stone stair chute to a lamplighted street filled with all-night vendors. Off her sickbed to join the midnight excursion, Jeannine notices, again, the walking edibles in cages, live monkeys, puppies, snakes, turtles, chickens, pigs, eels, and all kinds of fish, especially fat carp.

"Heavens to Betsy," she marvels, "these people will barbecue anything. Stick close to me, Doctor K."

"Pay attention," I rib, "we'll wok these dishes in Los Angeles."

"First thing is to get a bamboo basket," she says intently, "then we'll steam dumplings galore in the condo!"

"Be first dinner guest?" Henry chimes in.

Lacquered riverstones are the petty-cash items of trade—"Three Gorge Wonderful Journey" painted on rocks in Chinese—plus singed piglets, sliced pork ears, charcoaled duck, woven baskets, and wicker furniture.

"Like big mall, eh boss?" Henry says, taking my arm next to JJ. "Buy anything here, just like LA, you know."

I feel Jeannine stiffen. Growing up in the Sacramento valley, she defends California against all comers, especially the mall-bashers.

"Henry, you have to come to Los Angeles and see for yourself. We've got the freshest artichokes, the plumpest avocados, the sweetest oranges you can ever imagine. We just don't tie up live animals outside the markets."

"So not so fresh, huh?" Henry teases. Jeannine is doing her best to be a sport. It's not easy being the significant younger other, off-stage, especially with politics and personalities continually grating. Henry is, after all, another one of the guys, Chinese or no. My travel-mate has an edge, even a chip on her shoulder, about male privilege. None of the wives is buddy-type. Maxine spins in her own Sino-American orbit, here in China, which leaves Bobbi, a shy Oneida woman with three kids, twice Jeannine's age, as a woman friend. Sometimes I try to negotiate the tension, other times I just let it go, *chill out,* as surfers say catching the waves. I feel like a middle-aging Odysseus, adrift between Scylla and Charybdis, sirens in my ears.

"We may be seeing the Yangtze naturally for the last time," Harrison tells us. "In a year the Chinese will begin construction on the Three Gorges Dam downstream. It's tantamount to dissecting the Grand Canyon with several Hoover Dams." He waves out across the dark river. "The 475-foot dam will stretch 1.6 miles across the Xiling Gorge and flood the Yangtze. This 360-mile lake all the way to Chongqing will raise the river 360 feet. The water will engulf villages like Wanxian and displace three-quarters of a million people along the riverbanks. Think of it, a hydroelectric plant generating eighteen million kilowatts of electricity, 40% more than Brazil's Itaipu Dam, the world's largest today. Engineers hope to control the flood plains below. One hundred and forty thousand people died in the 1931 Yangtze rampage. China, Canada, and the World Bank are financing the massive project for the next eighteen years. And you know what a Sandouping butcher told *L.A. Times* reporters? 'I'll raise pigs for the construction workers'." Harrison twists his head to the side, squints, and looks away.

We wander the midnight streets with dazed awe, threading the melee and tourist bustle. Then as we came two hours ago, our party treks back down the thousand-year-old dark stairwell to the river. The docks spread out like lighted rice paddies, where gunnysacked piglets await barbecuing.

Jeannine and I get up three hours later for the first river gorge, *Qutang.* The two translators, Shu-mei and Sue Fan, stand on the bridge, peering into the night. We're wrapped in woolen blankets against the bitter wind, Shu-mei topped with my Mongolian fur hat from the Great Wall. The tour guide forgot to figure the switch to day-light savings time, so we wait in darkness for an extra hour. The river narrows, the walls jut higher, towering over us. We hear bats *chir-eep chir-eep.* The narrows are famous for wild monkeys and pirates. Red lights line the shoals to the right, green lights along the channel to the left. Our translators go below out of the cold winds, and Jeannine heads back to bed with congestion thick as chlorophyll mud.

Henry joins me at the ship's bow, when the women retire with my flashlight. "Mississippi like this, Doc Ken, this big crowded?"

"Well, not this populated, for sure, Henry. You have a great deal more land mass, six times as many people. And China is so much older than the U.S."

"Like to visit U.S.," Henry muses, "see malls, check Magic Johnson and Mickey Mouse. He call *Mi Lao Shu* here on TV, Sunday five o'clock, half hour show."

"You don't say!" I marvel, "lots of viewers?"

"Six hundred fifty million." The numbers drop from another galaxy.

Henry gazes off into the darkness, and after a time, breaks the silence. "You free, boss?"

"What do you mean, Henry, sure—free to shoot myself in the foot. In the States it's more what we're free *from,* than free to do."

"What you mean, boss, got snitch and soldier there, too?"

"It's a tricky thing, this freedom, Henry, it shifts with the political winds—but no, I don't worry about cops, or spies, or restrictions on where I travel. In the States we just get in a car and go. Our laws try to protect individual freedoms. And yet . . . it's complicated, this freedom."

"Not so complicated, here China. Remember Leshan conference? Silly men ask silly questions. Moment now, pretty free, talk and go, have you guys come, discuss writing. Abraham Lincoln and plaster Statue of Liberty popular now. Soldiers have more own freedoms, no one bug them—have girls, porn films, booze and smokes. Politicians have even more. Everybody own privileges. But Deng old boy, you know, short and tough, come through many killing with Mao, in jail, out, all that crap. If necessary, he force freedom back in can, just like Red Guard when I a kid. Not so long ago, you know. Not free here, Ken, not free like you. Truth still *come from gun barrel,* as Chairman Mao say."

"I'm sorry, Henry. Maybe someday." We both look out at the gorges and fall silent.

"Someday I come Stateside, eh? You help?"

"Sure, Henry, but what about your family?"

He takes a deep breath of the night river air. "Wife and kids? Don't worry, they know how to dog me. China be very hopeful if deadbeat fathers remain at large for long, if you know what I mean. . . ."

Henry exhales slowly, looking down at the river. "Mister Ken, please, I come and see what make John Berryman funny man. . ." He lets the phrase hang over the river. "*That funny money-man,* he call Wallace Stevens. I alway remember Dream Song blue lines, Berryman in Ireland, —*Mr Bones, you on trip outside yourself. / Has you seen medicine man?* I see medicine man in States, for sure, go with Indians." Henry sinks down inside his own thoughts for a few seconds, then brightens. "You know that poem, boss, end?—*These Songs not meant to be understood, you understand. / They only meant to terrify & comfort. / Lilac found in his hand.*"

"Yes, those are lines to die for, Henry, literally." I feel dumb, hearing Berryman come back to me on the night Yangzte. He killed himself by leaping to the frozen bank of the Mississippi as the Red Guard were terroring China. I don't know any more than Henry, on the other side of the globe, how to read the dark flash in the poet's lines, the leaping chant. It strikes me strange how poetry tries to cross consciousness, even language—*what is lost*, Frost said, *in translation*— how the loss carries over.

"Berryman was a wild guy, Henry, like your friend Ginsberg, only wilder. Whether he was free, or not, is a tricky question. Free enough to drink, carouse, and drive himself to suicide off a winter bridge. But it's a sure thing—the Beats, the gays, the bohemian crazies and manic academics—wouldn't stand a chance in China not long ago. Horses of a different color, we say. Still, you've got so much here, staggering resources, new technology soaring into the next century. You seem relatively free, now. . ." It's as much a question as a statement.

"Free, little now, yes, but I rather drink Yangzte than lose freedom to talk and go," he looks hard at me, "rather eat all cold mountain, boss." He takes another deep breath and swears, "I rather suck night-soil from honey-pot all day, than lose freedom, you get?" His question is left suspended over the river, going through the Three Gorges.

Morning brings the second and third gorges with more writers on deck. Harrison tunes in the BBC: "The U.S. navy has attacked three Persian frigates and bombed sections of Iran!" The existential cowboys ride loose again.

*

Telling Brush Strokes
If you are sick of sickness, then you aren't sick.
—Lao Tsu

Keep a firm position, the *I Ching* advises. No advance today, maintain ground.

A Chinese photographer on deck sees me throwing coins for the *I Ching*. He asks, through Henry's translation, "You know American Indianer diviners?" Well, yes, I've met some medicine people. "Chinese have healers and prophets pull out illness long-distance through 'EPS'," Henry inverts the letters. "They also know what you got in pockets."

Henry and his friend want to know about American Indian healing, so I tell them of the Lakota vision quest. "It's an initiation time, especially for young people, to go up on a promontory, or out on the prairie. They fast, chant, and pray for a focus in their lives, a spiritual path. All the four directions, or 'four winds' help here, along with the sky and the earth."

"Like stop-go-with-master, old ideogram for *Tao Te Ching*," Henry makes the connection. "Teacher and follower at crossroads?"

"The plains version is a little more formal, even. The vision questor may receive an adult name through a dream or an ancestor spirit. It can come through a visionary event. Near where I grew up, Crazy Horse, or *Sunka Wakan*, saw a horse above Scotts Bluff so spirited, so alive, that it hardly touched the earth." The Chinese lean in and listen carefully, interested in whatever they can pick up, even from a white man. "The ancestral spirits help with all this, the *Tunkáshila*, or grandfather stones—through isolation, fasting, chanting, and prayer down in a hole on a mountaintop. You prepare for this quest through an *inipi* or sweat ritual with your people, assisted by a medicine person. The people's *lowanpi* or 'sings' offer collective rituals for working out dream visions, healing petitions, and blessings, especially all-night *yuwipi* darkness ceremonies."

"Not like cell-block talk," Henry tosses in.

"No, spiritual, ceremonial, a kind of daily religion. There are rituals for all human events, from departures to homecomings, christenings to battle songs."

For several hours we throw the *I Ching* coins and decipher Legge's French-English translation of the ancient Chinese ideograms. We all try with broken English, invented Chinese, and intercultural chatter to decode each person's psychic index for the day. Double brightness, or fire over fire: the "boss" is told to punish the rebel chief and pardon the others. One woman has "late winter weeding" in store. Henry's friend is shown the "turned-over cauldron," someone will "wok new stew." Madame Fan, the group leader, comes up with a regal role in "empress," as Henry looks on diffidently. It all seems delighted play to a dozen or so Chinese, gathered on the deck above the Yangtze, a lost augury.

"Thinking behind ancient *I Ching* system," Henry says, "gathers oldest collective wisdom in China. Meditation originally drawn from heated turtle shells and *yin / yang*, then bones and bamboo slats, for vertical writing. Is said Confucius wore out bindings three times on *I Ching.*" His face darkens. "Mao have all texts destroy during Red Guard years. Now Changes Book only available in old library rare script." Henry stands there looking a bit helpless, with a smile on his face. "Sad to say, illegible to modern Chinese readers, more strange than Berryman, eh doc? Least, boss, we have English *I Ching,* from French guy paperback and you, here on Yangzte." Everyone nods and smiles shyly.

Meanwhile, our river cruiser sits in the just completed Gezhou lock, pilot project for the Three Gorges Dam. This is an upriver seaport the equivalent, perhaps, of St. Louis on the Mississippi. The river ladder drops the boat thirty meters, down to an alluvial basin and on toward Hunan and the sea. We're through the "three marvelous gorges" and churning turbid water toward the plains. The climate changes to moist humid air, tropically muggy.

By late afternoon, the river planes into a vast seabound aorta, China's lifeblood riding these waters, trade from all over the globe. The flatland spreads out jade green, the season coming earlier this farther south toward the sea. The soil has mutated from limestone and basalt grey, to sienna, clay, and sandy beige. China's commerce and agriculture floods onto this flattened heartland.

Writers writing and talking. Maxine is interviewed for the China press, while others draw ideograms with brush and ink, or just practice calligraphy.

"This *Hein-e-mann,*" Larry says, "must have the most complicated set of Chinese characters on record!"

Jeannine gets drawn into telling ghost tales on the foredeck, a story-trading session that goes on all afternoon, into the evening. I lean out over the bridge with Charlotte Salisbury.

"I've been writing diaries," Charlotte says, Bostonian quick, sharply angled toward honesty, "while Harrison has researched his studies of contemporary China."

"You must know the Chinese as well as your husband does," I venture.

"Oh, for many years, Deng Youmei, Lu Wenfu," she smiles wryly. "Many of our Chinese friends get more handsome with age, even younger."

"Harrison is quite handsome," I offer.

"What?"

"Handsome—your husband."

"That's nice. He never was before. Maybe it's my influence. Well, no matter that—just don't shake hands, pick your nose, or touch your mouth in Shanghai. They have a hepatitis A epidemic going there."

"I'll sit in my room with a baggie over my head."

Ten Swedes, a bedraggled but game lot from the Orient Express, join us after one hundred and seventy hours on a train from Helsinki to Chengdu. They had to stand up on Chinese rail from Chengdu to Chengquing, where they boarded our boat.

"In se-ven days they do noth-ing in our car. You should have seen the Mon-go-li-an bor-der ca-fes."

"Sing-ing Swe-dish and drink-ing Scotch whis-key."

"I'd say may-be twenty-five bot-tles—"

"Cul-ture shock! The Rus-sians and Chi-nese just stared."

"We've been on the Second Long March with Harrison Salisbury," Larry tells the Swedes. Still, our writers' community has congealed— an extended family of strays, loner poets, fringe interculturalists, rene- gade novelists, and shaggy-dog environmentalists. "It helped me to hear other ways of writing about so many different things," Bobbi says, thinking back on the conference. "I found my Indian sense of being alone was shared by other writers. At least we have that in com- mon, especially with the Chinese women."

"It's an old story," Bob suggests, "the stragglers who make up a wagon train." I think of my ancestors moving westward, pioneers, runaways, con men, tricksters, gutsy women and men. On this trip, our homes come with us, Chicago, Michigan, New Hampshire, Virginia, Wisconsin, Minnesota, Oregon. My own Los Angeles is a state of its own.

"Yeah, you're right, Bob," I agree, "Nebraska lies twenty years back for me, yet it constantly colors my worldview. Cornhusker vowels flat- ten my voice. All that potatoes and gravey tip my taste buds."

"So we each bring *there* across the water," Bob adds, "—*here*. We're like traveling windows." I imagine a jumbled chandelier of lights passing between cultures.

The engines drone with the rumble of underwater trolls, the river broadens and flattens. Reforestation has lined the banks with clover, aspen, and spring wheat greens.

"The Chinese on board ride 'second-class' in 'hard seat' passage," Shu-mei says with consternation. "They sleep on mats in the halls, wash with small towels, and eat their meals of noodles and vegetables. You see them drinking their jars of tea, standing or sitting on the metal stairs. They peer at our American-style meals from the port deck windows."

We feel like fishbowl exotics. The Swedes and two Chinese families share our foredeck status, complete with stuffed couch and segregated deck.

"Foreigners get charged four times what the natives pay," Shu-mei explains. "In a sense it's good Chinese business, though not much for promoting intercultural exchange. Ugly American rides on capitalist coattails of Chinese communist government!"

*

Comparing Notes
Why is the sea king of a hundred streams?
Because it lies below them all.
—LAO TSU

STRIPED TEAL TRAIL US BY MORNING. Seven seagulls cross the bow as we steam into Wuhan. From the front deck, Larry and I toast the Yangtze with a liter of Tsingtao beer. Barry gets interested in intercultural translations, Native America to America, as we discuss the problems of getting caught in the crossfire. He seems to want to bridge some small distance between us, like two explorers on drifting icebergs, reaching to shake hands across the chasm.

Maxine appreciates the inter-ethnic difficulties of our work. She's often adrift somewhere over the Pacific, between China and California. Max, Bobbi, Shu-mei, and JJ settle into telling more ghost stories on the foredeck. Jeannine recalls a time in her teen-age years when she was babysitting, and something or someone, was thumping around in the attic of an old house.

"I didn't know what to do, call the police, or scream," she says in a softly strained voice, "so I started singing jump-rope jingles and kicking the kitchen chair."

"Oh my goodness," Shu-mei says with wide eyes, "did it stop?"

"No, it got louder, then it started coming down the banister stairs..."

"Did you run home?" Max asks, holding her breath.

"I couldn't move, couldn't scream." Jeannine holds the moment, then smiles. "Then the kids' dog, a big old ridgeback, came bounding off the bottom stair into the room. I knew it wasn't a spirit or a burglar."

"That's better than my ghost stories," Bobbi says, "it's true."

Shu-mei, born and raised in Korea, says she "has no home." She lived in Taiwan, and now as a graduate student at UCLA, comes to translate cultures, looking for her lost home in China. The classical culture she so admires is receding, or has been suppressed in modern China with its utilitarian Maoist ethic, hard labor rebuilding, and politicized writing wars. The present lurch toward liberalism doesn't offset youthful ignorance of the masters, Confucius, Lao Tsu, Li Po, or Du Fu.

"Heinz Baby Food is advertized in gooey TV commercials," Shu-mei scorns. "Love Soap looks *hot* in a Madonna-style clip, a bathing beauty spun by shower water jets."

"L.A. Valley sleaze," JJ kibbitzes. "Chinese decadence may be on the rise."

How long before the Party moral majority lashes back? I conjecture to myself, like the Puritan push against maypoles at Merry Mount. The palisaded people are masses to be steered one course, then another, confused somewhere between. Jesse Helms and Strom Thurmond know about those political bromides back home.

We anchor in Wuhan harbor on the Yangtze and wait to disembark, trading addresses, anticipating the journey home. Everyone is a bit nervous about the flight from Wuhan to Shanghai tomorrow. If we get grounded again, there won't be another United Air Lines jet to Tokyo until next Tuesday, four days later.

"Count on Chinese air travel like throw *I Ching* for blind date," Henry mutters.

Harrison tells us that Madame Chen, head of the intercultural exchange program in Beijing, was sent with the men to the country during the Cultural Revolution, to do forced labor. Now she's the *boss*.

Madame Boss wants to hear about my work with Indians. "What is contemporary American 'native' life," she asks, "Lakota culture and religion, native history today?"

"Well," I search for the right word, "off-reservation it's a lot like the rest of the country, TV and pickups and frozen food, still mostly separatist on reservations. They have ceremonial and cultural responsibilities the rest of us don't share—Sun Dance, vision quest, sweat lodge, council meeting, extended kin, things like that."

She'd like to have my books, pictures of Lakota friends, maps, drawings of the Black Elk system—anything that would add to her Chinese translation of contemporary Native America in the journal, *Word Vision*. This would be my biggest audience ever, some five hundred thousand circulation. Still, I'll remain dumb to what is printed.

"Like read Berryman Mister Bones, eh boss," Henry observes. "Sound good, what mean?"

When people come together, whatever bloodlines, ages, genders, or politics, and work interculturally, they form personal bonds that transcend private boundaries. The center of gravity is constantly shifting. Our topics range from communism to ghost stories on the deck late at night, from writer's block to rice wine, from chopsticks to chapstick. But the human core, a sense of extended family, goes deep. Planes, trains, buses, and boats have ferried us all over China in three weeks. Banquet after banquet has offered countless toasts, from the mountains to the muddy plains. Challenges with Chinese writers broaden, even sharpen our collective sense of the art and audience, writing across countries separated ten thousand miles by ocean, ideology, and ancient history. Questions come up that didn't before: Are we blinded by politics, or craft, or our own concerns? We differ, markedly, about so-called "decadent" content.

Can a poet, Alice prods, write openly about sex?

What about an opposition party? Henry questions.

Or self-criticism? Jay challenges.

Clearly, we each have many more ways to see our trade. The journey opens our eyes wider to imagine other worlds, hearing voices silenced before this.

Bob challenges us as writers, Who holds us accountable tomorrow?

Does our writing serve anyone's needs, Barry adds, aside from our own?

And then there are *the people*, Maxine keeps stressing, folk as *real* culture. Does it matter how many people read our work? Who has the right to encourage, or to silence us?

Are aesthetes all snobs? Charles queries.

Larry wonders where writing fits next to men building roads, or women harvesting grain, or the bloodshed of revolution?

What constitutes classical literature, interglobally? Shu-mei presses matters of tone and form.

Alice asks again, Who determines beauty?

And I keep pushing how artists use humor interculturally.

If anything, this trip has opened what Harrison calls "the oyster shell of China" to the apple of America, our own seeds of growth into the next century. We'll see how soon either side closes, to digest the news and protect itself from too much of *the other*. If Americans disagree on so much about literature (form, function, voice, to audience), we can expect no less of writers in other cultures, politics notwithstanding.

VI

Wuhan, Two Rivers Away

What can I do? What can I do?
Take this bag of bones home and hide it in the mountains!
—HAN-SHAN, COLD MOUNTAIN

Ernie Whiteman

Yangtze Travelers at Boat Railing

Larry Heinemann and Jeannine Johnson

Roberta Hill Whiteman

Wuhan Riverport

A Feast of Writers

WE ARRIVE IN WUHAN BEHIND SCHEDULE, our luggage stuck on the second floor, late at night. In protest, Charlotte refuses to attend the banquet. Harrison stomps around the corridor in a raincoat and shorts, bare knees sticking out like sandcrab legs.

"Where's the damn luggage?" he thunders. "I want my bags, right now, or we're not going anywhere."

We spit-shine quickly and dash to yet another formal banquet, an exquisite state sampling of Hunan cuisine. Chicken, duck, pork, spinach, and assorted vegetables in savory sauces—less spiced than Szechwan cooking, each with a tang of its own, perhaps twenty dishes, along with a tart plum wine and *maotai* sans the sorghum bite.

"*Gan-bei*," my host tells me, over *maotai* "white and dry," a lightly flaming cognac.

"Bottoms up," Harrison chortles, still fuming, then croaks, "*Gan-bei*."

Xu Chi sits next to me at the big table and speaks broken English. Now in his mid-seventies, he was "sent to the country" in 1974, but "harbors no bitterness." Mr. Xu had been an intellectual his entire life, twenty years in Wuhan by then, and the Guard did not physically punish him. The "moderate labor," he says straight-faced, "improved my health and attitude." His temperance surprises me. Is this party line, pork-barrel tolerance, or simply a personal truth? I have no cause to doubt Mr. Xu.

Poets for centuries have come where the Han and Yangtze rivers join to commemorate the Taoist Yellow Crane. The temple is an uplifting, seven-layered pagoda whose "ears" or corners, hung with bells, resemble Mongolian herders' caps. I ask Xu Chi the yellow crane's significance.

"Yellow crane rise up and disappear. No meaning attached."

"Not longevity, like Yeats' long-legged bird?"

"Well, yes, but yellow crane not come back. . ."

"Like a poem?"

"Yes, like a poem, heh heh," Xu concludes. "But no need to go there now," he reassures me at 9 p.m. It's dark as coal dust, and the hotel is closed tight. "Just climb to twentieth floor at sunrise, look down on river, and then write poem." Mr. Xu has an affectionate "heh heh," characteristic of elder Chinese who endured revolutionary chaos the last half-century. His hearing aid, a cork-looking contraption, buzzes like a cicada.

After the gourmet feast, speeches, lotus seed dessert, sweet pancake, and *maotai* the likes of Courvoisier, Shu-mei leans over to whisper, "We've got a chauffeured car to the Yellow Crane temple. Come quickly. We'll write our poems." Sue Fan winks conspiratorially. Mr. Wei, the head delegate, has arranged for us to leave at 10:30.

*

Yellow Crane Pagoda at Midnight

Monkeys steal all the mountain fruits,
the heron fills his white bill with pond fish,
as I ponder a word or two of the immortals
under tall trees—mumble, mumble.
—HAN-SHAN, COLD MOUNTAIN

THE "GENERAL" IS OUR DRIVER, a classic Bogart character with long cigarette and FM jazz, piloting a state "Red Flag" limo resembling a 1950s black Packard. The bridge at 11 p.m. is crowded with trucks, bikes, and scooters, so we park on the sidewalk turnout in the middle of the bridge. I see a soldier crossing the crowded six-lane boulevard, passing the other way toward our limo. He's got a rifle strapped across his back. I motion to Mr. Wei, and he runs after the soldier, only to return smiling: "The officer welcomes us to break the traffic laws of Wuhan."

We hoof it toward the temple. "Damn," Henry says, "lock tight as brass drum." Mr. Wei wakes a night guard, and several minutes of conversation ensue. The next thing, we're single-filing into the deserted pagoda.

Laughing lions protect the entry stairs, dark fir and pines shadow the sky. The corner bells clang in the wind.

One circuit around the pagoda, a few lines scribbled in the dark. I give a Lakota necklace to Mr. Wei, a pack of smokes to our Chinese Bogart driver, and we're out the gate again.

THREE STANZAS, ONE STRAND

       I

Night writing: snake   bells   windy crane
rises above the Wan and Yangtze

We come eager to rhyme
and the line disappears

The guards sleep on
dark trees
bridge to Turtle Mountain
       II
Night train
and bike shadows
under the bridge
"Clarity"
       Xu Chi said
or was it charity?
       III
Over my shoulder
the trucks rattle on
man with a knapsack and policeman:
       "The officer
       welcomes us
       to break the traffic rules of Wuhan."

Tomorrow at sunrise
revise
soldiers and poets
blank pines   blurred lights   times change

*

Daybreak, Gone

AWAKE AT FIVE and to the top of the hotel by creaky elevator. Lights out on the top floor, all locks locked. I try to pry the lookout lounge door open just a crack.

Back down to the first floor. Nobody about. Guard asleep in the corner. Out to the dark reflecting pool to write a poem by flashlight, wind coming through the bamboo, single sparrow hurrying dawn.

Back up to the top floor. Pry the door open enough to catch predawn glow over the rivers. Back down to the reflecting pool.

If you don't learn poetry, Confucius said, *there's nothing to say.*

TWO RIVERS AWAY

No moon
in the reflecting pool
Night watchman
asleep
Tower lookout
locked
Yellow Crane flown.

I hear Wuhan
on the river
windy sounds
bamboo shivering by night
fretful dawn at daybreak.

Lost poet
the "four limbs"
do not move
and you cannot
separate
the "five grains."

Sparrows chitter
Waters ripple.

We steal into the pagoda
at midnight

Smudge hurried poems
by new pine greens
dark as Taoist jade,
an ancient pilgrimage.

"What would you have me say
to young writers, Xu Chi?"
He shakes his head.
The yellow crane has gone,
or was it "simplicity" he said?

Magpies chough—
strange words
clear lines
lucidity.
Steam whistle

in the distance.
Oh China! Confucian courtly
land of Lao Tsu and Mao
Old Li Po and Su Shih—

Beneath the noise, deeper waters.
The work goes on
surface riffles.
Dawn wakes a people

And thrushes chorus.
Watchmen stir
old men dream
classical forms.

Women graced as river willow
men virtuous as bamboo.
Yield and overcome.
Winged choir chirrups dawn.

—WRITTEN BY FLASHLIGHT AT THE FRAGRANT BROOK PAVILION
PREDAWN REFLECTING POOL, WUHAN, APRIL 1988

Watch the confluence of the rivers
from the top of the Tower
and your words will flow
like the ocher waters of the Yangtze,
so the story goes.

By the time our boat lands
it is late. Monks guard the Tower
gate and Buddhist bells tinkle
as trains run in the night.

At the Qingachuan Hotel, the poet,
Xi She, who for twenty years
dreamed the rivers from a pig farm
outside Chengdu, says, "Never mind.
The top of the hotel gives a better
view and the effect is just the same."

Next morning I ride the elevator
to the top floor then scramble up
a flight of stairs to the observation
deck. Through a window in the door
I look toward the rivers,
but the glass is dirty and
heavy smog floats over the valley, so
I can't tell if I am seeing the river
or not. I look again and see only
my own face staring back.

—Robert Rees

VII

Shanghai

In China, meaning is annulled, exempted from being in all those places where we Westerners track it down, but it remains standing, armed, articulated, and on the offensive where we are loath to put it: in politics.
—ROLAND BARTHES

Shanghai citizen

Nightsoil Collector

Shanghai Egg Man

City of Blossoms and Spring Greens

WE FLY TO SHANGHAI WITHOUT INCIDENT, though one of the tires on our C.A.A.C. prop jet is bald as my pate. "Hope there's one more landing in that sucker," Ernie says under his breath.

Late afternoon *I Ching* comes up "Encounter" with heaven over wind, anticipating a sudden meeting. Shanghai seems abruptly Western, almost Parisian, with tall, elegant pedestrians. Electric street-cars, buses, traffic lights, silk and velvet dresses, tailored men. "Developing Socialism with Chinese Characteristics," the airport bill-board announces. Modern high-rises, broad boulevards, orderly traf-fic patterns, leafing sycamore, cherry, plum, and almond trees. It's no wonder Red Guard terrorism ravaged these streets, trashing things Western, slavering to get a piece of the cake. Jeannine can't wait to shop for silk and pearls.

On the earlier trip, Bob wrote a poem in a silk factory, which he shows me riding the bus from the airport:

FASHIONS IN CHINA

At the Suzhou silk factory
> *young women in grey smocks*
> *muse over French fashion books*
> *dreaming up patterns*

Across a passage way
pigskin and fish dry in rows
weaving wave shadows on the factory roof

> *A young man in blue over and over*
> *pushes and pulls back red dye*
> *with the silk-screen print roller*

Down an alley
row on row of red canna lilies
decorate factory steps

> *The drying machine spills out silk*
> *looping and billowing*
> *in white canvas bins*

In the loom of a broken window
a spider spins out filaments
threading afternoon sun
> *Dreaming up patterns*

Our hotel stands elegant in an old French fashion. Grand pianos are placed about, attractive attendants, spacious and expensive state rooms. It's bourgeois with a vengeance, the hotel where Nixon stayed when he "opened" China to the States.

Shu-mei sits down for a cup of tea in the lobby, and I ask about the classics.

"Confucius is remembered as a gentleman with a sword at his right side," she explains. "*Wan wu* means the 'literary' and the 'swordplay,' coupled with *shong chuan* or 'both together'."

"So it's the Renaissance concept of *sprezzatura*," I try to splice *wan wu* through Italian, "roughly speaking, natural 'class'?"

"Sort of," she says slowly.

"Dueling with the right hand," I stay with the image, "penning verse with the left?" "All-around man, yes," she says. "Confucius collected the folk music of China two thousand and five hundred years ago, *The Book of Songs*."

"Pound called his translations the 'Odes'," I remember. "There's a Chinese edition, Beijing Panda Books, in the hotel gift shop, along with more scroll paintings. *Above all to be precise, | At the gulf's edge | Or on thin ice.*"

Shu-mei and I hire a cab to go to the center of Shanghai and buy musical instruments. We want a *paypei*, she says, but when we arrive, they have none. So we spot a three-stringed mandolin made of cherry, a "moon" box with a long neck called *yuechin*, that costs about twenty-three dollars. Then I see a *bangtzu* or cherry box with a striking stick, a wood clacker drum. Then a flute or *ditze*, much like the cedar love flutes the Lakota make—a dozen stops in a reed instrument. All of seven dollars, the *bangtzu* for five dollars, a three-piece Middle Kingdom band for the price of a cheap guitar. The moon-wine poet, Li Po, wrote many centuries ago:

> The dark is lazy, the moon bright. A recluse
> plays his pale ch'in sitting here lonely
>
> and suddenly cold pines begin singing
> all those chords born of sighing wind.
>
> Delicate flurries of finger-white snow,
> thoughtless emerald-stream clarities:
>
> No one knows it now. Those who heard
> a song this clearly disappeared long ago.

We return to the hotel, just in time to load into the bus and back downtown, stocking up on gifts to take home. A student at a local university, calling himself "Boba," glues himself to me in order to "practice English." The shops are filled with tea rooms, trinkets, jade, freshwater pearls, gold, carved wood, rosewood and jade chopsticks. In the "Friendship Store" for tourists, Jeannine and I drop our last R.E.N. on jade liquor cups and a lovely white jade stone with a green flash, slightly off-center. The streets are jammed with milling people, students, tourists, a wedding, and by now the expected call, "Hel-lo— change mon-ey?"

Jeannine and I stroll the anciently fashionable Shanghai streets. Golden carp swim in green ponds of water lilies. The filtered light softens all edges, as "Old Man" Lao Tsu says, *blunt the cutting edge, untie the knot, soften the glare.* Give in to the day, like no other day we have ever been alive, *yield and overcome.*

"So this is Paris of the East," JJ muses. "Do you suppose the steamed dumplings will top filet mignon?"

"Certainly better for a middle-aging girth."

"China has given us a work-out in that department," she says with a grin. "How's the belt-line today, Dr. K?"

"Another day, another notch."

The shops carry exquisite silk fabrics, and our fingers itch to touch them. JJ tries on a dress, bone-deep red, that it makes me think of carved lacquer. The finely etched patterns on sumac-resined bowls trace all the way back to the Han dynasty, almost two thousand years ago.

"Well, maybe Henry is right about malls," she admits. "I've never seen Los Angeles garment fabric of this quality." While she buys her silk dress, I run my hands through the ties and find several that would flag down a new fire engine. Red is China's color, long before Mao's little red book and communal politics, the color of passion and royalty. Pound's little Fenollasa book on the Chinese character says that five word-pictures make up "redness": rust, flamingo, cherry, fire, and blood.

The Grand Old Poets and Some New Ones

All day bright blossoms scatter my thoughts—
a white path of light stretches between us.

We made love our clouds-and-rain farewell,
then only autumn grasses along our path,

fall grasses and fall moths above,
all sorrows of you at day's end.

Will I ever see you here, or darken
this lamp as you loosen my silk robes?
—LI PO

WE TREK TO OUR LAST BANQUET OF APRIL FESTIVITIES and literary shoptalk. The grey-beige light, filtering through Shanghai streets, reminds me of European capitals, leafing gum trees lining boulevards of sunshine and shadow.

Wang Xindi sits to my right, wearing a gasket-like artist's cap and a bulbous hearing aid. He leans halfway down for me to speak into it.

"I've been learning about Confucius," I shout into his hearing aid.

"Tell the young wri-ters," he advises on his own track, "to write what-ev-er they feel—learn the forms la-ter. There's al-ways time for the clas-sics to catch up." He speaks in a singsong, nasal English that sounds like a late afternoon magpie. "Make your-selves at home," he says smiling. "Don't be ner-vous."

We launch into several dozen savory dishes. A duck skin, with plum sauce rolled in a thin pancake, gets the chopsticks clicking. There are crisp chicken pieces in light amber sauce, sweetly seasoned carp, steamed pork in dry mustard dressing, lichee and chocolate ice cream.

The white wine lights delicately on the palate, and we toast one another throughout the evening. I give our hostess, Madame Fan, a blue-and-white beaded Lakota necklace. She beams, blushes and hides her eyes, pleased to be embarrassed.

Mr. Wang has a cousin physicist at UCLA and a niece attending UC San Diego.

"Which forms do you write in?" I ask.

"All forms."

"Classical and free verse?"

"Yes, some are right for some things, oth-ers for oth-ers."

His English is staccato, syllable by syllable, precise and lyrical.

"Do you have masters to follow," I ask, "Li Po, Lao Tsu, Confucius?"

"Yes, all of them, but . . . Du Fu . . . he my man."

We chatter away like rattling cups, and the whole dinner takes on the tone of distant relatives gathering for Thanksgiving. Across the circular table with the oversized lazy Susan, the younger poet Li Hong Zhao looks at me intently and warmly. I return the writerly interest, making eye contact. To his right the older, silver-haired poet, Bai Hua, carries the presence of a wintry mountain in a temperate climate—genial, close-cropped, deeply grounded, austere.

As the banquet reaches a crescendo, the speeches begin. The head Shanghai delegate speaks of our "affinity" by temperament and trade. "There are no supermen," he says, "but ordinary human beings who face life with their backs toward death." This comes in Chinese, then translated into English, so as always we endure the translation warp.

"We also face happiness with our backs to pain," the speaker continues. "Shanghai is where the Cultural Revolution began, the suffering here most intense among intellectuals. The scars will not soon be forgotten. Now is a time to live up to modern changes and challenges, with our friends' help," the speaker adds.

"During the Red Guard madness, a minority of people rose to the level of deities," he says, "a majority sank to the level of animals. Human dignity now carries all of us forward."

For once, Henry keeps quiet, as the head speaker closes and everyone claps. "Shanghai offers one of many 'doors' to China," he says. "With heartfelt feelings these we welcome and bid you farewell."

There's a sense of the good life here in Shanghai—the better things and best desires. All these people, I realize, live by the word, curse to prayer, as we do. It's their daily bread, blood, and cherished covenant, violated by propaganda, betrayed by party cruelty, but still a sacrament.

Others rise to speak, offer welcome and toasts, open their minds. Madame Chen recalls, "On the boat, everyone was writing, reading, or meditating, thinking hard, through the Yangtze Three Gorges. This is a *working* group of American and Chinese writers," she underscores. I recall her doing Tai Chi exercises, three styles collapsed into one, on the sunrise riverboat deck. Chirruping birds and moving people—dawn memories of elders in the parks, the singing birds, my earliest sense of Chinese rebirth.

A woman stands up to eulogize her friend, "beaten to death on these streets during the Cultural Revolution." She says tenderly, "My daughter wrote about it in *Life and Death in Shanghai.*"

Sue Fan expresses her "deep pride in both countries, a sense of homecoming in China, and going home in California." She translates herself, as she speaks each tongue with a quiet, deep-seated dignity.

We break up and part for the hotel, exchanging cards and words through translators. Li Hong Zhao comes to me and Madame Fan, speaking quietly in Chinese to Fan. "He wants to say the time is too short," she says to me. "But during the meal your eyes met often, and your hearts were open."

Glancing at me, Mr. Li speaks in more measured tonal rhythms. Sue Fan continues, "He says he feels a great presence with you, and he knows you have many things to say together."

I'm stunned for the moment. "Tell him that I, too, feel the bond, and I thank him for speaking of it. We must write for our peoples—to talk across the waters."

We smile, as parting friends do at festivities, knowing the time is always too short, the words muted. We already long to return, but separation is imminent, perhaps permanent, given the shifting politics between our countries. Arrested in the moment, we bow with formal humility. Mr. Li works with the word. What he feels, I can feel. We both pray for a language of strength and peace. All this falls as word petals across a Shanghai dinner table.

*

Last Words, First Impressions

Our people take death to heart and do not journey far.
Though they have ships and carriages, they are unused.
Though they have armor and weapons, not one is displayed.
The people return to knotting ropes instead of writing.
Their food is simple and good, their clothes fine but plain, their homes safe;
Our people are happy in their own ways.
Though they live not far from neighbors,
And cocks crow and dogs bark across the way,
They leave each other peacefully growing old and dying.
              —LAO TSU

WE'VE MADE LASTING FRIENDSHIPS in this short time. Maxine, now *Tingting* to all of us, reaches up on her toes to hug me, and her eyes glisten.

"Our bond is being afraid of the same things," Barry tells me, pumping my arm.

Alice and I share a zany sense of the modern verse line, and certainly we'll talk more. Charles gives affectionate respect. Jay seems one of those quiet friends I'll know anywhere we meet. And Larry, my shirttail cousin in the Lincoln line, we hug like old bears in the Tokyo airport.

"Ride 'em hard and hang 'em high," he says with a big grin. "Don't forget to give a howdy when you're back on the ranch."

Bobbi and Ernie present me with a gold-lacquered turtle. "For my turtle brother," she says, then hands me the opening of a hand-written poem called "Traveling":

The moon on the rim of the world
skims westward over ripples of cirrus haze.
It is the orange sail of a junk
I follow, traveling in indigo twilight.

Do you know in order to sleep
I read Tibetan Poetry? Chinese History?
The sun wavers in unfamiliar air
quicksilver above the gearing down

of trucks leaving the nearby freeway.
Sometimes when I lift the lid of my cup,

tea leaves catch my heart in hidden currents
and I remember orchid petals

trembling in the Tea House of Du Fu
in his City of Brocade.

"I've already started to miss China," Bobbi says wistfully. The ache to return brings her the closing lines of the poem.

Sometimes I long for sweet-sour carp
and garlic shoots. Do you ever scour
the underground for books
on Indian nations beyond your eastern sea?

True to the drum and bell sound of my soul,
I dance these pictures into wind
and send them over the backs of ocean waters,
because I wanted you to know

every now and then I cannot sleep
until I touch my fingers to the earth
to feel if you're still rising
on the other side.

An electrical engineer just in from where he calls "Peping" joins us. "It's so good to hear English again," Mac sighs in relief and good humor, all 6'5" and 320 pounds. For two weeks, he's helped set up a power line system. "Private" American enterprise is working quietly with the Chinese People's Communist Government these days.

"Overseas Unlimited offers a contractor thirty to forty per cent over his wages," Mac explains. "You have to supervise Beijing apartment construction sites."

"If an American works outside the U.S. for six months and one day, he goes tax-exempt for that year. These people are great!" the builder sings out. "You want a concrete trench, and they're at it with a piece of rebar and a hammer!"

"And grunt work, man, all day long. The smell, the dust of burning coal, took me back fifty years to my Pennsylvania childhood." He's all good will, American ingenuity, and work ethic—a friendly admirer of Chinese hospitality.

"What did you guys think of the porcelain horses on the train? Some smell, eh? You know those toilets grow algae to fertilize the fields? And you should of heard me trying to explain a honey pot to the translator!" Mac is a corrective to the Sheraton V.P. in the baggage line, Harley, speaking in a Dallas accent of "party" thinking that chills his Chinese workers' incentive.

"Red-eyed envy, we call it. You give a bonus to one guy, and the rest resent him, gang up on him. American incentive just won't work. But the women," Harley swears, "they're the best workers. One girl I had, a real pistol, you know, but I couldn't reward her, or she'd be gone soon, I know it."

A Western newspaper surfaces, English in print like a lost friend turning up at the crossroads! The *Herald Tribune* reports that the Supreme Court has overruled Indian religious resistance to the National Park Service G-O Road in northern California by a 5-3 vote. The logging will carve up "Doctor Rock," a sacred Yurok mountain. Andy Warhol's vast collection of Indian artifacts will be sold at Sotheby's auction next week. The Reagan cowboys shoot up Iran, and Panama boils as the electoral primaries chug along.

Harrison looks aghast. "Charlotte, they're at it again," he mumbles.

Henry walks over, somewhat formally, and holds out his hand. I shake it, then hug him affectionately.

"Henry, you've been my main man. Don't forget our invitation to Los Angeles."

"No problem, Doctor Ken. You know what Berryman say, *This hard work, boss, wait for The Word.* Come to States real soon, no worry." His eyes moisten, and he turns away nimbly. I wonder if we'll ever see each other again.

"*Dok-shá*, Henry," I call out, as the Sioux say back home, *pay you back later.*

Jeannine puts a comforting arm around me. I've come to consider this Chinese translator, Xiao Chen, a decade-younger brother across the big water. Sometimes these connections have already been made before we meet, across continents, through histories, between cultures and tongues. I've felt this bond with men before, starting with my own brothers, childhood friends, my Sioux brother Mark, and teachers and students along the way. We work to trust the feeling of kinship, to honor what brotherhood we're given, momentarily, before time drops its curtain again. We are left to sift the memories, to write out the stories. *Mitak' oyasin,* the Lakota say, "all my relatives." A sense of honor and obligation comes through the blessing.

Time backflips seven hours, as the flight reverses the sun (racing with the earth's spin) and crosses the International Dateline, 39,000 miles up at 602 mph. Four hours of dark, then we return the same day, a day later—and an hour before we left Shanghai!

The jet loops down the California coast, homing.

VIII

Personal Statements

Prepared for the 1988 Chinese-American Writers' Conference

Young Friends Along the Way

Kenneth Lincoln at the Summer Palace

Jeannine Johnson in Shanghai

Harrison Salisbury

We meet once again this year, and I believe the time is propitious for a look ahead into the future and to cast an eye back to try and see whither we are bound, and from where we have come. We American writers bring to this dialogue two special qualities. With the exception of myself, we are a very youthful delegation, made up of men and women early in their professional careers; and we have in our delegation more than the usual number of poets. This gives us special credentials for looking into the future. Poets more than anyone else can sense the latest stirrings in the air, and often can reflect and express events yet to come, which are still invisible to more pedestrian spirits. No nation has a deeper, more brilliant, more lengthy poetic tradition than China. We sit at the feet of China's poets and her philosophers to learn man's history, his potentials, and where he is headed.

All great human movements, I believe, have been preceded by a generation of young creative artists who have a vision of the future. It was true in America, it was true in Russia, and surely it was true of China in the 1920s and the 1930s. And as for that revolution which I regard as the greatest in man's contemporary age, the Renaissance, that to be sure was foreseen by artists and poets and sculptors long before more practical men could assay the consequences of what was taking place. It's interesting and inspiring to those of us of the Western tradition to note that poetry was the handmaiden of China's revolution. The great leaders were not only men of action, guns, logistics, and strategy, they were poets, and their most deep and profound thoughts were written in the art of calligraphy, and in the form of poetry.

We bear a heavy responsibility. Our thoughts must not be limited by the strict logic of events, we must not feel hide-bound by constraints of the past nor by the harsh realities of the present. It's our task as writers to dream dreams which other men and women have not yet divined, to see shining goals which others may say are beyond our grasp, to think not of the insuperable obstacles, but to possess confidence that there are no insuperable obstacles. It may well not be true, as Chairman Mao once said, that an old man can actually move a mountain, but *many* men can move mountains—a real mountain, or a goal which may be even more important than that. China has shown us that she can stand up and we are in awe of that achievement. But that is just the first step.

If we Americans excel in anything it is in diversity. Our group today abounds in different styles and different attitudes. If we don't really represent a hundred different schools of thought, because there are only ten of us, it's only numbers which limit the differences which we have. We like that. We like to speak with different voices. We're very antagonistic to the One Big View. We like to have a hundred smaller views and pick amongst them, and possibly from that we can arrive at some consensus which has the strength of all the different views which the individuals possess.

We bring to this meeting a great admiration for China, a great admiration for her writers, for her remarkable traditions, for her contemporary achievements, and we are here to learn from you, if we may, and to let you, if you wish, learn a bit or two from us. We believe we are all engaged in the same endeavor, and that in friendship and talk, or debate and argument, we all shall benefit and somehow hopefully the future of the world may be made more secure and a new age of enlightenment may be brought a little closer.

I have on the wall above my typewriter a bit of Chinese calligraphy which is a poem written by Jiang Ji some 1200 years ago. It's a poem known to every Chinese here, every literate Chinese. It's called "Maple Bridge," and it's written about a bridge in Suzhou which was visited by the American and Chinese writers four years ago. I'll quote only a couple of lines from the Chinese poem. In a not bad English translation, I think, it reads:

> Beyond the walls of Suzhou
> From Cold Mountain Temple
> The midnight bell sounds
> Reach my boat.

On that occasion, on that visit, Gary Snyder, the American poet, who is familiar with lots of Chinese poetry, wrote an answering poem And I'll just read two lines from that poem, where it ends:

> And the bell sound has traveled
> Far across the sea.

I think that is about as good an example of the interrelationship of American and Chinese writers as we're apt to have, but I don't see any reason why a similar relationship may not evolve from this particular meeting. I like to think that this meeting at Maple Bridge symbolizes, indeed it is the bridge between China and America. And I like to think that here, so close to Emei Mountain, one of the sacred mountains of China, that we may erect between ourselves, maybe even this very evening in this great symphony of poetry which is about to ensue, another bridge between the two peoples and the two groups of writers. Thank you.

LARRY HEINEMANN

I WAS BORN AND RAISED IN CHICAGO, the second of four sons, and have lived in Chicago all my life. My father drove a bus, and my mother came from a large farm family. There were no books in the house as I grew up, and there was not much emphasis on reading, writing, or learning. So it's odd that I would become a writer. But then, my grandfather was a great storyteller, and my mother was a storyteller, so perhaps that is where I came by my love of stories.

Chicago is a large industrial central city of the American Midwest, the agricultural prairie. The city's history only goes back to the early 19th Century, about 1836, but has produced such writers and poets as Theodore Dreiser, Carl Sandburg, Richard Wright, Nelson Algren, and Saul Bellow.

As a soldier in the United States Army, I served a combat tour in Vietnam for one year. I have been writing about my participation in that long unhappy war and aftermath, and the inevitable personal reverberations for about twenty years. The Vietnam War was a benchmark of American history, if there ever was one, and as far as I'm concerned as a writer, it separates a generation of men: those of us who went and fought, and those of us who did not. In some ways the stories that I have to tell about the Vietnam War are very much comparable to what you call the "scar stories" from the Cultural Revolution. My first novel, *Close Quarters*, was published in 1977. *Paco's Story* was published in 1986. I am now finishing a non-fiction book about posttraumatic stress disorder, or certainly delayed stress, among the veterans of the Vietnam War. In World War II, delayed stress was called "combat fatigue." After World War I it was called "shell shock."

Finally, I guess, as a writer I am most interested in writing about ordinary working people—the reality of their lives as they work and raise families. I am interested in how the extraordinary events of war affect the human body as well as the human heart. And how ordinary people respond to and overcome, or not, the challenge of character. Or to use an American phrase, how they make it through the night. In writing about war, it is important to the spirit of the event to rely on frank language and blunt imagery. The pervasive ugliness of war cannot be conveyed in any other way. As a storyteller, and I prefer the generic term storyteller to writer or novelist, as a storyteller I feel compelled to make the reader *see* the story, and also smell, hear, taste, and feel, and for the reader to be involved imaginatively as well as viscerally in the hearing and reading of the story. No manner of expression or language should be permitted to be excluded or censored from storytelling or writing. Thank you.

HE SHIGUANG

Literature Belongs to the Man and Mankind
(transcribed from a handwritten MS)

LITERATURE, AS THE FRENCH PHILOSOPHER GENET ONCE DECLARED, is a by-product of human existence. As is always true in the past, the present and the future, we humans come into this world only to pass away from it once and for all. Our earthly existence is at once desperately short and infinitely long. There is an ancient Chinese saying which compares the passage of time to the instance of a galloping white horse seen through a crack in the wall. We can well imagine how time flashes by. But as the year moves through the cycle of four seasons and the day incessantly dawns on the night, time seems to us so immediate and ever-lasting. When we experience life, we not only confront time, space and daily living, but also confront our individual selves. Meng Haoran, a Chinese poet from the Tang Dynasty (7th century), once wrote,

> Man's life is full of changes both old and new,
> This coming and going make up the history past and present.

We have visited this scenic spot once more,
As our hills and streams remain here so nice and magnificent.

It goes without saying that a man's life flourishes and recedes rapidly. Whenever we are faced with the conflict between life and death, love and hatred, the individual and the society, our hearts cannot but be restless. I often feel, amidst nature and through winds and rain, the existence of a being independent of man's will. On these occasions, my feelings surge up and ideas come thick and fast. If I set pen to paper, I write what is commonly known as literary writing. Literature, therefore, is never an occupation open only to writers. Any human being alive can make it his/her own.

That human beings exist individually is beyond any doubts. Only when the individuals come together do we have human race and human existence. All sentiments that men are capable of, be it joy or sorrow, hope or despair, start with the individual. Without his/her feelings, there can be no sentiments shared by the whole society. If history attempts to record the common course traveled by mankind, then literature takes it upon itself to record the path taken by the individual man. So only when history blends with literature can we ever hope to make a complete and satisfactory record of human life.

Of course, the path taken by the individual is invariably linked up to the common course of the society. Eudora Welty, the American writer, has spoken about the relationship between these two. She says to this effect, to be regional means to be at a point where people, events, etc. can be specifically identified, verified in a genuine, precise and rigorous manner. Hence it is a trustworthy point where all sentiments and passions converge. The regional is closely identified with the sentiment; the sentiment is in turn closely linked to the regional. Historically speaking, the regional always stands for a certain sentiment, whereas a historical sentiment is always rooted in the regional. Thus, we have every reason to believe that "their regional" is a metaphor for the individual, and it is in the order of the individual, the regional, the national and the universal that man exists. Consequently, it is easy for us to see that as we set out to depict the individual, we are destined to end up depicting the nation and the world as a whole. We cannot write about the human race without first trying to write about the nation. On the other hand, if we write about the nation in a realistic and humanistic way, we would automatically be writing about mankind as a whole.

Since literature records the life of the different races in the past and the present, their external and internal worlds, their history and the present that results from history, it is obvious, then, that literature encourages, in a way that no other can match, mutual understanding and reference among people of different times and places. We have begun our lives on those lived by our forefathers. We shall in turn live out this life together with our contemporaries. It is equally obvious that the mutual understanding and reference among the individuals will contribute to the understanding of the regional, the national and even the universal.

By virtue of literature, people of both the past and the present have in fact been engaged in exchange and mutual reference all along. So there is all the more reason we should continue to advance the same cause with the same means.

MAXINE HONG KINGSTON

I AM AT A WONDERFUL AND RARE TIME that writers enjoy once in a long while. I finished a novel ten days ago, and mailed it away, and have not yet begun a next one. The name of the book is *Tripmaster Monkey—His Fake Book*; it is 750 pages long and I worked on it for seven years. I am happy to be among fellow writers, who will help me celebrate my freedom.

A "tripmaster" is a slang term for a master of a journey. And a "fake book" is fake as in not true, also a book of jazz melodies from which musicians can improvise. A "trip" can be a mental, geographical, or spiritual journey. The "monkey" referred to in my title is a reference to *Monkey—a Journey to the West*, the classic monkey; the title is a play on that classic. In my new book, the Monkey who took the Journey to the West keeps going and arrives in America. One of the paradoxes that interests me is that I am a Han person, a member of the largest race on Earth, and in my country, the U.S.A., I am a minority person. How does a minority writer speak in America, and still be true to her smaller community?

Now that China is working on policies concerning its minorities, I hope you will learn from our mistakes. The U.S. has treated its minorities shamefully, and is regretting it. There have been policies of slavery, genocide, relocation, quarantine. Artistically, minorities have been excluded from literature, both as creators and as sympathetic characters. To stay alive, minority people—all people—have to have freedom to write. "Freedom to write" is a goal of PEN International, an organization that we join as individuals. I am ignorant of the status of PEN in China, and during our exchange I hope you'll tell me about its work here. True literature reveals the humanity of individuals one to another, and it is created by the smallest minority, the individual writer, who needs the protection of the freedom to write.

Now a personal note: My family in China had a tradition that all the men sojourned in the Americas three or four times during their lives. My great-grandfathers went to Nicaragua, Hawaii, and Cuba. My grandfathers and great-uncles and uncles went to California. My father was the only man to make a one-way trip—to the U.S. in 1925. He came into New York harbor inside a crate, as cargo. He worked as a professional gambler and a laundry man. My mother, whose family were also sojourners, was the first woman in the family to emigrate to the U.S. She was a doctor, who ran a hospital in a cave during the Japanese invasion of Canton. She bribed her way onto a ship to San Francisco in 1939. She worked in the fields and in canneries and in my parents' laundry. She constantly tells stories—family history, Chinese folk tales, epics, and legends, including the chant of Fa Mu Lan, the woman warrior. Both my parents sing T'ang Dynasty poetry. My first language was Chinese, and the first stories I made up were oral and in Chinese. When I learned English, at about age eight, I began to write poems and fiction; the English language and written stories came to me simultaneously.

I wanted to write the adventures of my family, venturesome Cantonese people. I decided to do so without visiting China first. I would set down the mythic China—the Gold Mountain—which the Chinese Americans invented. I visited China after I wrote about here, and found a familiar place. I am relieved and happy to find that my imagination is true. As we travel about, China is confirming for me that the strong imagination can know reality.

We often hear that one is Chinese no matter how long ago one's ancestors left China. When I visited my parents' villages in Sun Woi, Kwangtung, my cousins kept welcoming me "back home." I am basking in the delight of being in a country where life and imagination come together.

Finally, I have some questions that are not in my prepared statement. I've been formulating them as we traveled. There are only four questions, and I would like to read them. Perhaps as the conference goes along, I will hear the answers to these questions. The PEN Freedom to Write Bulletin asks that writers watch over two Chinese writers. Their names, and I'll spell them, Fang Li Zhi, an astrophysicist, and Zhao Buo Ruih, the translator of *Leaves of Grass* by Walt Whitman. My question is, May we have news and reassurance about their safety?

My second question is, We've been hearing about the small ratio of Chinese women writers to men writers. I have an idea why this is so, and wonder if you could criticize my hypothesis. In the West, in general, women tend to write about interior self and about personal lives. Autobiography is the genre chosen by many women, including me. Can it be that in building a Socialist country you need a literature that is more external?

My third question is, I am very curious about how much the Chinese Writers' Association pays its writers. Is it comparable to a farmer, a worker, a government official?

For us minorities in the U.S., root-seeking literature is very necessary, because otherwise we are invisible, lost, and stereotyped in the mainstream. Lastly, Is root-seeking literature especially important to minorities in China, such as Tibetans and such as women?

Actually, I have a fifth question, and that is a request: I would love to hear the poets read the poetry in their own languages.

LIU SHAHE
On the Tri-Pillar Theory of Poetry

YOU MIGHT ASK ME, "WHAT IS POETRY?" "A garden in the air over the platform propped up by three pillars." This is my answer. From ancient times up to the present, both in China and in the West, all poetry may be generalized like this. In the twentieth century of China, I don't think it is quite necessary for the classical Chinese poetry, modern verse written in colloquial Chinese, or modern Chinese poetry to contradict each other like ice and fire. Have a little patience, ladies and gentlemen. If you look at poetry from the perspectives of architecture, you will come to agree that all poems are nothing but a garden in the air over the platform propped up by the three pillars. There is no exception at all.

What are the three pillars? They are the pillar of emotion, the pillar of intellect and the pillar of image. Without these three pillars, the platform cannot be propped up. You know, three points might fix a plane. Three pillars will fix a platform. Of course, it is quite all right to add a pillar or two in addition to the three pillars of emotion, intellect and image. However, it is essential to have the above-mentioned three pillars. Without any of them it would be incomplete. By emotion, I refer to the frame of mind which is the soul of poetry. By intellect, I refer to the wisdom of poetry which is the bone of poetry. By image, I refer to the picture of mind which is the feature of poetry. Poetry has emotion, intellect and image. So does man have soul, bone and appearance. How can any one of them be lacking?

In terms of "What is poetry?" we have different schools of theory, each definition is different from the other. It is impossible to come to a unified definition. That is because each school has a certain focus on setting up these three pillars. To them it is undesirable to keep the pillars equal in length; thus each pillar may emphasize its specific length. The 19th century European Romantic poets over-emphasized the pillar of emotion. They held that "Poetry is a vent for emotion." The weak point is often sentimentality. Readers are fed up with their poems teeming with tears. Both the American Imagist poets in the first part of the 20th century and the contemporary Chinese "Misty" poets emphasized the pillar of image a bit too much. The former held that image is everything. They did not think it necessary to have the other two pillars of emotion and intellect for support. The latter put out the image in a casual way, neglecting the other two pillars of emotion and intellect. Here, the weak point of the former is always some narrow-mindedness, which is hard to be presentable on grand occasions, while the shortcoming of the latter is that their poems are not arranged in order around a focal point. In contrast, the Chinese "Leaflet" poets in the middle part of the 20th century overstressed the pillar of intellect. They laid too much emphasis on the propaganda function of poetry. Their weak point is always a bit of dogmatism; the intellectual aspect is too apparent and the perceptual aspect is too weak. It would be rather dull to read their poems for several times. If we look at all this from the perspectives of architecture, the ups and downs of all these poetic schools are no more than the extension or shortening of these three pillars by turn.

What are the general reading public interested in? They are not interested in watching how the three pillars are extended or shortened. They would very much like to climb up onto the platform to watch the garden in the air. What is the platform here, after all? It is nothing but the language. On the platform readers might see flowers in full bloom without viewing the three pillars. It goes without saying that the emotion has to be true, the intellect has to be good and the image has to be beautiful.

Now let's come back to my topic: "What is poetry?" Ladies and gentlemen, you have gathered here, trying to get the essence of poetry. As some ancient Chinese scholar put it well, "Poetry is the expression of one's will." Then what is "will" here, anyway? It is actually the sentiment. To be more exact, it is the expression of one's emotion. Therefore we might say definitely that the essence of poetry is emotion. To be frank, I am here embarrassed for my lack of convincing points of argument. Ladies and gentlemen, could you forgive me for putting forward this ventured theory of mine before you?

You know, the temperament of ordinary people might be divided into three categories. The first category is the people of emotion. This kind of people would always express their sentiments full of emotion. The second category of people would always be quick for knowledge. The third category of people is called the people of the image. This kind of people are always very expressive in their description of things. As for the disposition of the poets, with the exception of some geniuses, they differ from one another in their strengths and weaknesses. That's why the style of their poetry is entirely different. The emotional type of poets are good at lyrics; the intellectual type of poets are good at displaying their wisdom; the imagist type of poets are good at creating images. Each has its merits.

I might give you some examples to illustrate my point. Once upon a time, three Chinese poets in the Tang Dynasty (618-907 A.D.) visited the Stork Tower (located in the present-day Shanxi Province in North China—translator's note) at different times. Each poet composed a classical Chinese poem and wrote it on the wall for appreciation. Later on, a noted Chinese scholar named Shen Kuo (1031-1095) in the Song Dynasty also visited this Stork Tower. He copied down the three Tang poems with the same title in his *Notes from the Dreaming Brook* (a well-known book of comments on science and literature—translator's note). Here are the English version of the three poems with the same title:

Ascending Stork Tower (I)

West of the Stork Tower lies a wall of a hundred feet,
The misty river and the hazy trees extend far and wide.
While flutes and drums have gone with flowing current,
The hills and streams stand with the sunset side by side.

I hate to see things flying away over a thousand years,
Yet a single day's grief is too long for me to know.
My cherished thoughts often go with my native paths,
No Spring is in sight; my heart is heavy with sorrow.

Ascending Stork Tower (II)

Behind the mountain the sun goes down;
Into the sea flows the Yellow River.
If you want to enjoy the scenes beyond,
Come on and climb up one more stair!

Ascending Stork Tower (III)

Towering above the birds' flight stands this sight;
In this world of man it is the tallest of all.
While the sky envelopes the vast plain on all sides,
The Yellow River rushes into the folded hills.

It is up to you, ladies and gentlemen, to make your own judgement.

Which poem is good at expressing the emotions, displaying wisdom, presenting images? It is no easy job to see the whole picture of a leopard by only glancing at one spot of it, as the Chinese proverb expresses well.

The way of poetry writing is diversified with each passing. And the art of poetry always gets something new with the passage of time. The three pillars' theory is always operating in a cycling fashion. Within the changes there is always something unchangeable. The coming and going of the three pillars of emotion, intellect and image is just like the merry-go-round shadows in a Chinese lantern show. That is the way of the world. Permit me to present this tri-pillar theory for your comments.

CHARLES WRIGHT

I FIRST STARTED WRITING POEMS—or what I thought were poems—in the Army, in Italy, in 1959, when I was 24 years old. I had tried to write fiction in my college days—stories, sketches—but they were never more than extended descriptions of landscape. In other words, I had no notion about how to write a story. At the Army Language School in 1958, I wrote what I thought was a journal for eight months, but which was really only whining and "inarticulate pang." The magic door opened when I read "Blandula, Tenulla, Vagula" by Ezra Pound in the spring of 1959 on Lake Garda outside Verona, on the site where the poem had been composed. That was it. The continuous desire to write that I'd had since high school had finally found its form: the lyric poem that was structured associationally, not narratively.

I had never been exposed to poetry at all in college. So I spent the next two years in Italy reading Pound and trying to rewrite *The Pisan Cantos*. I was also very much influenced by Pound's *Cathay*, translations of Li Po and other T'ang dynasty poets. I have continued to be influenced by these poets, in a deep and serious way. Back in the States, I got into the Iowa graduate school writing program on a fluke—no one read the manuscript I submitted. I knew after two minutes of the first workshop class that I had stepped into deep water, so I kept my mouth shut for two years. I probably learned more from that workshop than anyone who has ever gone there. I had a lot to learn.

They might as well have been talking in tongues. I needed an idea of history, of meter and tradition; I got all that, but also a great teacher who insisted that we reform our inclinations through craft.

I think poems should come out of one's body—and life—the way webbing comes out of a spider. I also think they should be as personally impersonal as a spider's web. I have tried very hard to get a kind of impersonal autobiography into my poems, without the tinge of "confessional poetry." Once the web is spun, the event that led up to it isn't necessary. The "I" in my poems is not, I hope, the merely personal. I hope it does go through a kind of sea-change into the richness of the impersonal, where the true and touchable voice actually lives.

Dante remains for me the great Buddhistic center of absolute attention and regard, the true magnetic field of seriousness toward which all real poems gravitate; the river of light is not a tributary, the songs rise and converge. When I read the complete *Commedia*, one canto a day, first the English translation, then the Italian, then the Singleton Commentary, it was the most glorious three months of reading I've ever done. I didn't write a line of my own during that entire time, I was so completely filled and fulfilled. By the time I got to the great Rose of Paradise, I realized the *Inferno*, which I had loved so much, was merely gossip—inspired gossip, but gossip nonetheless. The *Commedia* is ultimately a diagram for the salvation of the soul, a diagram and not a textbook.

But Dante is, ultimately, for me unapproachable. Emily Dickinson is the poet who, to this day, remains the only one who has ever "spoken" to me, the only poet who, when I read her, I feel as though I understand, I know, and have heard before, somewhere. She is the only one I've ever read who knows my name, whose work has influenced me at my heart's core, whose music is the music of songs I've listened to and remembered in my very body. Part of that, of course, is her genius. But another part belongs to another kind of genius, and goes back to country music, the music I heard on the radio in my childhood in Tennessee, the "white soul" music of the mountain people. That music, with its native tongue, keeps to the same theme, whether it's a coal-mining song, wandering song, love song, or gospel song: death, loss, salvation, departure.

My desk is my home these days and no particular place ever feels like what "home" used to feel like when I was growing up. As much as I love the landscape of my childhood, my landscapes have always been imaginary, invented and reconstructed. I look and I impose and then I decompose them and then I recompose them. The emotional glue—the cement of abstractions that hold reality together—gets worked in and becomes, I hope, an integral part.

But the South means a great deal to me. The look of it, the idea of it, the history of it. Of course, it's not really "The South" any more. Television killed all that in the homogenizing of America. All our character has become caricature now. TV did what Grant and Sherman never could: it finally ended the civil war. In most senses, that's a wonderful thing. The "burden" that Faulkner wrote under and out of seems gone. There's a new poetry uprising in the South, and in a few years it will be more apparent, I hope. If you're not local first, you're nowhere. Faulkner taught us that.

What I learned "in my bones" from the South is a tendency toward the romantic, an identification with landscape as opposed to what we think of as nature, a desire to subtract rather than add, a liking for lushness in a spare context, a dependence on memory as a condition of my present well-being, a love of style.

I've been told that my work got increasingly imagistic until I finished *China Trace,* and that since then the work seems more rhetorical, as I have lengthened my lines. I myself feel that the new poems are *more* imagistic; I hope there's more room for the image in the longer line. My basic structure pattern continues to be non-linear, imagistic, not narrative/rhetorical. It's true that I've added a narrative overtone, instead of the narrative undertone I used up through *China Trace,* the poems now have more of an anecdotal patina, but the canvas, the framework, the ground is always imagistic.

The following are some notes I've written to myself over the years:

All art is reminiscent. The best art reminisces about the future.

The image is always a mirror; sometimes we see ourselves in it, and sometimes we don't.

The image like a water drop contains its own world.

The image is what connects us to what's out there.

Poetry is the footprint of the story.

As a writer of poems, I've never had anything really except a good ear and bad memory.

Denunciation is stronger than participation.

All great art tends toward a condition of the primitive.

Everything must be temporary if it's going to be permanent.

All tactile things are doors to the infinite.

The secret of life is mathematics. It's an equation. If you don't believe it's the same way in poetry, that this piece of language, for instance, this description, equals the inarticulate ecstacy of being, then you believe in something different from what I believe.

Sometimes we think we're this, or we think we're that. But we're never more than servants to the language.

A metaphor is a link in the long chain that leads us to the invisible.

The love of God is the loneliest thing I know of.

If you can't sing, you've got to get out of the choir.

My poetic structures tend toward the condition of spider webs: tight in their parts, but loose in the whole, and endlessly repetitious.

All poems are translations.

I've never understood why sincerity and sentiment in poems automatically excluded music. Isn't it possible to have a poetic mind that has both music and sincerity?

Poems are considerations of considerations of poems.

Art tends toward the condition of circularity and completeness. The artist's job is to keep the circle from joining, to work in the synapse.

Good speech tends toward the condition of poetry, good poetry tends toward the condition of speech. The closer each comes to the other, the better each is. But they never meet.

The ultimate condition of art is inaccessible. Accessibility is only a matter of degree, a matter of form.

Style is everything and nothing at the same time, but mostly it's everything.

Form is the center of all things in poetry.

All my poems seem to be an ongoing argument with myself about the unlikelihood of salvation.

Form is nothing more than a transubstantiation of content.

All great art has line—painting, poetry, music, dance. Without line there is no direction, without direction there's no substance.

There is an organization for the universe, but it's not personal.

One has to learn to leave things alone. It's best to keep unwritten as much as possible.

Poetry is just a shadow of the dog. It helps us to know the dog is around, but it's not the dog, the dog is elsewhere, constantly on the move.

Some final observations. I consider poetry to be a spiritual activity. As such, it probably comes out of discontent, a yearning and emptiness that is temporarily filled by the expression of the poem. Poems are in a way prayers. Poetry cannot change or alter events, but it can change and alter people, as prayer can. It is music made out of words.

What differentiates poetry from prose is tone and rhythmic concentration. Actually poetry comes out of prose and seems to desire to return to it. The poet is not morally obligated to write political poems, though he may do so, indeed may even have to if he is so inspired. However, that does not mean the poet is not politically engaged or socially engaged. In fact, he is always socially engaged as he serves only to master the language itself.

Art is individual, not general. In any case, the true ideas of a poem are not those the writer brings to the poem, but those the poem offers after it has been written, whether by design or accident. Content comes from form. Form has meaning. Indeed, only form in art has meaning.

We could stake our art on the persistence of continuous inspection. By concentrating on things as they *are*, we can put meaning where it should be, in the picture itself, a reconstruction of the world as it is when we look at it. And if this seems simple, the simplicity could be deceptive. For the artist, the poet is a rescuer as well as a reconstructor. And what he rescues and what he reconstructs shows the difference between a truth and a lie.

DENG YOUMEI

FIRST OF ALL, I WOULD LIKE TO POINT OUT that though there has been a lot of unfair criticism of literature and writers from many ages, as far as I know up to now there has been no criticism of any writer for the language he has used. If any writer tries to restrain his use of language in my way I think it is more from consideration of aesthetics than anything else. Over the last two years, many novels have been written which contain language which has never appeared in Chinese print before.

For instance, one point, as a people we are very sensitive and wary about openly talking about sex. I would like to note that this doesn't mean that we're not interested in sex. We have one billion people, so you can see we're pretty good. But we do not have the custom, or we do not like to talk about these things or write about them explicitly. This isn't actually a national trait, but at one point this was carried to extremes. For instance, in my works whenever I wrote, came to talk about either dirty words or talking about the sexual organs, I would put two little crosses. And of course our Chinese readers are very clever; as soon as they see the little crosses, they immediately understand what this refers to.

Over the last few years, a new young group of writers have appeared. We call them the New Wave writers. They have purposely and unabashedly used many of these words that didn't appear before to show that they do not consider these things a taboo. I don't know how other readers feel, but when I read them, I certainly feel that this language is not very beautiful. Now from our cultural tradition we have always used poems, essays, novels and other writing to express a kind of emotion, a kind of feeling. When I write about a character who is coarse and uncouth, I don't avoid these words that he would use, the language that he would use. But if it is not absolutely necessary for the sake of the character to use that kind of language, I will try to choose something less uncouth or vulgar.

Mr. Lu Wenfu and I have a common trait in our writing, and that is we try to use the very vernacular, oral kind of language people speak. I write in the language spoken by the more common people of Beijing. Beijing has been the capital of our country for a long time, and so there are certain traditions. Even when they are cursing or shouting at somebody, they won't use very coarse language, they will use another way of expressing themselves. This is what constitutes the very special flavor, the local flavor of Beijing, and also contains a very special kind of humor. For instance, in the Beijing dialect if someone is very dissatisfied with somebody else, his strong expletive will be to say, "You're my grandson." People in Beijing use this word of "You're my grandson," but the real native Pekinger, the ones in Beijing who are the real Beijingers, don't use "grandson." They say, "Sir, your grandmother is praising you," which means that if your grandmother is praising you, you are a grandson. Now this kind of expression, this way of expressing yourself, cannot be replaced by using coarse or vulgar language.

So from my own writing experience, unless I'm writing about a character who will use uncouth and vulgar language, I will not try and make opportunities to use this kind of language in my work.

Mr. Wright said that if literature does not belong to a specific place, then it does not belong anywhere. Mr. Deng says, I completely agree with you. I think Mr. Lu and I probably have the same feeling. However, we've run into a bit of difficulty now. The problem has arisen that amongst all the works of Chinese writers translated into foreign languages, mine and his are the least translated. Many Sinologists and translators have told me that Mr. Deng, you works are really very special and unique, but they're very difficult to translate. I know Japanese, so I was able to read a Japanese translation of my work. But after I read the Japanese translation, I was disappointed to see there was absolutely none of that special flavor left, and that my works would probably be exactly the same as Mr. Lu Wenfu's works. The style sounded as if we were a reporter in one of those big newspapers in Tokyo. I believe that my works are special because of their local flavor. Without their local flavor, then there is nothing left of my work. However, this is often lost in translation, and I really don't know what to do about it. I wonder how you feel about this.

With regard to the question raised about whether American poets become poets intuitively, as you said, or because of external factors, Chinese poets have a special reason for asking this question. This is because for many writers above the age of 50 and for a certain number over 40, they have chosen the role of writer because of a sense of social responsibility. For instance Mr. Yixi Danzang—he's a friend of mine and I know a lot about him—when he was young, he had several choices ahead of him. At the time, he was the first Tibetan to study modern oil painting. In those days, all oil paintings were paintings of Chairman Mao Zedong, and the ones that were put up in the most obvious places were all painted by Mr. Yixi Danzang. He also had another opportunity to become a living Buddha. He recently went to a temple and one of the Lamas came over and wanted to touch the top of his head because he felt that that way he would be blessed. He decided to become a writer because after he had read a great many books, he discovered there wasn't a single Tibetan writer amongst them, so he decided that he was going to become a writer and he started learning right from the beginning. So that's why I would like to remind you that a great many Chinese writers write from a sense of social responsibility, or a sense of national responsibility. That's all, thank you.

ROBERTA HILL WHITEMAN

UNDERSTANDING MY WORK IS EASIER when it is framed by knowledge of my family and my people, the Oneidas, one of the six nations of Iroquois, or Long House people, whose homeland is in New York State and Southeastern Canada.

I've loved the power of words as long as I can remember. Yet my father didn't expect me to be a poet. I grew up in the shadow of my grandmother's life. Dr. Lily Rosa Monica Hill was adopted by a Quaker physician when she was five. A Mohawk Indian, she was the second American Indian woman to become a physician in the United States. She married Charles Hill, an Oneida farmer and musician and moved to his reservation. Though skilled in Western medicine and familiar with herbal remedies, she couldn't save her husband, who died of appendicitis when my father was seven. Through hardship years she raised six children and treated people, charging only enough to save their pride, and helping anyone who asked. She bridged the white and Indian world. An outsider, she helped, as our people say, to carry the village on her back. She possessed a phenomenal memory and loved to tell stories or recite poetry. When she did so, it seemed an invisible river filled with dreams swept over me from earlier generations. My father expected me to become a medical doctor, but I was not gifted in math. The invisible current of words sustained me.

My mother died when I was nine. My father raised my two sisters and me. My mother's death shocked me with the fragile luminosity of life. In our traditional ways, life and death are not separate, but are part of the natural order. Each one is thought of as a beautiful being. My mother's death strengthened me to feel empathy for people, animals, plants, as well as river, rocks, and stars.

Like many Indian people, I lived between two cultures that are almost opposite in their values and beliefs. Our parents and grandparents were sent to boarding school, which denied them their languages, prevented communal customs like dances, and split up families and clans. The present-day elders nurtured our cultural roots and kept them alive, sometimes at great sacrifice. During the 1960s and '70s these roots emerged following the civil rights movements. My story, *Fire Dragon, Fall Near Me Again*, turns on the conflict of two brothers, one who believes, yet feels defeated by the dominant American culture, the other who searches for contacts with a primordial being, which we call in our language *he who bumps his head*. He hopes for help in recovering an almost lost language.

My people see the universe filled with *orenda*, a spiritual energy that one can feel most powerfully in certain experiences when one is confronted with death, puberty, or birth. All other presences on earth are aware of this energy and follow through with their responsibilities for sustaining life. But mankind forgets. Our Great Law of Peace helps us to come together as one mind, our elders say, to increase this energy and to make us aware of the interconnectedness of life. Both the founders of Western democracy and Karl Marx, the founder of Communism, were influenced in their political philosophies by their knowledge of Iroquois culture. I search in my experiences for an awareness of our interconnectedness, which is a theme running through my work.

The 1960s and 1970s marked the beginning of the nationally recognized resurgence of Indian culture, made most visible by Indian writers who conveyed the continuing vitality of their ways of life. Some Indian writers felt that to identify their work as Indian, rather than as American, would place them at a disadvantage in publishing. In some ways this is true. Some critics and publishers expect certain characteristic content because they are unfamiliar with Indian experience. Luckily, innovative writers have been able to shake off some of these preconceptions. On the other hand, to identify one's work as Indian can provide an avenue for other Indian people who must make their way in a very confusing world. They need to know there are writers who can share and relate, empower and nourish their identity. In a true way both kinds of writers are needed; each must depend on his own perception of what is needed.

In our ways, all people in all life are related through an awareness of our kinship. This is one way of stating true understanding. The first is that all men and women are brothers and sisters, and the second is that we do not really know our own ways until we have come in contact with and understand another's ways. This is a practical understanding in order to protect and sustain us. We must respect one another.

We believe in the mysterious power of the imagination to give us new understanding. Because of our dreams, we also can sense the simultaneity of all time. Voices from the earth come through the soles of my feet, and I listen and sing with them. I must share what I have discovered, for I am made of the same material as earth, fire, air, and water. We have marvelous gifts as writers to bring forth and share the resonances of the human heart. To make the pathways of the heart and mind accessible to one another.

I am very honored to share with you and to be in such distinguished company. At this moment, through the people gathered here, the earth is united by rivers of our words. What we learn and share will follow through generations.

I have just a few questions, as my colleague Maxine had a few questions, that I would like to raise. I write by rhythm and sound, and it is language that leads me, and I gain a lot of help through singing and dancing and chanting. And I wondered how the Chinese writers look at creativity. What do they think are its origins? What methods do they use to enhance or strengthen or to weaken the writing process? And whether women are considered as creative a men?

My second question is, in the search for roots do writers wish to discover a spiritual understanding, as well as the social, political, and cultural understanding?

And I wondered if writers felt certain resistances to their work and its acceptance, and how they personally overcame this feeling of resistance to their work.

And my final question: In my work I've tried to merge the daily realities with the immediacy and power of dreams, and for that I've drawn on the oral traditions. Do Chinese writers foresee a merging of realism with the myths of their cultural roots?

YIXI DANZANG

IN RECENT YEARS GREAT CHANGES HAVE TAKEN PLACE IN TIBET. Every year the Chinese government has invested 900 million dollars for the reconstruction of Tibet. High rises, hotels, theaters, and asphalt-paved highways were built up three years ago. At present the number of tourists to Tibet is increasing with each passing day. We are now open both to inland China and the outside world. Tibet is surround by high mountains, great lakes, and rushing rivers, all above sea level over 4,000 meters. The country is noted for its beautiful sunshine, much warmer and brighter than Sichuan Province.

Most Tibetan writers today, including the Han and other national minorities, were nearly grown-up writers after 1980. Most are young people under thirty. Only a few Tibetan writers are over fifty. The Tibetan Writers Association was founded in October 1981; at that time twenty-two writers were accepted to be members of the Chinese Writers Association. I was one of them. At present, twenty-one have been admitted to the General Association in Beijing, that is, the Chinese Writers Association. Right now there are 124 members in the Tibetan Writers Association.

I began to write my first novel, *The Survivor,* put out by the People's Publishing House in Beijing in May 1981. It was the first novel written in the Han language by a Tibetan writer. Later on it was translated into the Tibetan language and broadcast by the Shanghai radio station. This novel has been published in French and English.

The three years from 1984 to 1986 were a golden time for Tibetan writers. Short story writers, novelists, poets, and playwrights have visited Yugoslavia, Romania, West Germany, Japan, Pakistan, India, and Nepal. We have established contact with French, Swedish, British, and Mexican writers visiting China. Through this we have promoted mutual understanding and friendship.

Generally speaking, the modern literature of Tibet started in 1951 when the peaceful liberation of Tibet was arranged with the Chinese

Central Government. At that time the leading writers were Tibetan Army writers. Most of their writing reflected the army life of the Chinese government troops. It was only after 1960 that the Tibetan writers began to realize their own historical mission, taking literary creation as a glorious undertaking. In 1980 the Democratic Reform of Tibet was completed. Through this reform, all the cattle, land, and property were equally distributed to the slaves by the Chinese government. So children of former slaves could afford to receive education in inland schools outside of Tibet. This gave them a chance to get in touch with the literature of the other parts of China and around the world. Therefore they could find out that their present condition was far behind other parts of China. During this era, quite a few Tibetan writers have been delivered from the restrictions and the fetters of religious influences. They began to try their hand at writing in the Han language. This is of course a step forward. We might say a new era began through some conditions and hard-working Tibetan writers.

Before 1950, most of the literary writings written in Tibetan language dealt with religious ideas or religious culture. Few touched upon modern ideas or modern pursuits. They did not realize its backward economic ways, nor did they know the superstructure, which was a stumbling block to their historic development. Besides, their mode of expression was rather stereotyped and dogmatic. It mainly focused on the form and application of classical Chinese language. If a Tibetan writer wanted to write poems, he had to follow strictly the model—this is a collection of Indian poems—mirror of poetry left over by our ancestors. Mirror poetry was a collection of poems by Indian poets. It could not have any error in rhyme or meter or diction or classical Chinese language. Once he was a little free to create something of his own, he would become feared, a great rebel against their old traditions. The same was true of fiction. The style of fiction writing also had a certain fixed pattern. That is, after a paragraph of prose there must be a stanza of poetic lines. Otherwise, it was not up to standards at all. Right now, restrictions and fetters have to be got rid of in a Tibetan literary creation, or else it is impossible to catch up with the literary work of other parts of China.

In our Tibetan Writers' Association we encourage our writers to create something of their own. That's why quite a few writings have not been restricted by any dogmatic rules, and they can have various styles or different means of approaches in their writing style. The Tibetan writers have put in great effort in close contact with the people to try to understand the Tibetan people, listen to them, and hear their views, so as to mirror their life. I think writers are necessarily short of mirroring our life. However, we writers could never be lacking the actual life. It's quite beyond our ability to give adequate description of the ideas, aspirations, and all walks of life in Tibet. It's extremely difficult for us to deal with the unpredictable changes. As you know, life is the mother of artistic creation. Even though some people like to put art into the category of sheer abstract things, but abstract ideas are nothing but the objective reflection of reality.

Last but not least, I would like to express my best wishes to the American writers on behalf of the Tibetan Writers' Association. You are surely welcome to visit Tibet someday and be friends of the Tibetan writers. Thank you.

JAY WRIGHT

POETRY REDUCES ONE FUNCTION FROM ANOTHER. In recent years I've been energized by the statement that the African leads us in music and in number. My reading of history impels me to think that music, speech, and calculation, the measuring of time and events, have been the complex relationships in which human actions in social and political relationship have been most glorious exemplified. I can set down basic elements of my theory, the one by which I am guided in writing poetry. Poetry is a concentrated, polysemous literary act, which undertakes the discovery, explication, interpretation, exploration, and transformation of experience. It differs from some other forms of speech such as that used by the legate, the chronicler, the mathematician, in that it handles its facts with more disdain, if I might put it that way, insisting upon spiritual resonance. It differs from some other forms of speech, such as that used by the preacher, the ritual chanter, the fabulator, in that it handles its spiritual domain with slightly more critical detachment than they do. The paradox of the extreme manipulative consciousness of the two domains, spiritual and material, imbue their association to produce what is at least a third and unique domain. This is what distinguishes poetry from other forms of speech.

The poem distinguishes itself by rhythmic ballad, accent, imaginative dissolution and reconstruction of its material. It has a rhetoric we recognize as something peculiar to what we call a poem. Irrespective of its line count, its imagery or the lack of it, its rhyme or lack of it, its metaphor or absence of it, its adherence to any accepted paradigms, what the new poem tries to do is to establish itself as a member of that class of things we call poems, and thereby establish a new paradigm, one that still serves to create the third domain.

Poetry has a functional value equivalent to all other forms of speech in a social and historical community. Putting things this way means that I consider poetry a social and historic responsibility. The poet cannot escape these. These responsibilities manifest themselves in the act of writing poetry and in the act of the poem. The "We" is the corporation of human beings who require and accept poetry's charter within them.

By concentrated I mean the kind of intensity and density that gives great weight to suggestiveness, to resonance. Polysemous here means capable of translation from one milieu to another. Can we say a poem discovers anything? Yes, we can. It first finds the experience in all its complexity to be revealed and talked about. I talk this way to avoid begging the question of givens. There are no givens in poetry. One does not recreate an emblematic state of anything. One works to create the act of becoming aware, attentive, active, and transformed.

Explication is analysis. Interpretation is the opposite of abstraction. Abstraction begins with a real thing and derives the concept. Interpretation begins with an empty concept and tires to find some real thing to embody it. You must notice the importance of an operation here, an act of fitting. These two last terms, explication and interpretation, should call attention to one of my basic assumptions, that naked perception, just seeing something directly expressed is miscreance in the highest degree. Every perception requires explication and interpretation.

Exploration means just that. The simple report of experience, if you could make such a thing, isn't good enough. Finally the whole process of making leads to transformation. The radical creation of experience. The making of a new body, a new heart, the bringing of a new spirit.

My sources, apart from the obvious Judeo-Christian ones, are in

Africa and the Americas. I'll turn to an elaboration of a European source. An historian taught Robert Duncan, a poet, that history and poetry have the same creative ground. Thinking about Helenic and Judeo-Christian thought and practice ought to assure us of the truth of that insight. The word history derives from the Ionian Greek *ahistoria*, learning by inquiry, the knowledge so obtained. That word stems from *historea*, to inquiry into a thing, to examine. Now for me, myth is a mode of knowledge. Traditional societies revere knowledge. Those who know the most, who think most acutely and accurately, who have developed a crucial ability to incorporate the many available forms of historical experience are the honored ones. I don't want to rehearse everything I've said in other places, but I should say that when we turn to ritual, the place where myth is often found, what we discover is I think what poetry embodies. Reverence and compassion, visual and auditory rigor, emotional and intellectual rigor, what I call the discipline of imagination, the freedom of rule, respect for history and memory, respect for vision and desire, and the ability to face up to the seriousness of life, and the inevitability of death.

Wilson Harris tells us that on society literature has profound and imaginative bearing wherein the life of tradition in all its complexity gives a unique value to the life of vocation in society. You can see that I keep coming back to the Americaness and Afrikanity, a division of history in literature.

My poetry looks for the basic human connections and experience, and that is why it's one which includes many voices. I'll say something last about the play.

The plays I have in hand derive their impulses from ritual in the fundamental dramatic expression found in myth. My way of placing an historical event in a different realistic context. Every element of theatrical structure is subject to rigorous inquiry during the play's process.

JIN YUN

I AM A PROFESSIONAL PLAYWRIGHT working at the Beijing People's Art Theater. My major area is play writing. Writing novel is my amateur job. People like to give us a humorous title, the "amphibious" writer. I would like to say a few words about playwriting. Some of my views and observations are related to the main topic of our discussion at this conference. In recent years, among the Chinese dramatic circles there has been talk about the so-called "crisis." Playwrights have explored new ways both in form and content one after another, trying to find out new ideas and means for the present reforms. As a result, a multi-form and multi-track development in the Chinese drama is underway. In this reform, Chinese and foreign drama have been mixed together through the interflow.

First of all, let me talk about the "crisis." I agree, there does exist crisis. However, it can be overcome, and it is being overcome. At present, the general ticket-selling rate is pretty low. You know, it takes great efforts to put up a play, but after a couples of performances you have to close it. The game is really not worth the candle. You might say it is the basic symbol of the crisis. Without performance of the play, there is no drama at all. During this period, there were also some plays being staged for over a hundred times. Among the well-received plays my poor work entitled "Lord Doggie's Nirvana" was popular with the audience. In the final analysis, it is a problem of how to win over the audience, how to improve the audience's appreciation ability. No doubt the production of drama and the attendance of the audience are synchronous. Therefore the reform, development and improvement should also be synchronous. With the change of the times and the aseathetic fashion, Chinese drama has to be reformed both in form and content. This is a demand common to the playwrights and the audience. Through the reform we can shake off the "crisis" for further development and boom of drama.

You know, Chinese plays are "imported goods." More than half a century after it was introduced into China, when it was trying to change and develop, Chinese playwrights would naturally turn their eyes to the West—the homeland of drama. They are trying to absorb some "suitable stuff" from the different schools of contemporary drama in the West for their own use. At the same time, since it has been imported to China, in order to keep its family line going on without interruption on this Chinese soil, the Chinese playwrights would also like to turn their eyes to the Chinese dramatic art which has a deep-rooted tradition, greatly appreciated for generations. They want to take some nourishment out of it to nurture the flowers of Chinese play.

Take the American drama for an example. I'm not going to say anything about Eugene O'Neill's work, or what a tremendous far-reaching impact they have on the Chinese drama. I'm just going to pick up Arthur Miller, the well-known American contemporary playwright, to illustrate my point. Mr. Miller came to China in 1983 to direct his famous play "The Death of A Salesman" for the Beijing People's Art Theater. It really hit the Chinese stage. Undoubtedly it was a pushing force to the Chinese dramatic circles going through a reform of their plays. To the Chinese audience, including myself, the form and content of that play is brand new. However, it was immediately echoed from among the audience. That play is of America, it is also of the world. Soon after that, when I was working on my own play "Lord Doggie's Nirvana," I was quite influenced by Miller's play.

The introduction of multi-theory and multi-schools of drama will surely be thought-provoking to Chinese playwrights in varying degrees. There is something in common when mankind wants to recognize life artfully and find the laws of expressing life. Based on this idea, I have found that there are striking similarities between the aesthetic principles of traditional Chinese drama and the Western modernist drama. Of course, this is not my own observation in the learning and exploration of new approaches, from the absurd, metamorphic, not-the-form-but-the-spirit, up to the free shifting from time to space. . .etc. They are interchangeable and can be merged and produce something with stronger force of life. That's why I have followed this principle in the creation of my plays: sitting on the present bench of China, extending my two hands for the best point of convergence from the ancient and modern drama both in the East and West.

The most important point to try to digest and absorb the best part of nourishment, rather than swallowing something raw and whole. I am not going to "take ancient stuff and suffer from indigestion." I am not going to import the "spare parts from the West and assemble them in China."

It would be a world thing if we could develop writing of high quality from one's own nation. The main topic for this conference: "The national and international features of literature," has clearly told us the dual characters of literature (including drama). It is international if it is really national. Just how I mentioned the easy acceptance of the American play "The Death of A Salesman" by the Chinese audience. It is a clear indication of this point. Though we don't have such a profession as a salesman in China for the time being. Nor have we heard of anybody dying in a traffic accident for the insurance premium. But this does not in the least stop the Chinese audience from understanding Mr. Willie, the hero in that American play, and sharing sympathy with his tragic death. Thus the Chinese audience would feel the uncertainty of human life.

You see, the "crisis" in Chinese plays can be overcome. And the prospect of the development of Chinese drama is quite optimistic. As a playwright, I think we have another mission: Since Chinese stage-wise directors have tried to find effective means for the stage from music—dancing up to magic and acrobatics to intensify our stage performance—we playwrights also have to develop the literary elements for improvement. Surely we cannot weaken the other elements to outshine or single out ourselves. On the contrary, we have to achieve something great in order to face the challenge. This would include a profound theme with colorful characters and excellent lines for our stage. I would like to know my American colleagues' comments. Thank you.

BARRY LOPEZ

MY WORK AS A WRITER has been shaped largely by the landscape I have grown up in and in which I now travel. These are for the most part remote landscape—the Mojave Desert in California, the Arctic tundra, the delta of the Okavango River in Botswana, the rainforests of the northwestern United States where I now live. In these places I encounter the oldest elements of human story—animals, the wind, the shape of a hill, the sound of an insect hovering over a flower. In being attentive to the natural elements of a particular place and then in setting them forth in an order that is not only dramatic but truthful, I hope to say something important about human questions, about dignity and compassion, or about the structure of history.

When I travel into the field, my companions are most often scientists

—archeologists, naturalists, anthropologists, and geographers. Their excavation of a prehistoric campsite or their detailed observations of an animal in the wild become the raw material from which I work. But the landscape itself, undifferentiated by science, is also a tutor; I spend days walking alone, trying to understand the landscape as one might try to fathom a personality. I read the journals of the early explorers in an attempt to understand the way people have construed these places historically. Often, too, I travel with indigenous people, with Eskimos and Indians, and am tutored in a knowledge quite different from the ways of Western civilization.

One thing I have learned in this kind of approach is that there is no single vision that can encompass something as fundamentally mysterious as a polar bear, or the Mojave Desert, or the Huanghai [Yellow] Sea. The scientist, the poet, the farmer, the hunter, the businessman or shopkeeper—each person contributes some insight. And it is here I believe, where we actually grapple with mystery, whether it be the complexities of human sorrow or the behavior of the wind in a certain valley, that we touch the foundation of literature.

I am keenly alert as a writer now to how human emotion grows out of certain spatial and temporal perceptions of the landscapes we inhabit. Hope, I think, does not grow only out of a certain juxtaposition of ideas in the mind, but is triggered as well by something in the physical landscape. How do we gain hope from our surroundings? What does it mean to write a literature of hope? Certainly it means you must look at the grotesque, at death; you cannot simply celebrate what is beautiful.

All serious writers, it seems to me, whether they are writing poetry or fiction or nonfiction, are looking at such large questions. They are struggling to uncover reality, to keep society from falling prey to the delusions of tyrants. The goal of the writer, finally, is to nourish the reader's awareness of the world. By telling a story, he or she hopes to clarify for a moment the fundamental paradoxes, the inescapable contradictions, the ineffable events of life.

In my own work I have gone back to the beginnings of story, to the undisturbed landscape, which was the first protagonist. In North America it is still possible to find such places, what a friend of mine calls "the unimpeachable sources." But though I sojourn in these places, and am often weeks on end in country you could say is still owned by the animals, I do not feel separated from society. I am an extension of society, and I hope what I am really doing in these places where human culture finds its roots is addressing the large questions that each of us turns over privately in his heart, as well as the questions that we address publicly. With a profound respect for language— for the beauty, the wildness, the mystery, the precision, the euphony of my own tongue—I try to do what every writer dreams of doing—to tell an interesting story well, to find those metaphors that will encourage wisdom to reveal itself, and so heal the human heart, elevate the human spirit, galvanize the human will—or merely remind us of the rich and intricate texture of human life.

At this moment it is my great privilege to be in the Middle Kingdom. As a writer who travels outside his community, it is my obligation to return home now and say as well as I can what I have seen, to face the terror of putting this mystery into words that will serve. I am daunted by this task, as daunted as I would be in trying to describe the life of a tiger. But I know that this is what writers have been trying to do from the beginning, to make not just the familiar but the foreign comprehensible. It is our affirmation of this task that makes us companions, no matter the difference in historical age of our countries, or the different lay of the land—one still half wild, the other tilled for centuries—that stretches before us.

LI ZIYUN
Sound and Fury

PERHAPS IT IS NOT EXACT TO APPLY FAULKNER'S TITLE to Chinese literature in the last ten years, but it is rather vivid, a disturbing and distracting time through the Cultural Revolution that broke out twenty-two years ago. After 1979, Chinese literature has progressed in fits of sound and fury. Only recently does Chinese literature seem to turn from the orderless to the order.

As China had practised denying of Western culture, demanding the literary work to serve the current politics and policies, the Chinese writers had fallen into a state of being closed to the world. Such a state had been carried to the extreme during the "Cultural Revolution." At that time, in a country of a hundred million of people there had been only eight "model plays" and two novels. The barren literary scene had turned into a desert. It was just in such a sullen atmosphere that a change appeared as a result of our country's new policy of "open and reform" in the economic field. A lot of bans taken for granted for decades were broken. For example, the writers had been allowed only to pick the subject matter of class struggle and describe the perfect heroes. However, in 1979 the government declared that a writer could choose what and how to write, and literature and art were no longer regarded as the mouthpiece of the current policy. You could imagine that the writers who had supressed for so many years burst into an exubrance of creation as soon as they got the freedom to write what they had not been allowed to. The bans were not broken all at one, but one after another. At the same time, the doors toward the world in the process of cultural exchanges also opened gradually. The process, however, was by no means smooth, but full of twists and turns.

The reason why I apply the phrase "sound and fury" to such a development is that, although the whole tendency has been one of freeing itself gradually from the interferences of the politics and approaching the law of the literature itself, the development has been too hurried. There is no longer a "still point," every writer has to explore along his own path of understanding. Every witer is worried lest he himself moves too slowly. A few are so anxious that they do not care as to what direction they are going.

The writers in the last ten years might be classified in such a way.

A lot of ambitious middle-aged writers have lost no time in making up for the waste time. They have broken up new ground for the subject they could choose to write, developed the technics to treat their subjects, and changed their styles.

The younger writers who began to play an influential role in the literary scene in the last seven or eight years are different from those middle-aged witers. They have not been so influenced by the traditional fossil of the literary mode. As soon as they appeared, they went their own way. Some have absorbed the ideas of the modern western literature, and some have explored the expression from the classical Chinese literature. They have brought with them a new climate to the literary world here.

There are some other writers who have shown a calm and cool attitude toward the fast developing situation. I do not mean that they have no intention to change, but they have been rather prudent toward their own creation. They have done a lot of thinking, showing no haste in looking for the subject matters as well as the technics most suitable to themselves. It certainly does not follow that they have got into a rut. Some have broken the new ground of psychological novels, some have introduced the stream of consciousness into the traditional narrative method, and have applied the method of realism in a new way. They have noticed the problem of combining the new technics with the traditional technics, and their styles have been consistent. Therefore their works do not give the readers a sense of unwarranted surprise. Of couse, most of these writers have their own subject matters over which they have pondered for a long time, and the development of their styles have been one of evidently consistency. Liu Binyan, Gao Xiaoshen, Wang Zhenqi, Zhang Chenzhi and Lu Wenfu, Deng Youmei, He Shiguang as well as the poet Liu Shahe——the last four are present here today——belong to the class.

And we can divide the development of our literature in the last ten years into several periods.

As our literature resurrected from the ruins of the "Cultural Revolution"—in ruins it indeed was, not only the literature and art like a wasteland, but the economy as well as the whole society in severe crisis, the literary works that reflect the situation of human existence and express the people's feeling can not refrain from looking at the crisis of the whole nation. Even at the time when the "Cultural Revolution" came to an end and the society began to find back its order with the reform in economy under way, the people still could not shift their attention from the politics and social status quo, as everyman had a stake in the reform. Therefore, when the writers got the right to choose their own subject matters, the first thing they did naturally was the protest against the feudalist fascism of the Gang of Four. They denounced the atrocities of the Gang of Four. They also set to explore why such a historical tragedy could happen to China in order to prevent it. From 1978 to 1980 appeared alot of poems, novels, dramas and films that were sensational for a period of time. These works were uneven in their artistic achievement, and some of them were even rather crude. But this "wound literature" gave voice to the feeling that had been surpressed for so many years, so they responded warmly among the broad masses of readers.

My American colleagues might feel that such a task was not up to the literature and art, but up to the political, the historical, and the sociological. However, in China people's fates are too closely related with the political and economical situation of the country. When the writers express the people's thinking and feeling, they feel it very difficult to avoid the social problems that directly influence the people. It reminds me of the western literature after the second world war. At that time, some western writers with democratic ideas and social responsibilities also exposed the the fascist crimes, fulminated against the war, and called for peace and humanism through their writings. For example, there appeared "literature in ruins" in West Germany. It called for the reconstruction of the country and human nature. It seems to me that the period of the Chinese literature just after the ending of the "Cultural Revolution" resembles some western literary works after the war. Although they were extremely popular for a time, they have been gone and past. However, owing to the characteristics of Chinese literature the reflection of the important social problems remains to be the subject matters for some Chinese writers. The so-called "fact-recording literature" of late—based on true facts, but undergone proper treatment of the writer—becomes more and more popular.

Around 1980, a lot of writers grew unsatisfied with reflecting the surface phenomena of the historical disaster and the personal suffering in it. They were no longer content with the explanations of the historical disaster in the term of personal factors. Some writers began to turn from the criticism of the personal behaviour to the study and anatomy of the behavior motives and psychology of the people of different types in the event. Such mental attitudes as compliance or resigned spirit came under the writers' attention. They started from looking for the universal spiritual attitude, and traced back to the flaws in the national cultural tradition, the moral behaviour mode which have influenced our national characters. At the same time, a lot of writers' conception of literature also underwent great changes. They got new understanding of the nature, function and object of the literature. These writers no longer took it as their responsibility to condemn the political abuses. On the contrary, they strived to write on the existent status quo and psychological activity of the characters. What is more, they strived to describe how the national culture of the long tradition had influenced the people's psychological strata—the subconscious and the unconscious. These writers called their own works "the literature of root-seeking," which reached its peak at the beginning of 1986. They drew on the literary technics from the western writers as well the eastern writers. In some cases we can even discover the influence of the classic Chinese novels. Among these works some were exquisite, embodying the various factors that form the Chinese cultural psychology. And some were mediocre, going so far as pander to the readers by exhibiting the disgusting habits of the backward area.

While the litrature of "root seeking" reached its peak, a generation of younger writers boasted of their "modern sensibility" and disowned the historical task and social function of literature. The majority of their works reflected the young people's frustration and bewilderment in the transition of the time. Most of the heroes (heroines) in their works not only discard the traditional value system, but also discard all values. They refuse to find meaning in anything, disdaining ideals, human kindness and relations. No matter how they tried to "make it new," as your Ezra Pound said, we might find in their works some ideas from Sartre and some influence from Salinger's *Catcher in the Rye*. In some cases they might be classified as post-hippie works. As the economic conditions and social background in China differ totally from those in America at the time of the sixties, most of their works seem to be superfical and pale, with the very few exception of combining originality with the characteristics of the Chinese society. Still, in these works we could sense the growing vexation among some Chinese young men.

Having made all kinds of experiments, some writers have felt a bit tired. Of course, those writers who had plans for a long period of time are still carrying out their works steadfastly. Some who were eager to set the fashion are now recruiting themselves and thinking in a deepgoing way. The nature of creative writing is something to be done with profound thinking instead of merely by individual talent. The originality of a writer is to be achieved through trails and trials. Therefore, it seem to me that the calmness over the contemporary Chinese literary scene does not mean anything like stagnation. Perhaps it is the beginning that the Chinese literature is moving toward a new height of maturity.

KENNETH LINCOLN
Have no twisty thoughts.
—CONFUCIUS

FROM NEBRASKA TO CHINA crosses the Tao of a lifetime: more than my own. The pilgrimage backtracks for millennia through global histories. Some forty-thousand years ago, Caucasoid natives migrated from Asia northeast; twenty-thousand and more years later, Mongoloid peoples crossed the Bering Straits into the Americas. The Western Hemisphere, our "New World" in effect, has been settling for four hundred or more centuries.

The Omaha Indians named my homeland *Nebraska* or "flat water," for the Platte River. A century ago, this shallow river led more recent European immigrants west to Colorado, Montana, Oregon, and California, where I now live. And I grew up on that "flat" prairie river, and then on the shortgrass tablelands above, in a small cattle and farming town named "Alliance," for two coast-to-coast railroads that came together. There homesteaders allied against the fierce weather, modest soil, windfall destiny, and wary Sioux Indians, Crazy Horse, Red Cloud, and Sitting Bull among them. Both sides rightly stayed, as the Tao Te Ching advises, "wary as men crossing a winter stream." The Lakota called the "whites" *waziya* for the "white-north" of winter snows; the word now means Santa Claus. The Whites have become *wasicun* or "fat-takers" to a tribal people whose self-given name, Lakota, means "allies." My family has been there four generations, sharing the work, allying against the odds, building the community, bridging differences.

My genealogical lines on both parental sides—the Lincolns and Whitmans, Johnstons and Giles—go back through the Ohio Fultons and Maryland Bradfords to the early voyages of the Mayflower. This was the spring-flower promise of America four hundred years ago. At today's end lies the autumnal challenge of reality, assassins' bullets and questions of freedom in a new, still unsettled country. What have we made of America, I ask, and what shall come? "No tool 'gainst tiger, / no boat for river, / That much, no more, / and they know it," the *Shih-ching* answers, in Ezra Pound's translation; "but above all to be precise / at the gulf's edge / or on thin ice."

As a writer and teacher, I lean on Robert Frost's "straight crookedness of a good walking stick." My sense of craft allies with words in a "native" or plain-style sense, and my flat-land upbringing speaks through me. Elegant basics are my text: wood, fire, earth, metal, and water, as the old ways have it. Past is still present, instructive. *Usa puyew, usu wapiw*, the Cree Indians say: "goes backward, looks forward," as the porcupine backs into its burrow with hindsight and foresight. Twisty or no, the challenges of reality, modernly and anciently so, seem no easy or small matter. And how we achieve these basics, the Navajo say, requires balance and beauty, harmony and goodness—*hozhó*. These multilingual tongues speak plurally for America.

But I sense the limits and contraries of language, too—the silences resonant between shadows of syllables, the spaces stretching between separated peoples. Words seem pointless, as we all agree, without bearing action, or integrity, or outcome. "A strong wind does not last all day," Lao Tsu said, riding into the desert to die in peace.

So why do we speak or write? What are the bodied consequences of speech or print? To reach across the mortgage each of us holds on mortality? to bridge cultures? to translate the very ancestral syllables that carry our breath one continent to another, one epoch to the next, one "modernity" to another? To what end?

In teaching at UCLA, I try to wake people up, as Buddha and later Picasso quipped, to whatever they're learning to see. By way of literature and language, my research addresses human needs that have not been thought through yet, from classroom aesthetics, to backwoods literacy, to alcoholism programs. My poems (after hours) seem small reminders of the lyric radicals of reality—the strange beauties, finally, of not-knowing too many things. "How aren't you?" the old masters quizzed.

My work as a writer is modernist with an old twist, Native American or American "native," in the presence of history and culture. Biculturally, I see modernism as history, the past as present. In such books as *Native American Renaissance* and *The Good Red Road* and the UCLA Native American Poetry Series, I have sought to reach across the Buckskin Curtain and have learned my texts from living natives today, ourselves and others. None of us is a relic of a forgotten or tragic past; we all stand as survivors and celebrants of an American heritage, deeply with us.

My present research concerns "Indi'n Humor," and it explores why "the people," as over a hundred American Indian groups variously name themselves, survive on the strength and resilience of their tribal humor. Neighbors with sibling immigrants, American Indians carry on hundreds of ways of life and language, culture and history, economies and ecosystems. They comprise two thousand distinct adaptations, reasonable and elegant, to all kinds of environment and circumstance in the Western Hemisphere. These thirty to forty million peoples have ancestors in Asia, adoptive families in America, and their own diverse and proud heritages. There are five hundred cultures with some two million Native Americans in the United States alone. Their ways may be models of the future for America, tested over many millennia, surviving beyond tragedies, viable today. Their lineages trace from America all the way back to China, and their lifestyles turn on certain communal concepts: the centrality of family, the grounding of homestead, the bonding of tribal tongue, a nurturing mother earth, a protective father sky, interconnections with extended kin and reciprocally related "others." These are known as two-leggeds, four-leggeds, wingeds, and roots, my adoptive Lakota say. In and through all this breathe the encompassing spirits that we variously invoke as the gods. The Lakota name this energy of the universe *Takuskanskan* or "the Power-that-Moves-[what]-moves."

And how do we speak humanly of such things, immediately to personal needs? "Finding the precise word for the inarticulate heart's tone," Confucius says in *The Great Digest*, as Pound translates, "means not lying to oneself, as in the case of hating a bad smell or loving a beautiful person, also called respecting one's own nose. On this account the real man has to look his heart in the eye even when he is alone." Lakota Indians call this respecting *cante ista* or the "heart's eye."

Perhaps our words come together as conditional prayers: each asks across the historical darkness for peace, health, long life, insight, and happiness. We make mistakes, and prayers break into laughter; we forgive, and retranslate, and try again. We go on. And all the while, our voices rise above the bones and dust, as Sitting Bull, for example, sang in the 1880s against an Anglo invasion he sought to live with and to negotiate:

I-ki-ci-ze wa-on kon he   So I longed to be a warrior
wa-na he-na-la ye-lo he   and now it is all over, so
i-yo-ti-ye ki-ya wa-on.   I know to bear against hard times.

ALICE FULTON

I GREW UP IN THE SMALL POST-INDUSTRIAL CITY OF TROY, which is located in northern New York State. Around the turn of the century, Troy was a thriving factory town, but by the time I was born, its glory days were done. As a child, I didn't know that Troy was not an exciting or pretty place to live, since I had never lived elsewhere. My parents were from working-class backgrounds, and although they were intelligent, kind people, they were not intellectuals. If they were to say what ambitions they cherished for my two sisters and me, I think they'd say that they only wanted us to be happy. Since we were girls, we were expected to marry, have children, and be supported by our husbands, yet we were also expected to go to college as a way of bettering ourselves.

Growing up in Troy, my exposure to the arts was limited to occasional museum visits. My mother, however, loved to read, and perhaps as a consequence my interest in books was encouraged. I soon learned that through reading I could escape or transcend limitations. I wanted to know everything about everything in the world, to encompass as much as possible within the confines of my head. At high school I'd skip classes and read poetry in the library, a very tame sort of truancy, but one that got me into as much trouble as far more indecorous enchantments. I copied poems by Emily Dickinson and Shakespeare in my own hand as a way of entering into the work and analyzing its structure. At some point I tried writing poems myself, discovering in the process that it was intoxicating to build things with words, which are, after all, both plentiful and undervalued. I was drawn to poetry for the

238

way it said intricate things beautifully, placing language in the foreground rather than merely imparting information or even telling a story. Prose can transmit a message clearly, without calling attention to itself as language or deviating from conventional usage. Poetry, on the other hand, is a richly subversive, consciously deviant use of words, and therein lies the difficulties and the possibilities. I still prize the formal aspects of poetry as highly as I do the content.

With that as background, I'll try to describe some of the subjects and concerns of my work. In some cases my poems include aspects of American culture, history or thought that are in my view often excluded from our poetry. America is a young country, and it's as if there hasn't been time yet for us to make sense of what we were and what we are. As remedy, some of my poems try to unveil, question, and explore the meaning behind those trappings often viewed as too trivial or crass for mention, from fast food to faith healers. Far from being empty or meaningless, such aspects of America are symptoms with their own weight and importance. Today's B-movie actor has a way of becoming tomorrow's President.

Many Americans have lost the orthodox religious faith of their parents, and I'm fascinated by the alternative faiths we find, and those we manufacture, in order to live and give our lives meaning. All obsessions are a form of religions, and my work explores amusements that become manias, desires that accelerate to greed. Rather than writing about European or classical cultures, as American poets have often done, I've written about the ways in which classicism has been interpreted in America. All over our country one finds aberrations of the classical: ranch houses with matchstick versions of Doric column, linoleum that looks like marble, cities with names like Troy, where I grew up, Athens, and Syracuse. Even the logo of the MacDonald's hamburger chain, the golden arches, is an appropriation of classical form.

One of the meanings of *Palladium*, the title of my second book, is taken from Greek mythology. The palladium was a statue created by Athena, which she flung into the ancient city of Troy. Having grown up in the American Troy, I'm fascinated by the disparity between the aspirations and the reality of such gritty, unbeautiful places, cities that having little sense of their own past or history need to borrow some of the grandeur that was Greece, if only in name.

Perhaps also as a result of my connection with Troy, New York, I find I'm intrigued with places, people, and experiences that tend to be regarded as peripheral or of marginal value. In my poems I hope to consider the most unlikely, least little things and events, and by doing so dismantle false ideas of centrality. I hope to question ethnocentricity, a stance that supposes one's own culture to be more important than other cultures, and I hope to do this by pointing up the arbitrary nature of our own, America's, cultural norms. And I'm especially interested in exposing, subverting, or offering alternatives to the patriarchal world view that subtly permeates much of what I hear, see, and read.

And this is one of the parts that is not printed, but during our discussions earlier, I think it was yesterday, the Nobel prizes came up and we talked about that for awhile. At dinner that night we had another discussion about prizes, and everyone seemed to agree, we all felt that prizes are often arbitrary and unfair, and many good writers are overlooked. And the point was made that China has been wrongly neglected and excluded. It's something I had never thought about before, but I think you made very convincing arguments, and I'm really here to learn and to learn more about China and Chinese literature.

I would like to mention another nation of writers even larger than China's that I think has been neglected also. I call them *majority writers*, rather than minority writers, and that is women, since we are a majority. I like that word because women are not only a majority in numbers, but also in the sense of a coming of age. In the list of writers who have received Nobel prizes, I don't know, maybe a woman has won one, but no woman was mentioned as having won for literature. And I bring this up just because my intention is to include those who have been left out, whether they've been Chinese writers, women, or men writers who deserve more appreciation.

One of the current limitations of the English language is the generic use of man and male pronouns. Although the universal *man* or *he* pretends to encompass everyone, when we read or hear those words, we tend to envision a male. To substitute *woman* for the generic *man*, or even better to create a new, inclusive usage, to be creative with words, is to question bedrock assumptions of marginality.

Through the implications of pronouns and subtext, my poetry tries to suggest alternatives to such prevalent hierarchies, and I want this effect to be almost unnoticeable, and therefore more insidious. I believe that poetry by definition leaves much unsaid. It implies rather than stating directly. In my view it isn't necessary to write didactic or polemical verse in order to have a political "message." Every utterance is political insofar as it voices some world view, and such casual philosophies support or undermine the status quo, whether we want them to or not.

War has come up many times during this conference, and I'm grateful to Larry Heinemann for bringing it up through the discussion of his work. One important question that was raised was the search for the source of wars, and the ways in which war can be eliminated. The sort of feminism that I am writing about or thinking about doesn't mean women trying to be like men, which I've heard several times, that feminism means women trying to be like men. In my mind that's not what it means. Why would we want to be like men? That would presume that men are in fact better, superior, all-knowing, wise, and so forth. But I think there is some hope that women can escape these stereotypes and take on a strength that will allow them to be leaders and assume more leadership. Hand in hand with that, there's a hope that men may assume some of the traits that have been associated with women, such as gentleness. And now I get back to the topic of war, because it seems to me that if men could assume more gentleness and women could assume more leadership, perhaps there would be a significant shift in power and we wouldn't have as much aggression. And thus the hope would be that the world would be a less aggressive place. In coming up with this, I've thought about women leaders such as Margaret Thatcher and Indira Ghandi, and I know that they're just like men, but I do believe that they are male clones, and the reason they're male clones is because of the system of patriarchy, and if we had another system, leadership could be different and you wouldn't have to be a male impersonator to be a woman leader.

I just have a few more thoughts. I've talked more about content rather than style thus far, and that's somewhat misleading. For me poetry is as concerned with how a thing is said as what is being said. A description of subject matter is insufficient description of poetics, so here are just a few of my thoughts on form. I think of each line in a poem as an independent unit. That is, I'd like each line to be interesting and complex when viewed out of context. And of course it must sing in chorus with the poem as a whole. And since my aesthetic is one of inclusion, indeterminacy, and multiplicity, I use enjambment and syntax to build variant readings within a poem. And I also create texture and metaphor through juxtapositions of tone and diction. One of my poems might sail along smoothly before suddenly borrowing legalistic language to create undercurrents of guilt and atonement, or economic terms might appear implying a subtext of commerce, credits and debits. So the registers of diction are in themselves a form of metaphor or metonymy. And though time-honored structures such as blank verse are useful tools, I'm more interested in devising new experimental forms, and last year, for instance, I wrote a poem that took its formal inspiration from the rhyme and patterns of Ethiopian poetry.

I would like to raise one question at the end, just one, and it's a question that I would only dare to raise among friends and family, and I do feel very comfortable with you people at this point. Earlier, Madame Zong in answer to Bobbi's question, said that she thought men and women were better at different things, and that men were better thinkers. And we talked a little bit about why. The reasons given were chemistry or biology, but isn't it possible that this might be a result of cultural education that encourages men to think and women to turn to less intellectual activities? Immediately I think of thousands of great women thinkers: George Eliot, Virginia Woolf, Emily Dickinson, many many examples. And I wonder, if you tell someone they are passive and emotional, that it doesn't become a self-fulfilling prophesy. It's just something I'd like to hear responses to, if there's time.

ZHONG PU

LITERARY WORKS ARE SUPPORTED BY MASS CULTURE, just like a boat on the surface of water. The boat rises as the water goes up. Chinese culture has made headway by leaps and bounds during the several great impacts. The Central Plain culture (historical culture) from the Yellow River Valley and the *Chu* culture (witchful culture) through the Yangtze River Valley have produced the colorful· *Han* culture after their interflow. The introduction of Buddhism to China in the seventh century during the Sui (581-618) and Tang (618-907) dynasties gave rise to the culture of the Sang and Song (960-1279) dynasties. In our modern history, the New Cultural Movement appeared on May 4th, 1919 through contacts with the West. During this movement, a slogan was put forward to promote science, democracy and modernization. We should say that this movement is still going on up to the present.

Classical Chinese novelists are good at using a simple and straight-forward style of presentation. The writers make characters alive in their writing with only a few strokes. Take *Dream of the Red Mansion* for an example, when Madam Phoenix fell a victim to some witchcraft. A knife in hand, she would kill chickens and dogs. Whenever she came across any human beings, she would "stare her big eyes, wanting to kill people." Here a few words were enough to describe her crazy manner, especially her behavior when she was under the spell of witchcraft. These novelists did not spend too much ink on psycholog-ical analysis. At that time they might not have special knowledge in this field. But a few words mean a lot behind the lines.

Most of the classical Chinese novelists often present their characters through the behavoir of their heroes. They pick out the most typical episodes, but never waste their ink. Again in this great classical Chinese novel, Yinchun and Xichun (granddaughters of the Jia house-hold) occupy not so much space. Only one incident was mentioned in the novel: When Yinchun could not put the arrogant servants under control, she did not bother to cross-examine them at all, just reading a booklet about Taoism alone. This typical scene fully expressed her cowardish character. As for the description of Xichun, the author did not write how she felt in her mind. He only wrote about some frag-ments of her conversation and a game of chess with a nun. This is enough to show her future road of life natural for a timid young lady to follow.

There is a world of difference between *Dream of the Red Mansion* and other Chinese novels. That is, the whole novel has some sort of roman-tic touch by adding a predestined story of wood and stone to the real-istic description. This was criticized by some critics, saying that this would weaken the power of the whole book, and turn the story into something entirely unreal. As a matter of fact, because of this misty and hazy portrayal, the whole novel affords food for thought. The affinity between Magic Jade and Black Jade is not a matter of vulgar retribution, but a force in the Great Voice.

If all these plots sound strange to our American friends, I would strongly recommend them to read this fantastic novel of *Dream of the Red Mansion*. We also have *Strange Tales* (Liaozai), a wonderful novel of ghosts.

Romanticism is my cup of tea. Among American writers, I have found Hawthorne to my liking. There were Chinese versions of his works even when I was still a child. I have read *Scarlet Letter* and translated "The Minister's Black Veil" and "Rapachini's Daughter" in Chinese for a magazine. This time I was really deeply touched by the author's dashing spirit. One of the major features of Hawthorne's fiction is his rich imagination which gives me full charm and admiration. As critics have it, half of his creation is a fable and the other half is reality. He himself claimed that his whole life was devoted to contriving "a neutral gound where the actual and the imaginery might meet." I think, this neutral ground has been searched by all those who are full of romantic humors.

One of Hawthorne's representative works is his "Young Goodman Brown," about a young man who went to a witches' sabbath. His conscience had been pricked all the way through. When he arrived, he found out that both gentlemen with good reputations and the shameless guys were gathered there. Even his pure newly married wife was among the crowd. This short story particularly showed some specific features of the author: his original sense of crime, his insight into the inner world of his characters and his imagination beyond human experience. All this has been artfully converged together on the flaming rocks of the gathering crowd of demons and ghosts. His powerful, mysterous atmosphere and his profound way of presentation really appeal to every reader.

In 1979, I produced my first short story entitled "Who Am I?" with the method of insight analysis. In my story, human beings have been reduced to an inhuman status. The hero of this story thought that he was nothing but a worm, his outside appearance had also changed. This sort of transformation has some previous experience in Franz Kafka's *The Metamorphosis*. This kind of worm is a Chinese worm. That could only be transformed in the cultural revolution in China.

My "Snail-like Swelling" deals with a person who has gone to hell in his vision. He came across Fan Wan, a noted Chinese minister in the Han Dynasty (206-220 B.C.), who was cruelly murdered. He saw Bruno burning through purgatory in a Flower Square in Rome. At the end of my story, he saw a long line, holding his own bloody head shining to light the darkness. But he could not tear himself away from his shield— the snail-like residence—until finally he was decayed in his own shell. In the process of writing this story, I had a feeling that my imagination started from reality, yet I was rather, free, confined by nothing.

Once a literary piece is written, it will have its own intelligence from which readers might find something they never expected to see. If that has been explained by the author, it will be too stiff and solid. Hawthorne seemed to have said: What is important is the piece of cake, but not the process of how it is being baked. Last of all, permit me to add one more thing to my chatterbox: In the process of my literary creation, while being mixed with the springs of life, I have found mighty support from the great, profound Chinese cultural tradition; I feel the support of the light shining from abroad. So I am very happy.

ROBERT REES

I CAME TO WRITING LATE, and it came to me slowly. My family was poor and my parents uneducated. There was in our home none of the arts; no music, no art, no literature. Although unsophisticated in arts and letters, my parents were good moral people. From them I learned the value of industry, integrity, sacrifice, compassion—what Faulkner called "the eternal verities." I also learned faith. Early I came to believe in love and to trust God. I still do. And that, perhaps as much as anything, defines me as a person and whatever claim I have as a writer.

I'm also defined by being a Westerner. My great-grandmother was part Cherokee Indian, and my great-grandfather a convert to the Mormon religion from Wales in the 1840s. He immigrated to America where he joined other pioneers who pushed handcarts a thousand miles across the plains to the Salt Lake Valley. Looking for a place where they could be free from religious persecution in the vast reaches of the West, they made the desert blossom. A sense of space one feels in the West is very much a part of me.

Faith and space come together for me in nature, where as Robinson Jeffers says that God has flung "rainbows over the rain / And beauty above the moon, and secret rainbows / On the domes of deep sea shells, / Not even the weeds to multiply without blossom." Jeffers concludes, "look how beautiful are all the things that He does, His / is the beauty of things." There is in that beauty, which at times can also be harsh and unforgiving, something mystical, mysterious, and deeply human. In one sense I believe it was created for us, and is one of our most sacred stewardships. Some of my writing focuses on this beauty and our relationship to it.

With so little culture in my home, it wasn't until I went away to college that I discovered for the first time what a poem is, and how words work. It was then that I came to realize with great joy and sometimes with great pain, that I am one of those who cannot escape imagination.

If we live in imagination, we have the ability to transform and at times to transcend the world. To multiply meanings, to comprehend correspondences, to make something which is dead come alive in our mind is to live in what Wallace Stevens called the "paradise of meaning." It is in that meaning that as writers we make the world make sense. It is also the way we can transcend time. I can read Li Po's words today, more than a thousand years after he wrote them, and for that moment I live in his mind, and he lives in mine.

In this way literature has a liberating and a healing power. Let me illustrate what I mean by this. I grew up in a home that was both racist and sexist. Although I had no social status or wealth, I considered myself superior to others by virtue of my race and gender. I first became disturbed by this when as a teen-ager I started reading the New Testament seriously. Somehow I couldn't reconcile my family's teachings with those of Jesus, and this was unsettling.

The process of breaking down and shedding prejudices required a conscious, labored effort, but it was greatly enhanced by the literature I read. For example, Richard Wright, Ralph Ellison, and James Baldwin helped me to understand that blacks are as fully human as I, and I am in as much need of their love as they of mine. What Ellison says at the end of *Invisible Man* could be applied to all human relationships that are marred by prejudice—until those who wield unrighteous dominion over others are free of their prejudice and feelings of superiority, neither they nor those whom they oppress can hope to be free. I believe, for example, that until men recognize the extent to which women have been and are held to be less than they are, men and women cannot be free to love one another fully. It is, I believe, the obligation of the writer to deal with these issues of human dignity.

Recently I've been reading a remarkable book entitled *Under the Eye of the Clock,* which won this year's prestigious Whitbread Award in Great Britain. The author, Christopher Nolan, paralyzed and mute from birth, could communicate only by subtle movements of the eye until he was twelve. Finally gaining enough control over his body to type with a stick strapped to his head, with tremendous labor that took up to eight hours just to type a single poem, he produced an astonishing book of poems entitled *Dam Burst of Dreams.* Until his dreams burst through that dam of dumbness, this mute glorious Milton had been storing in his mind what the Old English poets called a *word horde,* or *word treasure trove.* Calling on his vast storehouse of alliterative pairs, pungent metaphors, new-forged words, and what he calls "hollyberried imagingings," Nolan has written poems and poetic fiction that make anyone who loves literature glad to be alive.

I think our Chinese friends, many of whom had their voices stopped for years, and who had to store in their memories, sometimes for as long as twenty years, poems and images and phrases, can perhaps better appreciate Nolan's work that can we Americans, although all of us who have had our minds go blank for long periods of time, or whose tongues have been tied, can identify with him to some extend. As writers we are constantly working to make our dreams burst their dams.

Some writers are uncomfortable speaking about love, but I am interested in love as a serious subject for literature. We are all born wanting love, spend most of our lives trying to get it, and die not having gotten enough. It is love in its various forms and its multiple expressions that ultimately gives the world meaning for us. William Faulkner felt that the responsibility of the writer was to write about the human in conflict with itself. It is that conflict which most interests me as a writer. The following poem by Robert Hayden illustrates what I am trying to say. It's called "Those Winter Sundays":

Sundays too my father got up early
and put his clothes on in the blueblack cold,
then with cracked hands that ached
from labor in the weekday weather made
banked fires blaze. No one ever thanked him.

I'd wake and hear the cold splintering, breaking.
When the rooms were warm, he'd call,
and slowly I would rise and dress,
fearing the chronic angers of that house,

Speaking indifferently to him,
who had driven out the cold
and polished my good shoes as well.
What did I know, what did I know
of love's austere and lonely offices?

Theodore Roethke says, "Love calls us from the things of this world." I believe it also calls us to its lonely and austere offices, and it is my hope that as writers we will answer that call.

IX

Correspondences Over a Decade

"Magic" Henry Chen

Beijing Citizen

Birdman

A Writer's China

Chen Henry
Chinese Writers Asso.
Beijing, China
May 16, 1988

Dear Mr. Kenneth Lincoln,

How are you? I've got a piece of good news to tell you. After many years of efforts, I'm admitted to graduate studies in English in Kansas State University, at long last. The English Department there is generous enough to offer me a Teaching Assistantship, a scholarship and a PACE Award to cover all the expenses needed for a M.A. Degree in English.

Toward late April, just as you left, the Admission office notified me to register no late than June 8, 1988. I had to run against time to get everything ready for departure. But then, the English Department told me that my T.A. would begin in fall.

But what I'm thinking is that I can go to the States now and make good use of the 2 month's time to prepare myself both economically and psychologically. I'm expected to teach 20 hours a week at the writing center and carry 6-9 credit hours per semester. Obviously, this is no picnic. I can well imagine the tension and frustrations I'll go through at the very beginning. English, anyway, is my second language. And I know even for English native speakers, to pursue a M.A. Degree in English can be a tall order.

So if I can arrive at your country a little bit early and expose myself to English as it is spoken as well as to the society where the language is used, I'll certainly benefit a lot.

To this end, would you please help to find a live-in job for me? Any odd jobs will do, from being a waiter in a restaurant to a baby sitter at home, or any other clerical work. I can work any time between June 10 to August 20. I know it is as difficult as it is illegal, even more so when it comes at such a short notice. But perhaps you have some friends or neighbours who are willing to help. And it means so much to me.

I guess my letter will reach you sometime around June 1. So if you do find something for me, please cable back.

Your kind efforts appreciated

With best wishes
Sincerely yours
Chen Henry
The Chinese Writers' Association

June 15, 1988

Dear Larry and Edie,

We hit the ground skidding—one hundred and twenty students in modern American poetry, anguished over exams, papers, my absence, the TA's incompetence (or the other way around?). Anyway, I turned in my final grades, and there's momentary pause to re/collect, write a few letters, watch the Lakers get bumped off by Detroit, and prepare a syllabus for summer school—which I teach to pay my daughter's college tuition this fall. She graduates from high school next week, and my relatives are pouring in from New York, Nebraska, Berkeley, and parts unknown.

Last Friday, Xiao Chen ("Magic") flew in from Beijing. Two days prior, I received a telegram saying he'd gotten a scholarship to Kansas State for two years. He'd be here looking for housing, work, and loose women (we assumed the latter). So I've fixed him up with everything but the first two: it's been a sideshow of Sino-American relations. A friend promised some work, then fell through, another offered a place to stay, then qualified it. Henry has been on our couch for six days. This morning I took him to Bob's doorstep, where he'll camp for the next week, while Bob's family is in London. Meanwhile, the U.S. immigration cops are out with Dobermans, sniffing for illegal aliens working in shady restaurants, etc.

JJ has been giving Chinese cooking classes, reading scripts for a movie studio, and working eight hours a day more to save street kids from poverty, so she has her hands full, too. We're both angling toward half a year in Pisa, where some Italian friends are scamming for me to teach British fiction. Now there's a switch.

Actually, I'm on sabbatical come this fall. Some Nebraska friends have a fishing cabin for me to squat during August. My first breather from a wild year. I plan to take three fat notebooks from China and churn out a book, *A Writer's China*, which I've prospected with Harper & Row. It will detail a day-by-day journey with you-all through the Middle Kingdom, meeting *them*, cross-examining *us*. We'll see what comes of that. I've rewritten the *Indi'n Humor* book and shipped it off to Oxford.

We've been back and forth, feasting, with Shu-mei and her husband, Adam, recounting our misinformation on contemporary China. He's got the kind of droll humor you can light a match on, and she's even sassier here than in China.

I thought you might enjoy the enclosed pictures for your rogues' gallery of writers abroad. They bring back fond memories of our wanderings, endless banquets, toastings, roastings, talks, and those forgettable speeches by everyone. It was a blast, as they say out west, a real old-time round-up. Especially meeting you folks, in some way, like Old Home Week. I still hear an echo of "Mr. LINcoln" ringing across a crowded room and reach for my glass of maotai.

What did we learn? How to slurp down frog testicles without blinking; to say *ni hao* with a smile; to endure speeches without falling asleep; to enjoy ourselves on someone else's budget (not hard for writers); to blow our noses with our fingers (a childhood skill, actually); to spend funny money with a clear conscience. I learned many other things, too, to come out in the book.

I hope you enjoy *The Good Red Road*, here enclosed. We got *Paco's Story* in the mail, which I promptly piggy-backed into my class and read outloud from the first chapter.

Now that we've established these family ties, we need to start planning Fourth of July reunions. How about somewhere halfway, like Santa Fe? We'd be hard-pressed to find smoked duck and Tsingtao, but I know some fine little Mexican places where the green chiles and blue corn tortillas will warm your heart.

love from a lost cousin,
Ken

March 24, 1989

Dear Ken,

Got a letter from JJ at the Lannan Foundation asking if I'd like to come out to LA and give a reading—which I certainly would like to do—talked with her on the phone and said, book me.

Last summer, coming back from China, I was sicker than I have ever been in my life—hepatitis-A, probably from that train ride to Leshan, eh? Or maybe the *maotai*? Hep A is the one that doesn't kill you, though you wish it would, just scares you to death. Avoid it at all costs.

I had thought that I would be writing something about our China trip, but I couldn't get anybody interested in buying it. I had plenty of notes, but after writing about the trip in my journal, it just didn't seem to make much of a story. And last summer, too, Paul Theroux's *Riding the Iron Rooster* scooped me (and probably everyone else on the trip). Aside from the "Big Booder" in Leshan, the warriors of Xi'an, and that endless, magnificent trip down the Yangtze River, and the very good company, meals and all, that we shared—it was the two train rides that tickled me the most—chicken bones on the floor and all.

Then last fall I sat down to work earnestly on the books, one a Chicago novel and the other the non-fiction book about delayed stress. My plan was to alternate. The delayed stress book is not much fun—it's really depressing to hash over the material and explain it in such a way so that everyone will understand. And now, too, there is such a peculiar mood in the country about the war, Vietnam veterans running around in "K-mart" cammies and declaring the war a "good" thing. It's more than a person can stomach. I wanted to be able to juxtapose the grind of writing the book with the considerable comedy of the Chicago novel—which will be the funniest book you ever read. I wanted to work a month on and a month off, but it has not worked out that way.

Late in the fall I got an invitation to go to the Soviet Union with a group of Vietnam veterans to talk with Soviet veterans of the Afghan war—an opportunity I could not pass up. Nobody in their right mind travels to Russia in winter, but the trip took the first 2 weeks in December, and I have never been so rushed by conflicting images in my life. (Even the China trip was leisurely by comparison, but I think that was because I had more emotional investment on the Russia trip, soldiers and all.) It was an absolute worl-wind; here I was talking with guys young enough to be my sons, and if that weren't enough it was like looking at myself 20 years ago. They're hurt and bewildered and angry; young and tough and not about to take any shit from the government. One afghantsy (as they call themselves), talking about *perestroika* and *glasnost,* said that all the bureaucrats had to lose was their position and the privilege, all *they* had to lose was their chains. If Gorbachev doesn't pull it off, I'd say there's going to be trouble. Just a couple weeks before we were there 80 wheelchair afghantsy demonstrated in Red Square and got beaten up by the cops—and the cops in the USSR don't take no shit from nobody. Anyway, when I came back I went into this peculiar mood change—I don't want to call it a depression, because it wasn't. But I certainly didn't feel good. I worked more the better part of a month on my attic, getting it remodeled and ship shape to use for an office. (I'm sitting there now, with large, south-facing windows, a couple of roof windows on the slant wall over my head; the whole thing painted ceiling white so it's like being on the inside of a sugar cube; porch planking floor painted bright tile red—a deep shade of burgundy.) The whole thing is spacious like you wouldn't believe, and I've been writing my head off since.

Anyway, since the middle of January I've been working on an article about the Russian trip for *Playboy,* and it is now, finally, done. They wanted only 5000 words, and I cranked out almost 13,000—I am one of those people who thinks there is no such thing as a short story; the whole 2 weeks was remarkably complicated, what with a lifetime's baggage of what the USSR *is* in the first place, meeting these young guys in their early twenties, being uncomfortable in a *very* foreign country (even more exotic and crazy than China, strange to say; the food was just god-awful; hotel rooms stuffy and wildly overheated), going to the afghantsy memorial in Moscow, meeting mothers of men killed (and how betrayed they were; angry and bitter). We even ran into a large group of Vietnamese kids in the Moscow airport—and did *that* ever set some of the Americans off. Jet lag, *strange* food ("roadkill" sausage, day old bread, and Pepsi-Cola served at virtually every meal), the emotional roller coaster—every day it was some remarkable event. The afghantsy would come up to your hotel room and sit on the beds until the small hours, drinking that *righteous* Russian vodka (kept ice-cold so that it poured like a thick liqueur), and telling you the most heartbreaking stories of what they had been through. It took 2 solid months to get it all down and get it right. Then my editor and I have gone through it twice (I just talked to him this morning about the last of the changes), and now it goes to galleys. But an awful lot has been left out, which disappoints me, but that's the nature of the beast. The weird part of it was that I took a small thick journal (the kind that Barry Lopez had in China), a tape recorder, and many tapes, plus a camera and half a dozen rolls of film (I not much of a picture taker). But when I got there things were happening so fast that I couldn't take intelligent notes right then and there, didn't have any time to myself to write important things in the journal, and the couple times really powerful conversation occurred I couldn't bring myself to whip out the tape recorder—it seemed like such a violation of the intimacy, of the power of what the person was talking about. Some hot-shot journalist *I* turned out to be! Anyway when I finally sat down to work, I was positively amazed by how much I could remember. All the materials too particular and specific, and long-winded, to go into the article, go into the non-fiction book.

So here I am, finally back to the Chicago novel, which is a hoot!, as the fella says.

Then in the middle of all this I got an invitation to go to Vietnam with a delegation of writers next November. The Viets have begun translating work by American ex-GIs, and apparently they've already started with Willam Broyles' *Brother in Arms.* No word about the royalties. I'll be going with my very good friend Bob Mason, the guy who wrote *Chickenhawk.* The conference with Vietnamese writers will take a week in Hanoi, but he and I plan to stay over and travel south. He wants to go back to Pleiku and the A Xiao Valley and I want to travel to Ho'ville and Tay Ninh. It should take another week, but I think I might just stay longer if I can. The visit should make the best last chapter for the delayed stress book I could have. A lot of ex-GIs are going back nowadays.

I want to have both books done by the end of the year, then I'll finally have Vietnam out of my house, once and for all, and something else to put up at readings except Paco. And I've been dwelling on the war for over twenty years, and that's enough for one person, wouldn't you think?

We're been north and west, but never south along the coast, so we'll probably swing down through LA, and we'd love to see you guys. What you do think?

See you soon.

Your Cuz—Larry

From the book
Tell the World: What Happened in China and Why
Troops were advancing on Tiananmen Square from east and west. Residents and students from other parts of the city, concerned about the thousands of demonstrators still in the square, walked toward it. Passing the Xinhua Gate of Zhongnanhai, they saw soldiers washing the pavement with water. The students from the Institute of Politics and Law who had been sitting there a few hours earlier were nowhere to be seen. . . . .

At four-forty, just as the students were starting to retreat out of the square, a red signal flare ripped the night sky. Searchlights suddenly bathed the square. Students found that they were surrounded by armed soldiers wearing helmets. Some of them had already set up a line of more than a dozen machine guns, aimed at the students. Other soldiers rushed in among the students and beat them with electric cattle prods and rubber-covered steel clubs. They tore their way up the base of the Monument to the People's Heroes, and forced the students down, beating them until their heads were bleeding. As they reached the ground level, the machine guns opened fire.

By now the square was surrounded on three sides by armored vehicles or tanks, leaving only one exit.

The students began to retreat from Tiananmen Square, moving westward toward Xidan. A tank caught up with the students from behind. First it fired tear gas, then it ran over where people were most crowded. Witnesses say that at least thirteen students were crushed in one spot alone. Judging from the remnants of their clothes, people could tell that five of them were women.

As the sun rose on June 4, the morning clouds were red. The soldiers continued to fire until they reached the diplomatic area at Jianguomen. More than three thousand people were killed in Tiananmen Square and on the streets of Beijing.

After the killing, there were massive arrests nationwide. People who were involved in the Democracy movement were executed in Beijing, Shanghai, Chengdu, Changsha, Wuhan. The Communist Party of China boasted that it had smashed a "counterrevolutionary rebellion."

From June 4 to the beginning of August, 120,000 people who were involved with the movement were thrown into prison. And 20,000 were imprisoned in Beijing alone. Secret arrests, interrogations, and torturings were conducted in the darkness. The maniacal Gang of the Old cried in delirium: "We must catch them all! Imprison them all! Kill them all! We must pluck out the weeds by the root!"

The world must not forget China, China in the spring of 1989. If executioners like Li Peng and the Gang of the Old are not punished, how can humanity have a moment of peace?

—LIU BINYAN, IN COLLABORATION WITH RUAN MING AND XU GANG

TRANSLATED BY HENRY L. EPSTEIN

June 10, 1989

Dear Ken;

That monster shake really visited L.A! When the earthquake hit California, my thoughts went to you immediately. For all the damages, it didn't cause any casulties, which is what the Chinese call "fluke within bad lucks."

The other day I got a letter from one of my friends. I found out that he didn't get my previous letter to him in China. It struck me that my last letter to you also got lost in the mail since I mailed them on the same day.

Everything is fine with me. My teaching is getting better, as is deemed by my students. Ironically, they accept me not because of my hard work, but because of my leniency in grading. When I followed my departmental rule of grading to the letter, I was fighting single-handedly with a class of rebels in open mutiny. Later on I found out that I was the only one—slave of rigid rules. Now that I loosen up the grading to a reasonable degree, I see smiling faces all over. Another cultural difference. With best wishes.

Henry Chen

From the book *Tiananmen Diary: Thirteen Days in June*

As I have been writing these lines I have talked to some of my Chinese friends. What is there to hope for? They shake their heads in despair. "This is only the beginning," they say. They think of it in terms of the unthinkable: the Cultural Revolution in reruns, China sinking back into the sloth of warlordism, fascism.

I fear they are right. I confess I was one who thought the students in Tiananmen could change the mind of stubborn men who run the country. Yes, even that of Deng Xiaoping.

I was as naive as that young man from Nankai whom I met in the square. I thought he and his comrades were the wave of the future. Like so many Americans, I was very proud of the youngsters, so brave, so idealistic.

Now I know that China is still ruled by her three great symbols: the Yellow River, the Great Wall, and the Dragon. The Yellow River is believed to have given birth to Chinese civilization thousands of years ago in its rich alluvial soil and to have established China as a river country, not an ocean country. She still lives by the yellow river waters, not the blue of ocean seas, turning inward instead of outward, as did the men of the Renaissance and the privateers of Queen Elizabeth. Not yet have the people and their rulers begun to see that the Great Wall keeps the people in, as well as invaders out; that the walls and courtyards in which they contain themselves, the great magenta walls that surround the Forbidden City and Zhongnanhai, confine minds as well as bodies. And the Dragon is still supreme, China's benevolent dragon that protects the nation, protects the throne, protects the dynasties, protects the people—so long as they do not threaten its order.

—HARRISON E. SALISBURY

November 23, 1989

Dear Ken,

Thanks for Giving. Thanks for giving me the chance to cruise L.A., to know you better, and to milk those who dared to park their cars near China West, that restaurant on Picco Boulevard.

When I watched T.V. the other day, I was relieved to know that the earthquake was far away from L.A. I remember last year when I was there, people were talking nervously about an imminent earth-quake and those who could afford it flocked out of California for safety. One year too early, though. Who is that guy who made the prediction? A Dutch?

In this letter I'm not going to complain about the heavy workload a graduate student has to shoulder. Got a more frightening monster to grapple with this semester: Freshman English. To work with a whole class of American teenagers fresh from high school is not like teaching English to my "comrades" in China. The young American comrades here don't always listen to their commander, and sometimes they even blame their higher-up for their own mistakes. The other day, a black girl student, who had had more than ten unexcused absences so far, came to my office and complained to me about her grade. She said she had shown her paper to four of her friends, and they all said it was at least a C paper. So the D+ grade I gave her confused her. I told her there was nothing confusing here. Since her friends took a D paper for a C essay, it tells why they are her friends but not her English instructors. Then she started accusing me of being responsible for her bad grade in this course. It never occurred to her that the grade was what she earned rather than what I gave. I felt so frustrated that I almost told her the whole truth: I had to keep my windows open when I graded her paper—it stank.

In fact, it is a lot fun to teach. The sense of self-fulfillment after each class makes up for the pressure I feel as an instructor. Many times on my way to my office after the class, I felt so great that I just wanted to kiss all the passers-by. Too bad the Kansans are not ready for this yet. Now, everything is fine except for one thing. No matter how hard I tried, I can't remember the names of all the students. I have no trouble with the most beautiful girls, but when it comes to others, I am just at a loss (J.J. must be the first name you remembered in class). Oftentimes, I had to finger at one of them and demanded "You answer the question!"

I learned a great deal from teaching, more than I do from my own courses, in a way. Last time I asked my students to do a paper of causal analysis, and I learned so many things from what they handed in—older people coming back to college, classical cars reclaiming the road they once owned, and American enthusiasm about physical fitness (Is J.J. still going to the gym class?). Teaching has not only deepened my language awareness but also helped me gain some insights into the American culture. And I got paid for all these. What a deal.

Bob Rees called the other day. He got everything ready for the Sino-American Writers' Conference, but heard of no word from the bureaucrats on the other side of the globe. He was reluctant to push them for a response in fear that they would send over those hard-liners instead of China's Allen Ginsberg, or Yevtushenko. He has had enough of the Russian roulette. Who knows. Maybe Bob is right. Even "magic" is no longer a compliment in their book. I guess they prefer interpreters who are "undaunted," "revolutionary," and "double-speaking."

So I am very hesitating as to what to do after graduation, which is the coming summer. I don't know if I should go back home or go on to my Ph.D. program. It might be difficult for me to get assistantship from other universities since Kansas State University doesn't sound as impressive as Harvard or Stanford. I am thinking of doing practical training for a year or so, as is allowed by laws here. I can teach either English or Chinese, or I can do any other kind of language-related jobs. But I am told that people get appointment in teaching through contacts rather than application. I'd appreciate it if you can give me some advice.

One trouble international students face after living here for a couple of years is that they not only learn English but also pick up American values. They become aware of and are torn between the differences of values in two cultures. If each time after President Bush makes a speech at the news conference, the Americans are forced to study the speech and discuss its significance for months on end, the American people would have a revolution, too. Then the thought of "political study" at home (The fanfare nowadays is about why the decadent, degrading, and nasty capitalist topless and bottomless are jeopardizing the grand blueprint of the Four Modernizations of China) makes one feel ridiculous and cheated. All one wants to say is "kill me now!"

Not long ago, I read from a L.A. newspaper that Maxine Hong Kingston got a literary prize, and my impression is that it is quite a prestigious award. Good for her.

Remember me to J.J. and Rachel.

With best wishes and have a nice Thanksgiving Day.

Magic (Henry) Chen

November 15, 1993
Santa Fe NM

Dear Henry the Info Spec,

So you're housed in New England at last. My guess is it's a pretty place—cold, indeed, but civilized. Some parts of the world, like LA, are neither. An incendiary mess. Traffic that makes the Beijing bicycle brigade look like ducks out strolling.

I'm camped in New Mexico. My UCLA class is Friday mornings, so

I hop a plane on Thursday afternoon and fly back Saturday morning. Not a bad way to put beans on the table. I'm trying to learn to write something marketable, like a sex manual for septegenarians (by the year 2000, they tell us, a third of the population will be retirement age), or an underground classic on how to grow marijuana indoors with t-v screen irradiation. It's a good thing my income does not depend on this.

Spent the spring in Europe, lecturing in France, Italy, and Germany from the new Indian humor book. Rachel, my daughter, went along, and now she's working as an au pair in Paris. So I'm flying there mid-December for two more weeks of dissipation and middle-aged escapism.

And, my God, you zigzag across America. Canada isn't in my horoscope too soon, as far as I can tell, but you never know. Never thought I'd be going to China a few years back either, and look how that turned out. How did it, now?

News: JJ got married to a nice guy. I couldn't have picked a better one. In fact, I said so at the wedding, over several glasses of wine. She's happy, I think, working as a food editor for an LA newspaper.

Larry Heinemann and I stay in touch, but not much from the rest of the merry pranksters. Once in a blue moon I run into Maxine or Barry. Bobbi Whiteman and Alice Fulton cross my trail occasionally. The others scattered to the four winds. Bob Rees, last I heard, was in Lithuania converting ex-Marxists to American Studies.

I don't have an E-Mail code, as far as I know. If I do, it's a mystery. I do have a friend here in Santa Fe with a FAX number. What the heck is E-Mail?

You can see I'm stuck back in the 60s.

Well, Mr. Magic, I hope that you like the northern woods. Come to New Mexico some day. You'd like it here. Cactus, blondes, tequila, longhorned cattle, and sagebrush.

You'll find me at home. Be well, stay in touch, and do good work.

—Ken

March 7, 1997

Yo, Cousin Ken,

Hi and howdy from the friendly confines. Edie and I have been crewing for friends of ours. Their boat is a few decades old, and basically moves like a brick; we never go out of sight of land, and the race course is pretty much always the same. Edie especially has caught the sailing bug.

So we decided to raise the children first, sell the house, meanwhile ordering a boat from the Hunter-guy here in town, and have it delivered to the Granville beach a couple blocks east of here. He's to anchor it off-shore, call us from the pay phone at the cafe there (we're packed and ready to go!), tell us the boat's here, and we reply we'll be right down. We get a cab, arrive with all our stuff, and go aboard. Before we do anything we christen the boat "Gatherer," so that on the fantail the name appears:

Hunter

Gatherer

We motor through the locks at the Chicago River, cruise around the Loop, head south toward the canal to the Illinois River—through Peoria, etc., to the Mississippi near Alton just upriver from St. Louis. Then we make for New Orleans where we pause to top off and make for the open water of the gulf and take up the life of pirates; make enough money to set sail for St. Martin's. We sail into that harbor, tie up at the wharf, *nail* the hull to the woodwork, cut the masts down at the deck wood, and retire once and for all. I take over the forward compartment; Edie takes the aft spaces; we share midships; I write my pirate memoirs; Edie writes hers.

Some plan, eh? (I may have told you all this before.)

*

Still at work on the train book, though I am beginning to see the wood of my desk. Harcourt/Brace bought the paperback rights to *Close Quarters* and *Paco's Story,* so those two books (which have gone out of print at Penguin) will be back in print soon; these will be reprinted simultaneous with "my next book." I've been horsing around with the Vietnam train book for the better part of 5 years, and, Cousin, wouldn't you say that enough is enough? Time to cut to the chase. The story I told you about in LA finally came out in *Atlantic Monthly*—"The Fragging"—a war story, absolutely the last thing I ever thought would happen (on two counts). Firstly, it's a war story, something I promised myself ten years ago I'd never do again; I thought I had my fill of war stories. And secondly, it was published in *AM,* something I never thought would happen in *this* lifetime (didn't think my work ran to their taste). The story is a milestone of sorts, anyway—I haven't had a piece of short fiction published since 1981, when *Harper's* printed an excerpt from *PS,* and people wrote in cursing me up one side and down the other, and canceling their subscriptions. That didn't happen this time, though the several letters the magazine got in response were two to one against. One letter, especially, is (as Mark Twain once said) a daisy; four and a half pages of tightly constructed rant (how dare I denigrate such a venerable institution as the Citadel, etc.). The very dictionary definition of a lifer; I've waited 30 years to tell this clown off. The editor asked me if I'd like to respond, but where does one begin, Cousin? Let it go; there are bigger fish to fry.

Earlier this year, Preston and I spent two weeks in Vietnam—my first trip back in five years. Went with a delegation of writers that included Maxine Kingston (and fulfills a promise I made to her on the China trip). She was just blown away; Preston (now 17) was also blown away. Got to show Max a magnificent sunrise at China Beach (5 o'clock in the morning); no one there except a couple fishermen tending their boats, some Viet joggers (of all things), the water glass smooth, and the sun coming up like thunder. Maxine ran up and down the beach, hop-skipping-and-jumping, windmilling her arms and whooping like a kid. On several occasions at concerts arranged by the Vietnamese, the young women singers would flirt shamelessly with Pres, and (God bless him) about all he could think to do was blush literally to the ears. We must have visited a dozen and more pagodas, temples and shrines; from the Nui Den Hung north and west of Hanoi in the Red River valley (see "Story of 'The Geese'" enclosed) to Nui Ba Den (and the Ba Den Temple) just east of Tay Ninh in the south (more about that below). I didn't intend the trip to be organized this way, but the whole two weeks became a religious pilgrimage. This trip was, overall, easier than the others I've taken; didn't have to *pay attention, take notes*, be *on*, if you know what I mean. All I had to do was sit back and let 'it' come to me. When we got home, Edie said that I was "mellow." I certainly *felt* better and had less trouble with jet lag, etc., than on previous journeys. I think it helped that I knew what I was looking at, and knew what it was that I wanted to show Maxine and Preston and the others. Without knowing or planning it, I think that I'm becoming a Buddhist; some guy asked me about this lately—why a Buddhist?—and I said (to make a long story short) I liked the part about not having to take a test. I was raised Lutheran and Lutherans take a *serious* test.

Didn't take many notes; certainly didn't keep a travel journal—just let the thing wash over me; much like the China trip, just let it happen. And I came away with an appreciation of Vietnamese spiritual life, something I hadn't seen before. And it gave me the *end* of the book; which is basically a meditation on what happened 30 years ago at war, and what has happened since.

*

Now, on another matter, and the actual nub of the letter.

As I said, among the places I visited was Nui Ba Den, what the French called the Black Virgin Mountain, near the city of Tay Ninh (where I had soldiered 30 years ago). Nui Ba Den has always loomed large in my memory of the war, in my imagination and my writing about that time of my life. I vividly recall many a morning awakening to the sight of the mountain becoming visible as the dawn light gathered and the sun came up. It was a remarkable presence, as remarkable a sight as the spooky mountain islands of Ha Long Bay or Marble Mountain or other such places in the Central Highlands. I am sure that I am not the only ex-GI who served near Tay Ninh who remembers that place. I have traveled all over Vietnam, and when asked where I served during the war, I mention Nui Ban Den, and every Vietnamese, north and south, young or old, knows of the mountain. At the bottom is a monument to the more than 10,000 men and women from round about Tay Ninh who died during the war.

In a country overwhelmingly of the Buddhist faith, the mountain is regarded as sacred to the memory of Ba Den ('ba' is a mode of respectful address to signify a matron over 40, ma'am). I have heard several legends about the mountain—all antique. One story goes that Ba

Den's husband was killed in one of the many wars of Vietnamese history; she so grieved his loss that she wanted to join him; she climbed the mountain to be as close to heaven as she could manage, then committed suicide. Another tells of Ba Den and her soldier-husband who lived at the foot of the mountain; while her husband was away fighting she was captured, raped many times, and died of shame. A third story relates that Ba Den, unknown to anyone in those parts but remarkable for her spiritual simplicity, was a devout older woman who visited the place to pray and meditate; when she died the mountain was named to honor her anonymous and humble piety.

The story I favor is this: a young woman Ba Den was to marry a soldier, but on her wedding day her husband-to-be was called away to war and never returned. Yet Ba Den waited for him, cried so hard and long that her family thought she would lose the sight of her eyes, and, as legend has it, she *became* the mountain.

In any case and whatever the story (the elements and point of the story are very Vietnamese), a pagoda shrine was built to the memory of her faithfulness and devotion.

To reach her pagoda shrine you ascend a rocky path to a stone stairway. It is a solid kilometer, and quite a hump. At the top of the stairway, perhaps half way up the southern face of the mountain is a temporary shrine. The original pagoda, destroyed during the war, is being rebuilt. It is not a static artifact and hardly a tourist site, but a functioning Buddhist temple, a place of pilgrimage and worship.

I would like to assist in the rebuilding and am writing to ask you to help me. If you would like to contribute to the restoration of the Ba Den Pagoda, a place of unique spiritual significance to the Vietnamese people, send it to the Ba Den Fund, c/o me. In a country where the per capita income is something like $250 a year, even ten or twenty dollars goes a long way, but a larger contribution would certainly help the construction along (send what you can, Cuz). If you would like to include a small personal object or message with your contribution, please feel free to do so; just remember that any personal object has to be hand-carried (by me) up the side of the mountain. It will be presented to the pagoda priests when the fund is delivered.

Keep your topknot tight and your utensils clean.

> Hoa binh,
> Larry

The Story of "The Poem"

I am not a poet; I'm too long winded, perhaps not calm or introspective enough for the work, and besides I'm one of those guys who thinks there's no such thing as a short story. Every poem I ever wrote either became a novel or part of a novel, so why fight it. I tease poet-friends of mine that all I know about poetry is that every line begins with a capital letter and every other line rhymes; some get the gag and some don't.

But "The Geese" is different; the first piece of work I've ever written that poets I admire and respect have told me, Yes, Larry, this is a poem: write a bunch more and you've got a book.

The story of the poem begins the spring of 1986. I had been working for eight years on my second novel; I had just quit my teaching job of fourteen years and needed to finish; we needed the money. During Spring Break, Don Bodey (a carpenter/writer friend of ours; wrote FNG) loaned us his place on a bit of lake in northeast Indiana. The kids would haul out Bodey's row boat and paddle around the lake, trying to catch a box turtle (any box turtle); I would squirrel myself away at the bench of Bodey's work shed and write; Edie would set up on the big-puzzle card table and type. Edie had been typing my manuscripts since 1968, and was a superb editor.

That spring was record cold. I turned on the typewriters first thing so the machines would have a couple hours to warm up enough to work. One morning I stood by Bodey's boat house, the moon was setting, the sun was rising, and two geese flew over the place and settled on the lake in front of me. I am a city kid and had never seen the likes of that before. How can a body not be moved by such a thing?

Although it did not occur to me to sit down and write the poem for six years, the image, that long moment at 6:00 am at the edge of Bodey's lake was unforgettable.

*

American writers are supposed to take long jaunts to Europe— England and Ireland, Portugal and Spain, Scandinavia, Italy and France. I keep winding up in Southeast Asia. Not long ago I was invited to join a group of writers and poets going to Vietnam to help the Vietnam Writers Association celebrate its 40th anniversary. It would be my fourth trip. I am in thrall every time I go, now; the food is terrific, the women are beautiful, and riding the trains is all kick. I have good friends there, perhaps the best of friends: poets and writers, painters and sculptors, scholars and musicians, curb-side bicycle repair guys, and folks met on the street; some veterans, some not, some too young to have any memory of the war.

Vietnamese literature (in the broadest sense of the word) goes back to the third or fourth millennnia BC, and everyone knows the stories, legends, traditional oral poetry (ca doa), the written literature (which dates from the 10th Century, AD), and can recite their own (and others') work by heart. Because Vietnamese is a tonal language, their poetry is like song (and spiked with classical references).

On my first return trip in 1990, I met Hanoi University professor of American Literature Nguyen Lien (Vietnamese names are expressed family name first, then the given name, Chinese fashion). During one conversation I asked him what his job was during the American War (as the Vietnamese call it). He said that his "task" was to go to Beijing and learn English, then go to the University of Moscow and study American literature, and *then* come back to Hanoi, go out on the Ho Chi Minh Trail, and give lectures on Whitman, Twain, London, Fitzgerald and Hemingway, etc., to the troops moving south. Professor Lien asked me in all earnest seriousness what Vietnamese literature the U.S. Army had taught me? I had to push myself way from the table, throw my head back and laugh right out loud. (Apologies later to Professor Lien.) The honest guilelessness of the question could only provoke robust, derisive laughter from an American. The very idea of the United States Army giving anyone classes in literature of *any* sort is a mellow and ironic absurdity of the richest kind, and makes a body *need* to laugh out loud—haw, haw, haw.

During the war the North Vietnamese People's Army newspaper (*Van Nghe Quan Doi*) routinely published poetry. Its American counterpart, *The Stars and Stripes*, did not (that I ever heard); the thought would never occur to those people. North Vietnamese soldiers were encouraged to keep journals, write poems and songs, or whatever else came to mind; Americans were discouraged by direct written orders from keeping journals—even from saving letters, for that matter.

Writing and poetry, "story" in the deepest cosmopolitan sense, have always been important to the Vietnamese. Vietnam was a mature culture centuries before Europeans discovered soap and water.

During my previous trips to Vietnam Huu Thinh, a tanker during the war and editor of *Van Nghe*, had always asked me to contribute an essay or a brief story. *Van Nghe*, a weekly tabloid format (like the *American Poetry Review*), has translated and published the work of many Americans.

In 1990 I wrote about my first visit to Hanoi (a place at one time in my life strictly forbidden even to my imagination) and the irony of Vietnamese hospitality; distinctly different, you understand, from the home-welcome I received in 1968 when the raw ambivalence of Americans was at its most touchy extreme. The distinction was so sharp that it was already a cliché among ex-GIs returning to Vietnam. This at a time when the only lights in the streets of Hanoi at night came from the sidewalk shops, hot water in the hotels and guest houses wasn't available until 7:00 am, and round-eyed white guys like me were assumed to be Soviet Russians. *Lien xo* ("lean so"), we were called many times. The Vietnamese don't like the Russians almost as much as they don't like the French or the Chinese. Russians, the southern Vietnamese said under their breaths, were "Americans with no money."

In 1992 I wrote about train travel in Vietnam (I'm a train buff) and, since it was late November, the family-holiday ritual of Thanksgiving; and what it meant to spend Thanksgiving in Hanoi where I am included in an extended "family," if only as kin of the distant-cousin kind. The Vietnamese put great store in the hierarchy of family relationships, the give and take of loyalty and respect and responsibility. It is not for nothing that Ho Chi Minh was called Bac ("Uncle") Ho.

An appellation of the greatest veneration and affection; Washington, Lincoln and Roosevelt all rolled into one.

But this trip, March of 1997, I would give Huu Thinh my poem, "The Geese," which had been gathering dust in my drawer.

My 17-year-old son, Preston, and I arrived in Hanoi and joined the other American writers, Maxine Hong Kingston among them. Huu Thinh said my poem would be published later that week. I was tickled, not to say flattered, my first published poem, by God; translated by Nguyen Ba Chung, an ex-patriot scholar and poet from Boston whose father was killed by the French and whose mother still lives in Ho Chi Minh City.

Thursday, March 20, we traveled northwest of Hanoi to Nui Den Hung. *Nui* means mountain; *den* means temple; *Hung,* the first Vietnamese dynasty, which legend dates at 3000 BC. A fair translation would be the Mountain of the Temple of the Hung Kings. The *oldest* surviving part of the temple—the praying stone—dates from the 3rd century BC.

*

It didn't occur to me until we were walking up the mountainside steps among the crowds of pilgrims and peddlers hawking bundles of incense and Chinese-made trinkets that March 20 was thirty years to the day since I first arrived at Tan Son Nhut outside Saigon to begin my year's combat tour. Without a doubt the worst year of my life.

We enter the temple by stepping over a foot-high threshold and joined a close crowd of serious worshippers come to pray. The altar is way at the back where a life-sized Buddha sits, lit only by several tall, skinny candles and what little light that comes under the broad porch eave, in the door, and through the crowd. To each side of the Buddha are two tall bronzes of cranes standing on the back of turtles. The crane and the turtle are emblematic of an *old* Vietnamese story about the faith of friendship; about everyone getting what they need. In front of the Buddha is a bronze bowl, about the size of a wedding punch-bowl, filled with sand. Here the worshippers plant their handfuls of incense—joss. The sharply pungent smoke, thick as the smolder rising from a yard-leaf fire, fills that little room; strings of gray ash litter the altar and the stones underfoot. There is also a flat platter for the Offerings, usually given in 100, 500, and 1000 Vietnamese Dong notes (pennies, nickels, and dimes), and plates of fruit and giftwrapped sticky-rice cakes offered to the dead. At the side a monk dressed in a workaday brown robe stands next to a bowl-shaped temple bell, holding a wooden clapper. Every time someone steps out of the crowd and reaches up to place their joss, the monk strikes the bell, and that deep and solid reverberating *boom* stills the room to the darkened rafters, despite the close softness of the crowd.

There is a constant murmur and hubbub.

I could not stand on Nui Den Hung at the altar of the praying stone thirty years to the day I first came to that country and not think back on what happened then.

Thirty years ago I was scared to death and thought I was going home in a bag. And, take it all around, I was not a pleasant person and the war was not a pleasant business; what happened then not pleasant to recall. I was not a very good soldier. I have no medals; I never did anything brave in front of anyone who lived to testify. Going home without a scratch seemed plenty good enough. The thing done with, not done well, you understand.

And how can I stand there holding my own hefty handful of joss— always an odd number; an even number is unlucky—the rich and sharply piquant smoke rising in my face and hair, and not think of my life since; especially with Preston standing next to me? The good things come into your life. The blessings sought; discovered; stumbled upon; given to you—as if *pushed* into your hand. Beginning with the simple fact of your life; any soldier will tell you that. You haven't blown your brains out; you haven't boozed yourself to death; Agent Orange hasn't incinerated your liver with cancer; you aren't in the Lifer's Club at Joliet (or Walpole or Parchman or San Quentin or the like).

A long moment I stand there in daydream; so long, in fact, it becomes a meditation. Preston eyes me with deliberate curiosity; he has never seen me stand thus. When I step forward to plant my joss, the monk nods deeply and signifies with a long wink, and whacks the bell a righteous lick.

*

Back in Hanoi at the guest house hotel, copies of *Van Nghe* were waiting in the lobby with my poem inside. I am a poet at last; I am 53. I smile big and brag to everyone. The young woman at the front desk, a student at the university, asks to copy it in her journal, "for study." The next day, our last full day in Hanoi, we go downtown to the old market neighborhood to shop—what Preston calls "Scoop Day." At the newsstand across Dinh Tien Hoang Street from the Lake of the Returned Sword, near the Water Puppet Theater, I stop to buy an armful of *Van Nghe*. Standing next to me is a gentleman in a trench coat and beret, a Hanoi native. We strike up a conversation. He asks if I speak French. Not a word, I say. But I am a poet. I open the newspaper to the middle page and there is "The Geese." He is impressed. He says he is a concert pianist, just returned from a world tour, and pulls out an album of photographs of himself playing in Moscow, Copenhagen, Berlin, Paris, Rome, London and Dublin. A pleasure to meet you, I say. We shake hands. We are both veterans, fought in the south, and lived to play the piano and write. We both agree that life is a grand thing. I tell him he must come to Chicago and play with the symphony; I will come and bring all my friends. He buys a copy of *Van Nghe* and asks if I would be good enough to sign the page with my poem. I am more than glad, and wish him health, prosperity and long life. I finish with an unreadable whirligig signature. *Hoa binh*, peace.

My first customer.

All that morning and into the afternoon I make a thorough pill of myself. I cannot help it.

I importune astounded sidewalk peddlers trying to sell me collections of stamps and picture post cards, the cooks at the funky, no-name cafe where we stop for *bun cha* (noodles and beef, which Ba Chung says is famous "for blocks"), fellow tourists eyeballing made-for-the-trade souvenirs, kids hawking lottery tickets, shopkeepers selling hand-embroidered t-shirts and toy helicopters made of Coca Cola and Heineken beer cans. You're a poet? they ask. Yes, I say, look here. And I whip out a copy from under my arm. See? Everyone looks at me with blinking astonishment. They read the poem and rhetorically "ooh" and "ah." Foreigners are supposed to shut up and *buy*, not harass them into buying a poem. The shoe shine boys assume that I am famous.

That evening the big potatoes of the Writers Association host a formal dinner. Twenty-five or thirty people sit at a long table. Crab and shrimp, chicken and duck; at the end of the meal plates of food, glasses and bottles, chop sticks, and napkins are scattered everywhere. For the many toasts we drink Remy Martin. The aperitif glasses are state-dinner elegant; the Remy Martin is tasty.

Our official host, poet Pham Tien Duat, stands up and announces to one and all that *Heinemann* has a poem in the current issue of *Van Nghe,* and would I be good enough to recite it for everyone. Duat is a veteran of the Ho Chi Minh Trail. Aside from being a soldier, then a journalist, one of his last jobs during the war was to travel up and down the trail, giving readings of his own and others' poetry to keep up the spirit of the soldiers moving south. In 1973, he wrote "White Circle," arguably the most famous poem of the war:

> Bomb smoke climbs in the sky in black circles,
> white circles rise on the ground.
> My friend and I go on in silence,
> the silence expected after war.
> Friend, there is not greater loss than death.
> The white mourning headband takes the shape of a zero,
> inside that white circle
> a head burns with fire.

—FROM *WRITING BETWEEN THE LINES*, EDITED BY KEVIN BOWEN AND BRUCE WEIGL, UNIVERSITY OF MASSACHUSETTS PRESS, 1997; TRANSLATED BY NGUYEN QUANG THIEU AND KEVIN BOWEN. REPRINTED WITH PERMISSION.

Every kid is taught the poem in school.

In 1993, he stayed a week at our house on his first visit to the U.S., and was much taken with Chicago's gangster history; I tell Duat, for instance, that Chicago invented the "drive-by shooting." He is slight, like most Vietnamese, with gray hair and sparkling, almost giddy eyes; a trickster's eyes.

*

Everyone at the table insists I recite my poem. How can I refuse?

It just so happens that I have brought a couple good cigars and three pints of Jack Daniels on the trip. The cigars, in screw-top tubes lined with cedar, for the hell of it. The Jack Daniels, because on other visits there is always one dinner or other when someone brings out a bottle of *lua moi* (new rice wine)—very strong stuff; the only wine I've ever had to drink with a beer chaser. I've told the Vietnamese that Americans call this "moonshine." Tonight there is no jug of new rice wine, but there's plenty of Jack to go around.

I stand, hauling out a cigar and the pints. I hold up one of the bottles and slap the label. I tell everyone that, like new rice wine, Jack Daniels is traditional American moonshine, and proceed to tell some bullshit story I do not now recall about the origin and tradition of sour mash whiskey manufactured on the sly; why we wait for moonlight; full moon; quarter moon; new moon; and so forth. Several of the Vietnamese poets in the room have made careers writing about moonlight. War by moonlight; love my moonlight; writing by moonlight; the garden and moonlight.

While Ba Chung translates, I take out a cigar and poke the lip-end with my pocket knife. I light it and smoke.

I tell briefly about the visit to Nui Dan Hung on the thirtieth anniversary of my first trip to Vietnam as a rifle soldier; how it was to stand there at the praying stone with my son.

Ba Chung translates and I smoke.

There are many ex-grunts in the room; among the Vietnamese there are men and women who spent all of their adult lives as soldiers (some from late adolescence to middle age). They know what anniversaries mean. Vu Tu Nam, one of the moonlight poets, joined the Viet Minh in 1947; he is a poet, novelist and writer of children's stories; past head of the Writers Association; now a member of the Vietnam "House of Representatives"; on a recent trip to Chicago in winter he remarked about the clean look of the moon over the lake on one of those evenings when we say the hawk is out (nights when a northeaster blows so hard, so bone-numb cold out of Canada, that it snatches the breath clean out of your lungs.)

I say it is not the least of the ironies of the war that I became a writer *because* of the war (the same as any number of others I know who are also veterans); that my old man was an ordinary working stiff, a bus driver, and if not for the war, I would be driving a bus—or something like; that I became a writer because I wanted to understand what I saw, what I did, and what it was I had become.

Ba Chung translates and I smoke.

Our war, I say, will always be a source, a font, the well-spring of my work. I have often wished it were not so, but how can it be otherwise? I will always be able to reach back and touch it one way or another, and find "story." Whether it has anything to do with the war or not.

Ba Chung translates and I go for the whiskey.

Now, I say, it is time for the toast and crack the seal. Everyone takes up their aperitif glasses and throws out the Remy Martin. As I understand it, everyone assumes they are in for a treat. I go around the room and pour everyone a shot of Jack. I say that I learned long ago to celebrate every good thing that came into my life, and lately it is the publication of my first poem. Then I wish everyone health, prosperity and long life.

Ba Chung translates and everyone in the room knocks back the Jack in one shot—*wham*—neat and hard. A peculiar expression comes over everyone's face. It basically translates as, "We threw out the Remy for this?" Moonshine turns out to be moonshine all over the world.

And now, I say, "The Geese."

I give the poem, gesturing with both hands; we're in a large room with a tight echo. I pause at every period, every stanza, for Ba Chung to translate; I wait, tipping ash and pouring shots of Jack. This evening I am a poet among poets. I knock back shooters and smoke my cigar down to the lips.

THE GEESE

Cold April.
Bodey's Lake,
Indiana.
Passover,
Six a.m.

Takes an hour
to start the fire
and make the coffee.
Hot cup stings
my palms
and fingers.
Shoes soaking
in the grass.
Wear my cardigan sweater
Edie made
of skein-ends;
knitted as her hand
came to them.
Sweater is thick
and heavy,
but warm;
a riot
of colors.

This morning,
I have the lake
to myself.

Across the way:
across the lake,
just over the farmhouse
kitchen garden
the full moon sets.
Fat and flat,
big as a tea cup saucer

held at arm's length;
color of a thick
slice of snowy ice.

Behind me:
back of Bodey's
handbuilt cinderblock cottage,
just over the pasture grove
of hickory and bur oak,
the sun rises.
Huge and yellow
orange,
and warm,
thank God.

Hold my coffee
with both hot hands
and sip deep,
sweet as brass.
Sun and moon,
both large lights,
opposite
and poised
on the horizon.
An amazing moment,
even *I* know that.
When such a light
touches such a heart,
what happens?

Mated pair
of geese who live
on the pasture pond
fly over the house
and yard,
honking and crying,
loud.
Low enough to hear
the air fiercely
hushing over their
wings and backs;
close enough to hear
the sharp,
hard breathing
as they work.

Cruising side by side,
they ease down;
touch and coast

into the wide
shivery wedge
of moonlight;
make straight
for the shoal reeds.

Long wakes
like arrows;
with feathers,
the patina
of old silver,
clean to the tip.

From: Chen@ufo.ugha.edu (Chen, Henry)
To: Lincoln@humnet.ucla.edu (Lincoln, Ken)
Date: Tues, 01 April 1997 14:16
Subject: *Are you there?*

Ken, I got this email address from the Internet, but not sure if this one works. If you get this message, please drop me an e-note. I am in Maryland now.

Henry Chen

03 April 1997
Re: *Are you there?*

Dear Magic, Well sort of— I've been seeing old friends and relatives in Nebraska and Colorado, over the quarter break. Got a new book, *Men Down West,* just out from Capra Press in Santa Barbara, California. Essays on growing up in the west—cars, guns, fathers, women, war, brothers, LA, and single-parenting Rachel. My version of Larry Heinemann's war stories.

Wouldn't you just know it? I've started rewriting the China book, and you're emerging as a character. So it's good that you rang on E-mail, however you found my so-called mailbox. I'm still green to virtual reality, somewhat how you felt coming to California.

I've thought of you often, my friend, hope you're fine, hi & howdy and all that. Let me know how it's going. I'm irregular at this Internetting, but eventually I'll get back on-line to you.

Am now living in Santa Fe and commuting to UCLA part of the week, then back to paradise. TurboProf, the students call me. The old condo is still my LA hang-out in Culver City. Remember that beat-up futon? If all else fails, you can find me at UCLA, as always.

yr. Beijing Buddy, Ken

04 April 1997
Re: *Are you there?*

Ken—very excited to hear from you. Now I can harrass you with email messages. Beware!

I remember not only the futon in the condo, but also the day when Magic Johnson played during the final NBA game in 1988. And I didn't watch it! Now that I'm a basketball fan, I always regret that I missed that game when you were watching TV in your room while working out on a rowing machine. That was my first week in America, feeling baffled, confused and lost because of, as I understand it now, culture shock. I wasn't in mood to do anything. It has been a long way making the transition from one culture to another.

I still remember vividly days when I sat in shadow behind that Chinese restaurant along Pico, enjoying California gentle breeze. I also remember how I politely talked people into paying me one dollar for parking at the lot of our neighbor's instead of paying 2 at that snack bar. Of cause I also rember how I got intimated by that Los Angeles Lawyer. Looking back, I feel fearful. If someone filed a suit against me, I would end up in big troubles. Only people like me who are so ignorant of law could do those stupid things. As Chinese saying has it: only a calf is not afraid of tigers.

Days in Los Angeles are so memorable. For one thing, I was free from all heavy academic stresses that are piled on graduate students, international students in particular. I didn't have to worry about dead line of all paper. Here, I would say, life is easy, but living is hard. Gone are good days of getting paid by doing nothing but sitting in lawn chair outside with *Man's Search For Meaning* in one hand and Coco Cola in other.

My advisor told me not to get panic. I'm learning how to not study that hard and pay less attention to grade. "Done is good," as they say. So my next letter will be probably on how I spend whole day swimming, playing, frolicing and what else? Philandering? Oh, no, Deng Youmei doesn't like it. Anyone from China is not expected to do it. Besides, I've to keep a clean record.

I'm doing fine now (and feeling at home, too). Last January, I moved from Kansas State to Univ. of Maryland, for a bigger pay check. I still do the same thing as I would in any other counseling: answering questions, searching, consulting and teaching. Does naming make a difference? According to Confucius, and many other word players (isn't it true we have no street cleaners these days?) "sanitary engineers" have taken over.

The only problem is that my new fiancée is still back in Kansas (she is also a counselor), so I have to travel back and forth each month to visit her. She tries to find a job here, but it's hard to find an appropriate one. Someday, you'll meet her when we visit L.A.

So now my English name, Henry, is official? It sounds innocent, phonetically speaking. Keep me posted.

KENNETH LINCOLN

Your "paradise" must be resembling mine a lot, except for the weather. I'm beginning to question my move to Maryland, not so merry in winter.

Any plan for the summer? Teaching in Italy again, or going to Nebraska? Since you don't have to switch cars with JJ this time, you don't have to worry about breaking down on the road. Still remember when the front wheel came off your sportscar? How time flies. "This girl has grown into the wife of someone else," as a Chinese line says. And I have been here for nine years.

Henry

Dear Ken,
September 3, 1998

Thanks for your working draft of "A Writer's China." If there is one thing I have to say about writers, it's their memory—tenacious, photographic and everlasting.

I just came back from a trip to China. So much have changed since your last visit there. Even I had trouble recognizing all the places I was so familiar with before. Changes are everywhere, not just physical surroundings. People are much more open-minded than ever before, about making money, that is. You can hardly meet anyone in China today without engaging in some sort of talk about doing business. Everyone wants to be an entrepreneur, and self-claimed business men/women are everywhere, which you can tell by the cellula phones, beepers and other electronic gadgets they carry with them. Getting rich is not just glorious these days. It is a must; it is about survival. It has become almost the meaning of life for many. Sometimes, I felt out of touch of the reality there. I found myself a stranger once again.

If you ever come East for conference, visit or anything, let me know. It has been ten years since we last saw each other.

Take care,
Henry